PRAISE FOR

She's Not There

AND

Jennifer Finney Boylan

"This surprisingly buoyant memoir about a sex-change operation is a frank and funny tale about gender, friendship, family, and love."
—Sara Nelson, *Glamour*

"Boylan's description of femininity, as James becomes Jenny, is fascinating and often hilarious."
—*Washington Post*

"Her thoughtful approach to her own tale succeeds in bringing to life the seemingly impossible dilemma of the transsexual.... Fortunately for her readers, Boylan has a very active imagination. "
—*Chicago Tribune*

"In addition to being a complete delight, this book should make us all question what we mean when we use the words love, marriage, and friendship. Jennifer Finney Boylan is a great gift to womanhood."
—Haven Kimmel, author of *A Girl Named Zippy*

"[A] candid and exuberantly funny memoir of self-actualization.... In simple and direct language, Boylan describes an extraordinary metamorphosis. A superb primer for understanding the transgender impulse, *She's Not There* feels at once liberating and regretful, embracing honesty in all its messy forms."
—*The Onion*

"Intelligent and funny . . . this unusual memoir [is], first and foremost, one amazing tale. . . . Boylan has a gift for transporting the reader, even one who has never felt this particular sort of gender claustrophobia, to a place where it can be imagined. . . . True and courageous."
—*Seattle Post-Intelligencer*

"Honest and humorous . . . her quest for identity gets to the heart of what it means to love and be loved."
—*Lifetime* magazine

"Poignant yet often comical . . . a remarkable story that straddles the seam between humor and tragedy."
—Associated Press

"The best, most satisfying reading experience is a serendipitous coming together of reader, writer, and book on an almost visceral level. When it happens, there is a kind of 'click,' an emotional engagement that enriches the whole undertaking and makes the reader feel somehow privileged. Boylan is a gifted storyteller . . . sustained by zany humor, a fine sense of the absurd, and an optimism that seems to defy all odds."
—*St. Louis Post-Dispatch*

"In writing as sheer as stockings, artful without artifice, she explains the process of becoming Jennifer. . . . Serious, real, funny. Told so disarmingly that it's strong enough to defang a taboo."
—*Kirkus Reviews* (starred)

"What makes the book so appealing is Boylan's honesty, optimistic but never cloying tone and wry humor. . . . The reader comes away with a sense of wonder and hope."
—*Hartford Courant*

"Boylan's well-written and informative book is a worthy contribution to the body of work on this subject."
—*Booklist*

She's Not There

A Life in Two Genders

Jennifer Finney Boylan

Broadway Paperbacks
New York

Photographs on pages 1, 85, and 301 are courtesy of the author. Images on page
169 are courtesy of Colby College. Photograph on page 219, copyright © 2002 by
Bruce Strong. Photograph on page 279 courtesy of Colby College Communications;
photograph by Brian Speer.

Library of Congress Cataloging-in-Publication Data

Boylan, Jennifer Finney, 1958–
She's not there: a life in two genders / by Jennifer Finney Boylan;
with an afterword by Richard Russo.—1st ed.
p. cm.
1. Boylan, Jennifer Finney, 1958–   2. Novelists, American—20th century—Biography.
3. English teachers—United States—Biography.   4. Transsexuals—
United States—Biography.   5. Gender identity—United States.   I. Title.

PS3552.O914 Z477 2003
813'.54—dc21
2002038235

ISBN 978-0-385-34697-9
eISBN 978-0-385-34698-6

Printed in the United States of America

Book design by Caroline Cunningham
Cover design by Honi Werner

10 9 8 7 6 5 4 3

Second Paperback Edition

For Katie Finney

(1948–2002)

Contents

Unlike Some People I Could Mention
Foreword to the Updated Edition, 2013   xi

PART I

Mr. Fun Hog 3

Hurricane Ethel 19

After the Bath 29

The Failures of Milk 47

Come Down in Time 51

Monkey Orphanage 59

House of Mystery 69

PART 2

Bright Star 87

The Troubles 110

The Ice Storm 119

Wibbly Wobbly 133

Boygirl 146

PART 3

"They Aren't Like Jellyfish at All" 171

Some Pig 185

Persons Such as Themselves 202

Drunken Noodles 213

PART 4

The Yankee-Doodle Girl 221

Conundra, or The Sick Arab 244

Explosive Bolts 252

The Death of Houdini 259

The New Equator 267

Afterword: Imagining Jenny
by Richard Russo 279

The Life at Sea
Epilogue: Ten Years Later
by Jennifer Finney Boylan 303

Imagining Grace
by Deirdre "Grace" Boylan 319

Providence always did put the right words in my mouth, if I would only leave it alone.

—Huck Finn

Unlike Some People I Could Mention

Foreword to the Updated Edition, 2013

Rereading *She's Not There* in preparation for this tenth-anniversary edition put me in mind of an old Amish expression: "Ve are too soon olt und too late schmart."

I know there are plenty of people who, looking back at their younger selves, have had occasion to think, *Man, what you don't know could fill a book.* I'm unique, however, in that the book filled with the things I don't know is an *actual book*.

She's Not There was the first in a trilogy I wrote about gender. The second, *I'm Looking Through You* (2008), concerned my parents' allegedly haunted house and the ways in which the living, too, can wind up haunted, especially by the phantoms of their younger selves. The last in the series, *Stuck in the Middle with You*, is being published by Random House concurrently with this updated version of *She's Not There*; it focuses on the challenges faced by my family. It also addresses the differences between being a mother and a father, and considers the time when I was betwixt and between the binary poles of gender, the parental version of the schnoodle or the cockapoo.

My boys—six and four when this book was begun—are now a college freshman and a high school junior, respectively. It's my hope that having a father who became a woman has, in turn, helped my sons become better men.

Looking back on my life from the vantage point of my fifties, I'm aware that the woman I have become in middle age is perhaps less the result of hormones than of a lifetime spent telling stories. It was the writing of these books that, more than anything else, helped me understand the narrative of my own life, and those of other women like me.

When I was a teenager I searched the library in vain for the story of a person I might resemble. To whom could I turn? Tiresias? Jan Morris? The Amazing Kreskin? Without much in the way of dependable narrative or contemporary myth, there were ways in which I felt, back then, as if I did not exist. Talk about phantoms! Surely, if there were no books about lives like my own, I was fated to live a life in which I could only be invisible.

There are lots of good books about people like me now. There are memoirs and textbooks by Jamison Green, Leslie Feinberg, Helen Boyd, Donna Rose, Susan Stryker, Julia Serrano, Chaz Bono, Deborah Rudacille, and many, many others. All of these stories have helped change trans issues from something extraordinary to something more commonplace, from a single, simple narrative to a series of messier ones, moving us toward a time when, as Robert Hunter once wrote, "things we've never seen will seem familiar."

I have left the original text of this memoir virtually unaltered. The one exception is that I've changed the word *transgendered*, which freely inhabited the original, to *transgender* or *trans*. These have become, in the intervening years, the preferred terms, and I'm fine with that.

Other than that, the original draft stands unchanged. Unlike some people I could mention.

This updated edition contains two new sections: a new chapter from me, bringing some of the story up to date, and a short afterword from my spouse, Deirdre, who is called "Grace" in this book.

Given how public our lives became after the publication of *She's Not There*, it was tempting to change all the pseudonyms and replace them with everyone's actual names. But at this hour it struck me that this would only be confusing, and might lead some readers to mistakenly conclude that in the last ten years everyone I know—following my curious lead—has changed his or her identity.

My own identity, after all these years, has wound up less altered than I had expected. It should not have been a surprise, perhaps, but in some ways the most shocking revelation after ten years in the female sex is that mostly I am the same person I always was, gender notwithstanding. As my wife, Deedie, notes in her afterword to this updated edition, "the strength of our love for each other never fundamentally changed . . . as Jenny used to say, it's the same monkeys, different barrel."

It has been a long journey, made possible by my loving spouse, my remarkable sons, and the creation of these tales. It is only because of these gifts that I have left a phantom's life behind, and have at last become something solid.

I am also put in mind of the story of James Thurber at a party in Paris, in which a woman informed him how much funnier his stories were in French. "Yes," lamented Thurber. "They tend to lose something in the original."

Jennifer Finney Boylan
Belgrade Lakes, Maine
2013

Part I

Atlantic City, New Jersey, 1974.
"I'm so sorry," she said. "The milk didn't work."

Mr. Fun Hog

(December 2001)

There they were, two young women standing by the side of the road with their thumbs out. They weren't warmly dressed, considering that it was December, in Maine. One of them had green hair. They looked to me as if they were in trouble, or about to be. I pulled over, thinking, Better me than someone else. The world was full of characters.

"Can you take us to Augusta, ma'am? The Middle Road?" said the one whose hair was not green.

"Yes, of course, I'm going right past there," I said. "Climb in."

Soon they were in the car and we were driving west. The smell of pot wafted from the women, and I thought about the fact that my purse was on the floor in the back next to Green Hair.

"Wow, lady," said the girl next to me, looking at all the equipment in the minivan. "You sure have a lot of stuff. What is that, a guitar?"

"Synthesizer," I said. "I was playing at a Christmas party at the Samoset Resort last night. I was sitting in with the Roy Hudson Band."

"Whoa, I know them," said Green Hair, suddenly impressed. "You *play* with them? They're great. The Roy Hudsons used to play at Colby when I went there."

I glanced in the rearview mirror to get a better look at her. Something in her voice was familiar. "You used to go to Colby College?" I said. I was about to say, *I'm chair of the English Department there,* but hesitated.

"Yeah," she said. "A couple semesters, a long time ago. Couldn't hack it."

It was possible, although not certain, that Green Hair was named Ashley LaPierre, who'd been a student of mine back when I was a man. Looking at her now, all I could think was, *Wow, she's really changed.*

The class Ashley had been in was Love, Literature, and Imagination, the introduction to fiction, poetry, and drama for nonmajors. I loved teaching that course and sometimes did it as a great big lecture class where I stood at the front of the room and sang. We read a wide range of stuff, most of it having to do with people trying to find the courage to do something impossible. We talked a lot about the journey of the mythic hero, about the slaying of dragons and the attainment of illumination.

I used to stand at the lectern in my coat and tie, waving my glasses around, urging students to find the courage to become themselves. Then I'd go back to the office and lock the door and put my head down on the desk.

Ashley LaPierre had dropped out of Colby in the middle of that semester, which broke my heart. I remembered she'd been a fine writer, though, shining in both my class and Richard Russo's fiction workshop.

Now, six or seven years later, Ashley—assuming it was she—didn't seem to recognize me, which wasn't a surprise, seeing as how I didn't use to be female. I was wearing blue jeans and a coral knit sweater. My long blond hair fell just above my breasts.

"So what are you girls up to?" I asked.

"We was walking into Augusta," said the one next to me. "Pickin' up this pit bull."

"I'm Jennifer, by the way," I said.

"Stacey Brown." The other girl didn't introduce herself. Stacey punched in my lighter.

I wanted to say something about how we didn't allow smoking in our family, but I decided not to. The car was full of amplifiers and sound modules and monitors anyway, and I'd just spent a night playing songs like "Hey Bartender" and "Mustang Sally" for a bunch of tattooed millworkers. It didn't seem like the time to start lecturing these girls on the dangers of nicotine.

"You live around here?" I asked. Ashley was looking out the window.

"We live on a farm," said Stacey. "We got five cats, three hens, one rooster."

"Any eggs?"

"Nothin'," said Stacey.

The lighter clicked out and she lit up a cigarette from a pack of generic smokes.

"So you live out there by yourself?"

"Yeah," said Stacey. "Since our boyfriends went to jail."

I looked at Ashley in the rearview mirror. She smiled for a moment, as if at some happy memory. The smile accentuated her apple cheeks, her bright, shining eyes.

"Who owns the pit bull?" I asked.

"We don't know, some guy who calls himself Speed Racer. He's got a brown trailer. We saw the dog advertised in *Uncle Henry's*. We been thinking about getting a pit bull for a long time."

The smile faded from Ashley's face.

One day Ashley LaPierre had come into the office I shared with Russo to talk about a paper she was trying to write on "The Love Song of J. Alfred Prufrock." She was wearing gigantic black boots with clunky heels. Her eyes fell upon a poster of the Marx Brothers on the wall above the file cabinet. "Who are those guys?" she asked.

"The Marx Brothers," I said. "Groucho, Chico, Harpo. You've never heard of them?"

She shrugged. "Nah. Anyway. This poem? Prufrock's Love Song?" She spoke with that feminine-inflected voice that makes every statement sound like a question. Occasionally I brought the symbolism of this inflection to my students' attention, especially when I asked for their names and they answered me as if they weren't sure what they were. *Megan? Heather? Ashley?* "Say your names as if you are proud of them," I'd urge my students. "Your *identity* is not a question."

Now that I was female, that same inflection often snuck into my own voice, a fact that both amazed and infuriated me. *Hello? I'm Jenny Boylan?*

"Yes," I'd said to Ashley. "We talked about it in class." I'd been sitting at my desk chair, next to my computer. I'd been wearing Dockers and a tweed jacket, a blue Oxford shirt, and a brown tie. It seemed like a long time ago. I had a mop of brownish blond hair and small round wire-rim glasses, a fountain pen, stubble.

"See, that's the thing," Ashley said. "The way that opens, *Let's get out of here, the both of us, while . . . whatever . . .*"

" '*Let us go then, you and I, / While the evening is spread out against the sky / Like a patient etherized upon a—*' "

"Yeah, yeah," Ashley said. "See, in class we were talking about how, like, that's him talking to this girl, right? Only I don't see it that way at all."

"No?" I said. "Well, how do you read it?"

"I think he's standing in front of a mirror," she said. "And it's like he's this person cut in half, you know, it's like he's got this half of him that everybody thinks is cool, like he's Mister Fun Hog, but in fact he's totally scared of everything. It's like he's got this person he's invented and then there's this other person who's really him and he's trying to talk to this other person, trying to, like, convince him to get the hell out of there."

I nodded. "So you feel that J. Alfred Prufrock is torn in half?"

She looked at me as if I hadn't read the poem. "The fuck yes," she said. "Don't you?"

I nodded again. "I do." I was having a hard time concentrating. "So is he crazy?"

"Crazy?" Ashley said. "Hell no. Everybody feels like that. Don't they?"

We drove toward Augusta in silence. Every now and then I'd ask a question or make some clever observation, but mostly I just let things stay quiet. Back when I was a boy, I'd hitchhiked lots of times, and there was nothing worse, sometimes, than a driver who was determined to make you talk.

We got to Middle Road in Augusta, and I drove down the street first one way, then another—but there was no brown trailer. "Are you sure it was Middle Road?"

"Middle *Street*," said Ashley.

"Do you have directions?" I asked.

"Yeah," said Stacey. "It's like you go down this road and then there's some sort of intersection or something?"

We let this sink in.

"Why don't we call?" I said, and pulled in to a Mobil station. Stacey looked at me, embarrassed. "Here," I said, pulling a quarter out of the cup holder. "My treat."

As Stacey went off to the pay phone, I sat in the car with Ashley. I suddenly had this unbearable urge to turn around and say, *Ashley, it's me, Professor Boylan. Remember? I'm, like, a woman now?* I had this sense that, for the first time, there wasn't some kind of invisible wall between us, that for the first time I could actually be *known* by her. But that wasn't true. There were all sorts of walls between us, even now.

I turned on the radio. A chorus of voices singing in a cathedral. Thomas Tallis's 40-Part Motet.

Stacey came back to the car. "Okay, I got it," she said.

I headed out into traffic. "What do we do?" I said.

"You go, like, along some way, and then there's some kind of, like, turn or something, and then there's some other road?"

I nodded.

I had a hunch where Middle Street was, and we drove through Augusta, Maine's hard-bitten capital, toward Belgrade.

Two little girls were playing in the front yard of a row house.

"Go on, play, little girls," said Ashley. "Enjoy it while you can."

"Yeah," said Stacey. "They don't even *know* the shit they're in."

"You got kids, Jenny?" Ashley said.

"Yes, two boys. They're seven and five."

"You have 'em by cesarean?" she asked. This wasn't the question I was expecting.

"Don't ask her that," said Stacey. "Jesus, like it's any of *your* business."

"I just think it's interesting," said Ashley. "All my friends are cesareans, *all* of them. Don't you think that *means* something? It's like, all cesareans have this *thing* about them?"

"I wasn't cesarean," said Stacey.

"Actually, the thing cesareans have? *You* don't have it."

"My boys *were* C-sections, actually," I said, although I didn't want to mention that I wasn't the one who'd actually gone through labor. "And I was one, too."

"I *knew* it!" said Ashley. "I'm psychic!"

"Psycho, you mean," said Stacey.

"Lucky you, having boys," said Ashley. "You don't have to worry about all the *shit*."

"Yeah, well, boys have other things they have to worry about," I said.

"As if," said Ashley.

I drove down Middle Street and hoped, in a way, that I wouldn't be able to find the trailer. It was already clear that a pit bull was the very last thing these girls needed in their lives, that it was the only thing I could think of that might make their lives any worse than they were already.

I had to get up to Colby by early afternoon, to meet the Russos for dinner, then introduce Richard at the reading he was giving at the college that night. His new book, *Empire Falls*, had come out the previous summer, and the Colby reading was ostensibly the last stop on the year's long reading tour.

I was looking forward to introducing Russo that evening. It would be my first official reintroduction to the college community since I'd switched from regular to Diet Coke. I knew the reading would be packed, too, the room likely to be filled with a few hundred people. It would definitely be an occasion. To make it stranger, everyone knew that Rick had been my closest friend back when I was a man. As a writer—and as a man—Russo was something of a tough guy. Having his best friend turn into a woman hadn't struck him as a great idea at the time.

I pulled up in front of a brown trailer. A pit bull was chained to a tree.

"This looks like the place," I said.

"Okay," said Stacey, getting out of the van. Ashley was still staring out the window. Stacey took a few steps toward the trailer, then looked back at us. "Lee?" she said, irritated.

"Coming," said Lee, and opened her door. I thought, Is that what she calls herself now, *Lee*? I still wasn't sure it was even the girl I had known.

Before she put her feet on the ground, Lee said, "Listen, Jennifer?"

"Yes?"

"Do you mind coming along with us?" She looked up at the trailer. "In case this guy is sketchy?"

I nodded. "Sure," I said.

As it turned out, the trailer was *way* sketchy. Four busted-up cars sat on cinder blocks. An old red truck was pulled up next to the back door. On the back windows were two decals. The first one said, SHOW US YOUR TITS!

The second one, in Gothic script, read, YOUR COLLEGE SUCKS.

Stacey knocked on the door and waited. No one answered. She knocked again.

The pit bull came over, snarling and bouncing and wagging.

"Aww," Lee said. "Pretty girl."

I had no idea whom she was referring to. It didn't appear to apply to anyone present. Then she knelt and started petting the pit bull, which in turn licked her face. "Pretty girl," she said again.

Stacey kept knocking on the back door of the trailer. I looked around the yard, which was all mud. There was garbage and rusted pieces of metal and broken auto parts in every direction.

"I guess he ain't home," said Stacey.

She came over to where we were standing and looked at the dog. "Wow," she said. "She's great."

Lee looked up. "What do you think?" she said. "You think we should just *take* her?"

We all thought about it. The guy was *giving the dog away*, after all. Still, it seemed odd that he wouldn't be here, especially after Stacey had just called him on the phone. Was it possible we were at the wrong house? If we just took the dog, it was entirely possible we'd wind up getting arrested for dog larceny. These girls seemed to be exactly the kinds of characters to whom such things happened.

"Wait," said Stacey. "Something's moving in the house."

We went back to the door and knocked again. Stacey turned to us with a look of urgency. *"He's only wearing a towel,"* she said.

Lee looked at me urgently. *Please, save us,* she seemed to say.

But I didn't think I could save anybody anymore.

Speed Racer, clad only in a towel, unlocked the door. "Sorry," he said. "Didn't hear ya. Come on in. Let's get some clothes on."

Well, yes, that sounds good, I thought. He vanished. Then Stacey and Lee and I looked at one another and considered our next move.

"I guess we just—go in?" said Lee.

"Uh-huh," I said.

They let me go first.

A moment later we were all standing in a filthy kitchen. Dishes were piled high in the sink. There was a calendar of a topless woman on one wall, and my first reaction was, What's the deal with men and nudie calendars? Is it just so they can show everyone how stupid they are? Then I caught hold of myself. I sort of remembered what the deal was.

The young man came out a few minutes later. Camouflage pants and a NASCAR T-shirt. Military haircut. "So," he said. "You see her?" He meant the dog.

"Yup," said Stacey.

"She's been fixed," he said, trying to provide any other relevant information. "Got all her shots. She's pretty nice." A look of trouble darkened his features momentarily. "Ah—one thing. You don't wanna move a remote control around too fast in front of her."

"Okay," said Stacey.

I tried to imagine the consequences of waving a remote control too swiftly in the dog's presence. They were bad, very bad.

"So," said Speed. "You all sisters?"

We all smiled, although I was privately appalled. I didn't think that Lee (with the green hair) looked very similar to me.

"No," I said, smoothing things out. "We're just friends."

Stacey looked at me as if I had just delivered a great compliment instead of a bald-faced lie. Lee, for her part, looked at Stacey, and I could guess what she was thinking. *See?* she thought. *I told you cesareans were cool.*

"You all *look* like sisters," Speed said suspiciously.

"Well," I said a little more firmly, "we're not."

"Whatever," he said. "You want the dog?"

"Yeah, I guess," said Stacey.

"Okay," said Speed.

Then we all stood there for what seemed like a long time, no one talking, no one moving. At that moment I realized neither of the girls was wearing a bra. I rather wished that they were, I thought as Speed Racer licked his lips.

Then Lee said, "Could we, like—borrow a leash?"

Speed Racer nodded and said, "It's in my truck," and a moment later we all followed him out to the mud pile where his red pickup with the SHOW US YOUR TITS! decal was parked, and we stood by as he dug around in its innards. Beer cans, floor mats, and old bags of fast food fell into the mud.

"Here ya go," he said at last, and put the leash into Stacey's hands. The leash was bright red and made of what seemed to be an extra-heavy-duty material.

Stacey went over to the dog and put her on the leash. I looked at my van, still filled with all of my rock-and-roll gear, and wondered where the pit bull was going to go. "You wanna make sure she's near a window," said Speed Racer. "She gets sick."

"Okay," I said. "Stacey, can you sit in the back, have her sit in your lap?"

"Yeah, sure," she said.

We all looked at one another. It was time for us to go. Speed Racer was looking at us with a kind of hungry expression. I opened the driver's-side door, but just as I was about to climb in he said, "Hold on, ladies."

I stood there with my hand on the door handle. Lee rushed to the other side of the car.

"I said *wait*, goddammit." Speed was now turning red, and he looked scary. It was official: the three of us were all frightened now. I looked at the pit bull, pretty sure she wasn't going to be on our side.

"Yes, sir?" I said, hoping that even now, politeness would be counted in my favor.

"You can't go yet," he said. "I'm not going to *let* you go yet."

He started walking toward me. And I thought, fleetingly, about how little upper-body strength I had now. If it came to a fight, it wasn't going to be a very long one, even with the three of us against him and the dog.

He came closer. I saw the muscles tighten in his jaw. I held on to my car key, hoping I could use this as a weapon if I had to. It wasn't the way I'd imagined my death. After all these years, I'd wind up stabbed near a trailer next to a truck with a decal that said YOUR COLLEGE SUCKS.

The dude got closer, and closer, and then—put his arms out and hugged the dog.

"Good-bye," he said to the pit bull. And started crying. "Good-bye, sweetie pie."

Stacey and Lee and I looked at one another. Lee grinned as if pleased.

Speed Racer was crying so hard now, he was shaking. "You be a good girl," he said, again meaning (I presumed) the dog.

"Listen, mister, she's going to be all right," said Stacey. "She's gonna live with us on our farm." I tried to put her first sentence together with the second, tried to figure out the connection, but failed.

"Okay, okay," said Speed Racer, "you should just go. I don't wanna have to—"

Then he turned away midsentence and walked straight back into the house and closed the door without looking at us.

Stacey got the dog into the backseat, and Lee sat up front this time. I noted that the window next to the dog didn't open. I thought about what he'd said about how the dog got sick sometimes.

I started the car and headed back to the road. The car lurched in the potholes.

"We forgot to ask her name," said Stacey.

We drove on a little farther.

"You think we should head back?" Stacey asked. "Ask him what her name is?"

"No," Lee and I said in unison.

I drove back to 27 and headed south. "I'm going to let you girls out at the Wal-Mart, okay?" I said. "You should be able to get a ride from somebody there."

Lee looked back at the nameless pit bull and Stacey. "Man, you sure got a lot of stuff," she said to me.

"Yeah, well, keys mean a lot of equipment."

"Must be fun, being a musician. Playing in bands, meeting guys. You meet a lot of guys, playing out?"

I thought about the night before. I'd gone to the women's room during the break to find a long, long line. While waiting for the stalls, all the women were talking to one another, looking at ourselves in the mirror, fluffing up our hair with our fingernails. It made me smile, thinking about the same scene in a men's room—everybody deadly silent, not looking at one another, concentrating on the business at hand as if soberly standing atop the bridge of a mighty intergalactic star destroyer.

There was one girl sitting on a chair, smoking a cigarette. I still thought this was a kick. Women's rooms often have a little place where you can sit down and smoke, presumably just so you can have a few minutes away from your freakin' husband. There are no such places in men's rooms, ever. Men always ask, *What took you so long? What are you chicks doing in there?* Now, after this long voyage, I finally know the answer. *Having a few precious moments away from you, darling.*

While I was in the stall, I heard some women scream softly, then some laughter. When I came back out, I looked at the smoking girl. "What happened?" I said.

"You'll never believe this," she said. "But some guy just tried to walk in here. In the *ladies'* room!"

"A guy?" I asked. "What did he want?"

"Beats me," she said. "God only knows *what* they want."

I looked at Lee. "I don't meet that many guys, playing out," I said. "Fewer than you'd think.

"Listen," I said to Stacey and Lee, "can I ask you girls a question?"

"Sure," said Stacey.

"What are your boyfriends in prison for?"

"Well, mine's in for assault and battery," Stacey said. She sighed. "Some guys, you break up with them, they go totally apeshit."

"I don't know what mine's in for," said Lee. "A couple days before he took off, he asked me if I'd still love him if he ever went to jail. I said sure, whatever. Then right after that he says he's going to go visit his aunt for a while."

I vaguely remembered the boy that Ashley LaPierre had been dating at Colby. He was a Canadian, from Nova Scotia, who played for the ice hockey team. I remember he told me once he was going to quit hockey for good. When I asked him how come, he pointed in turn to his knee, his ankle, his ribs, his knuckles, his wrists, and so on, and said, "Twisted, broken, broken, replaced, torn, sprained." He pointed to his thigh. "My leg I broke *twice.*"

I remembered the last time I'd seen Ashley, the day she came to my office to tell me she was dropping out of school. She'd sat there in my office chair, next to the poster of the Marx Brothers, crying.

When she finally took her leave, I just sat there and watched her run down the hall. I didn't suppose I'd be seeing her again.

But I was wrong. Here we were, six or seven years later, and I was a woman, and she was the owner of a secondhand dog.

"You ever think about going back to college, Lee?" I asked. "It doesn't have to be Colby."

"I don't know," she said.

"I know it's none of my business," I said. "But you should give it another try. Maybe you'd surprise yourself."

Lee nodded. I was expecting her to roll her eyes and grin that grin I'd seen before. But she didn't. She looked as if this were advice that no one else had ever given her before. I wondered if I had let her down six years before, by not doing a better job of discouraging her from dropping out.

We were almost at the Wal-Mart. "You know, I had a teacher at Colby who made a big difference in my life once," Lee said dreamily.

"Bullshit," said Stacey, from the back.

"No, remember that guy I used to talk about, the writer?"

"Who?" Stacey said.

Then Lee smiled, the name clicking into place.

"Russo," she said. "Richard Russo." Lee shook her head. "Man, he was some teacher."

I nodded. "He's not at Colby anymore," I said.

"Aw, too bad," said Lee. "What happened to him?"

I smiled. "They made his movie, *Nobody's Fool*? You ever see that, with Paul Newman?"

Lee just shrugged. "I don't go to movies."

I pulled up in front of the Wal-Mart. "Okay," I said. "You wait here, somebody'll pick you up, take you back to Freedom."

"Hey, thanks for the ride, Jennifer," Stacey said. The dog jumped off her lap, and she got out of the van. Lee waited for a moment longer.

"Listen, thanks for helping us deal with that Speed Racer guy," she said.

"I was glad to help," I said quietly. "You take care." I so much wanted to take her hand and say, *Goddammit, Ashley—it's me!*

"Hey, Jennifer," she said. "Can I ask you something? A favor, like?"

"Sure."

"You think I could, like, ever call you up sometime, you know, just so I could talk?"

"Sure," I said, caught off guard. "That would be fine." I wrote my phone number on a piece of paper and handed it to her.

She stuffed the scrap of paper in her jeans pocket. "It's like, sometimes there just isn't anyone who—you know. . . ."

"You give me a call whenever you like."

I looked out the window at Stacey. The dog was peeing next to the Wal-Mart sign.

"Okay," said Lee, and got out of the car. "See ya," she said.

I turned in at the Civic Center to make a U-turn, and while I waited for the light to change, I checked my purse. The money was still there.

Across the street from me were the two girls with their thumbs out. Stacey was yanking the nameless dog along on its thick red leash.

I drove back home and just barely had enough time to unload the keys and the amplifier and straighten the house before heading up to

Waterville to meet Rick for dinner. I changed into a black twin set and a red-and-black faux-Japanese print skirt. Black hose and flats.

We met at a Mexican place in town, Rick and Barb and I, plus Rick's daughter, Kate. I was sorely in the mood to drink a margarita, but the last time I'd had a margarita before a fiction reading, I'd gotten lost on the way back from the restaurant to campus, which was only about a mile away, on the same road. I wound up on the other side of the Kennebec River in the parking lot of the closed-up paper mill, which is about as far away from a fiction reading as you can get.

When I got to the lecture hall, I found it packed, just as I'd expected. People were already sitting on the floor. I scurried around, trying to find a few more folding chairs, then went up to the podium and welcomed everyone.

"Hello," I said. "I'm Jennifer Boylan, and welcome to the Colby Visiting Writers Series."

I gave Russo an emotional introduction. I talked about the time the two of us shared a small office at Colby and spent our afternoons telling jokes, talking about the Yankees, and lamenting the fate of comic writers in the publishing world. It was a time, I said, when working in the English Department was like living in the barn in *Charlotte's Web*, when each day seemed full of "the nearness of rats, the love of spiders, the smell of manure, and the glory of everything."

Then I said, "Ladies and gentlemen, my best friend, and the country's second best novelist, Mr. Richard Russo."

Rick came up to the podium, and the two of us hugged, and I put my head on his shoulder. Then I sat down, and he said, "Thanks, Jenny."

After the reading, a long line of readers snaked out the door, each waiting for his or her turn to get Rick to sign a book. While I waited for him to finish up, someone came up to me, a young woman I vaguely recognized from somewhere.

"Hello," she said. "I'm Carolyn Dorset? I used to work as an assistant in anthropology?"

And I thought, *Say* your name, Carolyn. Don't *ask* it.

"I'm Jennifer Boylan?" I said.

"Hi," she said. "I know one of your students. She says you're a wonderful teacher."

"Thank you," I said.

"Now, there *used* to be a *James* Boylan on campus," she said thoughtfully, as if she were remembering someone she had known a long, long time ago. "Are you his wife?"

"No," I said. I felt a little dizzy. I didn't know what to say to her without lying. "He's gone now," I said.

I stood there for a moment, wondering what I could tell this anthropologist about James Boylan, who wasn't with us anymore. It made me feel a little sad. Carolyn saw the shadow cross my face.

"Oh, I'm sorry," she said. "Is he . . . ?"

Then I smiled as I thought about Ashley, hitchhiking with a pit bull toward Freedom.

"What's so funny?" she asked. "What are you thinking about?"

"Nothing," I said. "Someone I used to know."

Hurricane Ethel

(Late Summer 1968)

I was born in 1958, on June 22, the second day of summer. It was also the birthday of Kris Kristofferson and Meryl Streep, both of whom I later resembled, although not at the same time. One day when I was about three, I was sitting in a pool of sunlight cast onto the wooden floor beneath my mother's ironing board. She was watching *Art Link-letter's House Party* on TV. I saw her ironing my father's white shirt—a sprinkle of water from her blue plastic bottle, a short spurt of steam as it sizzled beneath the iron. "Someday you'll wear shirts like this," said Mom.

I just listened to her strange words, as if they were a language other than English. I didn't understand what she was getting at. *She* never wore shirts like that. Why would I ever be wearing shirts like my *father's*?

Since then, the awareness that I was in the wrong body, living the wrong life, was never out of my conscious mind—*never*, although my understanding of what it meant to be a boy, or a girl, was something that changed over time. Still, this conviction was present during my piano lesson with Mr. Hockenberry, and it was there when my father and I shot off model rockets, and it was there years later when I took the SAT, and it was there in the middle of the night when I woke in my dormitory at Wesleyan. And at every moment as I lived my life, I countered this awareness with an exasperated companion thought, namely, Don't be an *idiot*. You're *not* a girl. Get over it.

But I never got over it.

Our house had been built in the middle of a tract of land that had been a failed Quaker settlement in the 1800s. In the 1960s, the remains of the cobblestone road threaded through the thick forest, connecting the ruins of five or six stone houses. Most of the old mansions were missing their roofs. Trees grew through the living room floors. In the center of the forest—which was known as Earle's Woods—was the elaborate, destroyed mansion of Pennsylvania's former governor. The mansion, which had been gutted by fire, still had a lot of its old furniture in it. The burned-out house stood on the banks of a lake where sometimes I went fishing by myself. I had mixed feelings about fishing there, though, in spite of the giant brown trout that occasionally jumped out of the water and made a splash that echoed in the woods like a gunshot. It was scary, sitting there by the lake, the burned house on the bank behind me. I felt as if I were being watched.

Sometimes I played a game in the woods called "girl planet." In it, I was an astronaut who had crashed on an uninhabited world. There was a large fallen tree I used as the crashed-and-destroyed rocket. The thing was, though, that anybody who breathed the air on this planet turned into a girl. There was nothing you could do about it, it just happened. My clothes turned into a girl's clothes, too, which should give an indication of exactly how powerful the atmosphere was. *It changed your clothes!* Once female, I walked through the cobblestone woods, past the abandoned houses, until I arrived at Governor Earle's mansion, which I started to try to fix up. It took years, but eventually I had a nice little place put together. By the time astronauts from planet Earth came to rescue me, I had grown into a mature woman, a college professor, occasionally playing piano in blues bands, kissing my children good night as they lay asleep in their beds. My rescuers would say, "We're looking for James Finney Boylan, the novelist. We found his rocket all smashed up back there in the woods. Do you know where he is, ma'am?"

"I'm sorry," I said. "He's gone now."

I did not know the word *transsexual* back then, and the word *transgender* had not yet been invented. I had heard the word *transvestite*, of course, but it didn't seem to apply to me. It sounded kind of creepy, like some kind of centipede or grub. In my mind I sometimes confused it with the words that described cave formations: What was it again—transves-*tites* grew down from the top of the cave; transves-*mites* grew up from the bottom?

But even if I had known the right definitions for these words, I am not sure it would have made much difference to me. Even now, a discussion of transgender people frequently resembles nothing so much as a conversation about *aliens*. Do you think there really *are* transgender people? Has the government known about them for years and kept the whole business secret? Where do they come from, and what do they want? Have they been secretly living among us for years?

Although my understanding of exactly how much trouble I was in grew more specific over time, as I child I surely understood enough about my condition to know it was something I'd better keep private. By intuition I was certain that the thing I knew to be true was something others would find both impossible and hilarious. My conviction, by the way, had nothing to do with a desire to be *feminine*, but it had everything to do with being *female*. Which is an odd belief for a person born male. It certainly had nothing to do with whether I was attracted to girls or boys. This last point was the one that, years later, would most frequently elude people, including the over-educated smarty-pants who constituted much of my inner circle. But being gay or lesbian is about sexual orientation. Being trans is about identity.

What it's emphatically *not* is a "lifestyle," any more than being male or female is a lifestyle. When I imagine a person with a *lifestyle*, I see a millionaire playboy named Chip who likes to race yachts to Bimini, or an accountant, perhaps, who dresses up in a suit of armor on the weekends.

Being transgender isn't like that. Gender is many things, but one thing it is surely not is a *hobby*. Being female is not something you do because it's clever or postmodern, or because you're a deluded, deranged narcissist.

In the end, what it is, more than anything else, is a *fact*. It is the dilemma of the transsexual, though, that it is a fact that cannot possibly be understood without imagination.

After I grew up and became female, people would often ask me, How did you *know*, when you were a child? How is it possible that you could believe, with such heartbroken conviction, something that, on the surface of it, seems so stupid? This question always baffled me, as I could hardly imagine what it would be like *not* to know what your gender was. It seemed obvious to me that this was something you understood intuitively, not on the basis of what was between your legs, but because of what you felt in your heart. Remember when you woke up this morning—I'd say to my female friends—and you knew you were female? *That's* how I felt. *That's* how I knew.

Of course, knowing with such absolute certainty something that appeared to be both absurd and untrue made me, as we said in Pennsylvania, kind of *mental*. It was an absurdity I carried everywhere, a crushing burden, which was, simultaneously, invisible. Trying to make the best of things, trying to *snap out of it*, didn't help, either. As time went on, that burden only grew heavier, and heavier, and heavier.

The first time I remember trying to come up with some sort of solution to the *being alive problem* was about 1968, when I was staying in a summer house in Surf City, New Jersey. A hurricane was blowing up. My parents were away, watching my sister ride horses, and I was being tended by my dipsomaniac grandmother, Gammie, and her friend Hilda Watson, a tiny woman from North Yorkshire who was as deaf as a blacksmith's anvil. Since it was nearly impossible for Hilda to hear even the loudest sounds, most of the time she sat in a chair wearing a startled expression; when she was aware she was being spoken to, she made a soft whooping noise, similar to the squeals of a guinea pig. Also there was my eccentric aunt Nora, who liked to make sock puppets as a gesture of love. One time she made me, out of one of my father's black socks, an octopus with a mustache and a red top hat.

On the day the hurricane hit, I had taken a walk underneath the boardwalk. It was as close to infinity as I could imagine under there, the row of pylons and boardwalk stretching as far as I could see. All around me were the echoes of the ocean and the howling wind and the seagulls and the rain, the smells of creosote and tar.

I was "taking a big walk." On the *big walk* I was going to try to *solve* whatever it was that was wrong with me. I walked down the dark tunnel of the place beneath the boardwalk, trying to figure out what the deal was with being alive. I knew I wasn't a girl—by then it was clear that girls and I were different. And yet, clearly enough, I wasn't a boy, either. What was I? What was going to happen to me if I didn't stop wanting to be a girl all the time?

That afternoon under the boardwalk, as the hurricane blew up, I tried to think about what I could do to solve the problem. This whole wanting-to-be-a-girl-all-the-time business was eating up a lot of my time. But what could a person do, if she wanted something impossible?

I got as far as a fishing pier, and I left the tunnel of the below-the-boardwalk place and climbed out on the jetty next to the pier. Waves were already crashing up angrily against the rocks, and rain was starting to fall. The wind whipped my hair around. I sat on the farthest rock and looked out at the sea and watched the ocean for a long time.

And then I thought, *Maybe you could be cured by love.*

Even *then* I think I was aware of how corny this sounded. Still, I believed it to be true. If I was loved deeply enough by others, perhaps I would be content to stay a boy.

I walked back to the apartment with this newfound awareness surrounding me like a caul. I would start with my grandmother. I opened the door to find Gammie and Mrs. Watson playing gin and drinking vodka. Gammie was describing the night of my father's conception. "Best screwin' I ever had!" she shouted. I stared at her.

"What's with you?" Gammie said.

"Nothing," I said. Mrs. Watson was listening to the Zombies on the AM radio. The song was "She's Not There."

But it's too late to say you're sorry / How would I know, why should I care? . . .

It was odd that Mrs. Watson—or any of these women—would be listening to the Zombies, as they were all classical music fans.

"Why is Hilda listening to WFIL?" I asked, curious.

"Sssh," said Gammie. "She thinks it's classical."

The disc jockey, Jerry Blavat—"the Geator with the Heater"—broke in. Surf City was being evacuated. Everyone was encouraged to get in their cars and head for higher ground. The hurricane would arrive by nightfall.

"We have to leave here," Aunt Nora said.

"What?" said Gammie.

"They're evacuating the island," my aunt repeated.

"Oh, are you going to fall for *that*?" said Gammie. "Nora, *you* are like a scared *chicken*!"

"They say we're in danger," Aunt Nora said.

"Oh, shut *up*, Nora," said Gammie. Outside, the wind howled against the windowpanes.

"Whoop? Whoop? Whoop?" said Mrs. Watson, and adjusted her hearing aids, which suddenly blasted with feedback. She looked as though she'd just received an electric shock.

My grandmother shouted to her deaf friend. "Nora says we should LEAVE. Like SCARED CHICKENS."

"We aren't leaving?" Aunt Nora said, disappointed.

"Cluck cluck cluck," said Gammie.

I just stood there, looking at my grandmother. I liked her enormous gaudy earrings and wondered how old I'd have to be before my parents would allow me to get my ears pierced. Then I remembered. I wasn't going to be thinking that way anymore.

"What's with you?" said Gammie.

"Nothing," I said, and went to my room.

I had brought with me to the seashore a magic kit I had been given for my birthday. I sat cross-legged on the wooden floor and messed with it. There were all sorts of tricks to learn. There was the disappearing egg. Card tricks. A set of sponges that traveled through plastic cups.

I sat there for an hour or so trying to get the disappearing egg to disappear. It seemed easy enough. You put the egg in the holder, then you covered it with the lid, said a few magic words, and lifted the top. With the proper amount of pressure, the egg would adhere to the ovoid lid and become hidden in its depths.

But I couldn't get the egg to cooperate. I broke the first one I tried and had to go out to the kitchen and get the carton of eggs out of the refrigerator, as well as paper towels to clean up the mess. I had to move stealthily in order not to be seen by Gammie, who, if she saw me stealing eggs, would insist that I come over and sit on her lap, where she would pinch my cheek and announce that I was "Gammie's little apple."

I struggled with the disappearing egg for a long time. The problem was that the egg wouldn't stick to the lid; it kept falling out and smashing on the floor, calling the credence of its disappearance into question. I tried lining the lid of the chamber with adhesive tape in order to make it stick, but this didn't work, either.

For a while I wondered if the problem was my magic words. I'd been using "Abracadabra." The instruction manual invited the apprentice sorcerer to make up her own magic words, so I tried the trick with a variety of alternatives as well: "Presto change-o." "Voilà."

And so on. I even tried being imperious with it: I COMMAND YOU TO DISAPPEAR.

But it didn't disappear.

By ten o'clock that night, the wind was screaming outside. Rain hammered against the window. I lay on my back in bed. Gammie had forgotten dinner, which was fine with me, since when she did remember it would unquestionably be a big potful of chicken à la king. She loved to make chicken à la king, made it every time she baby-sat me. Since her full name was Ethel King Redding, I assumed they'd named it after her.

Gammie, Hilda, and Aunt Nora were out in the living room, having this discussion:

GAMMIE: Hilda, do you know where you'd GET *(inhale, pause, exhale)* if you went—directly—EAST—from Surf City?

MRS. WATSON: Whoop? Whoop? Whoop?

GAMMIE: EAST!

AUNT NORA: I think we should leave. I think we're in danger!

GAMMIE: If you went EAST from Surf City, Hilda! Where do you think you'd get?

MRS. WATSON: Hm. Whoop? Mm. England? Whoop? Is it England you'd get to?

GAMMIE: SPAIN!

MRS. WATSON: Oh, no, I don't think it would be—

GAMMIE: SPAIN!

MRS. WATSON: Portugal? Perhaps Portugal? Whoop?

GAMMIE: SPAIN! That is where you would wind up. SPAIN!

I came out of my room and stood by the card table.

Aunt Nora said, "I think we should leave. I'm afraid!"

Gammie looked at her and rolled her eyes. "Don't listen to her, Jimmy. She's just a chicken. A SCARED CHICKEN! Cluck cluck cluck."

"I think we should leave, too," I said.

"Oh, nonsense."

"I do," I said.

"If you think I'm driving back to Philadelphia in this pouring—"

Aunt Nora took a look at me. She saw something.

"I'll drive," she said.

"Oh, you will not," Gammie said. "Don't be an imbecile."

"Whoop?" said Hilda.

"We're going to pack up and head home," Aunt Nora shouted at Mrs. Watson. Mrs. Watson adjusted her hearing aids. They squelched. "There's a hurricane."

Mrs. Watson nodded. "Entirely sensible," she said.

"You all go," said Gammie. "I'm staying here."

"We're all *going*," said Aunt Nora. "Either you go, or you die," she said. For a long moment, Aunt Nora and Gammie stared at each other.

"Jimmy," Gammie said at last. "Go get the vodka."

Years later, Gammie announced that when she died, she wanted to be a cadaver. She donated her body to Jefferson Medical School. "When you're dead, you're dead," she explained. She talked her friend Hilda into being a cadaver, too. It was something they did together. At the time, I was horrified by this, by the idea of my grandmother's corpse being the private concern of a first-year medical student in Philadelphia, opening her up and holding her liver and her heart in his hands. Did he know, as he examined her innards, that this had been someone's Gammie, someone who once danced on top of pianos, whose first husband nicknamed her "Stardust"?

Now I'm less bothered by all this, though. Maybe she's right, when you're dead, you're dead. I don't know.

I looked out the back of Gammie's Dodge Seneca as Aunt Nora drove us into the storm. The boardwalk was visible as a dark shadow against the threatening sea.

"You're Gammie's little apple," Gammie said from the seat next to me, and pinched my cheek. The windshield wipers slapped against the storm. I looked at my grandmother's earrings and at Mrs. Watson's wedding ring. Thirty-three years later, after I became a woman, my mother gave me Mrs. Watson's ring. Hilda and Gammie had been dead for thirteen years at that point. The ring has two big diamonds and eight little ones.

"Whoop? Whoop? Whoop?"

Aunt Nora looked at me in her rearview mirror. "It's all right, Jimmy," she said. "We're going to be safe now."

After the Bath

(Winter 1974)

I had high hopes. My parents and sister had gone out. That left me alone in the place we called the Coffin House, built by Lemuel Coffin in 1890. It was just a few days before Christmas, and the war was over. This girl named Onion was coming over while my parents were gone. There were rumors about her.

We'd been living in the Coffin House only for a couple of years now, and it still didn't quite feel like home. The people who had lived in the house before us, the Hunts, had left quite a mark on the place. On the third floor, next to my room, there was one room that was kept locked. The ceiling was collapsing in the locked room. My parents used it as a storeroom. At night I'd lie in bed, waiting to hear footsteps on the other side of the wall, a door opening softly.

My parents took down the wallpaper in their bedroom and found, beneath the paper, old poems written in pencil on the plaster. One of them was a woman's lament for a man who had died. She'd signed her name: Mariah Coffin, 1912.

There were other stories about the Coffin mansion. Mrs. DePalma, who lived across the street, claimed that the people who lived in the house before the Hunts had kept a sick aunt in a back bedroom. When she was little, Mrs. DePalma said, you could hear the woman's fingernails scratching on the door at the top of the back stairs as she attempted to claw her way out. I'd been in that back bedroom, which didn't have any heat, and there were indeed scratch marks on the door.

Sometimes I'd go into the empty room next to mine and I'd put on some old dresses that hung in garment bags there. They smelled like mothballs. I'd stand around thinking, *This is stupid, why am I doing this?* and then think, *Because I can't not.* Then I'd take the dresses off and go back to my room and think, *You're an idiot. Promise you'll never do that again.* Then I'd go back into the storeroom, try on a different one, and think, *Idiot.* I kept busy for hours that way—had, in fact, been keeping busy that way for years now. But no one knew.

I'd had a car accident earlier that fall, on the first day of eleventh grade. I was showing my friend Bunting how to drive a stick, which he actually mastered relatively quickly. Unfortunately, a few miles down College Avenue in Haverford the car started fishtailing wildly, and within seconds it swung off the road, smashed into a fire hydrant, flipped over, soared off a small cliff, and disappeared into a ravine.

Other than that, school was going pretty well. I was in Mr. Prescott's Nineteenth-Century Poetry class, as well as one Mr. Meehan was teaching entitled The Individual Versus Society.

Bunting and I got thrown out of the wreck. I flew through the air. As I did, I wondered, *Okay, I'm about to find out if there is life after death—is there? Is there?* There was a crash and a gong and many layered curtains that I passed through on my way out, each one finer and more delicate than the one before it.

Suddenly I saw a dark blue form in the middle of a light blue field, and light was shining all around. A deep voice said, *Son? Are you all right, son?*

And my first thought was, Cool! There *is* a God! Excellent!

What this was, though, was a cop with a blue hat bending over me as I lay in the middle of the road on my back. I was looking up into the blue sky. My glasses had flown off in the collision, which was why everything was soft and blurry.

Bunting was okay. He was standing next to a fire hydrant, which was erupting like the fountain in Logan Circle. My ear was falling off. "You're going to the hospital," the cop announced happily, as if I were going to the circus.

Before I got into the ambulance, I insisted on climbing back down into the ravine to get my books out of the back of the Volkswagen. Coffin and Roelofs's *The Major Poets* was on the floor of the backseat. There was a little blood on the cover. Mr. Prescott was having us read "O Rose, Thou Art Sick!" for the next day.

I'd arrived at early adolescence having inherited my mother's buoyant optimism. In spite of the nearly constant sense that I was the wrong person, I was filled with a simultaneous hopefulness and cheer that most people found annoying. My mother had been levitated her whole life by a corklike faith in the goodness of people, by the belief that things would somehow "work themselves out."

This legacy of cheerful wit became the thing that sustained me and also, at times, burdened me. In spite of a sense of ever-present exasperation with my own body, I was rarely depressed and reacted to my awful life with joy, with humor, and with light. (In the nineties, when various critics reviewed some of my early novels, they would question how it was possible that the characters in these books could react to the conflicts in their lives with comedy. I never understood this comment. What else should they use to express their sorrow? Tears?)

Wearing my sister's and mother's clothes wasn't exactly satisfying, though. For one thing, it was creepy, sneaking around. Even *I* knew it was creepy. For another, the thing that I felt wasn't satisfied by clothes. Dressing up was a start; it enabled me to use the only external cues I had to mirror how I felt inside. Yet it was the thing inside that I wanted to express. I was filled with a yearning that could not be quelled by rayon.

Still, the nights when I was alone in the Coffin House, "being female," were always a great relief for me. For a few short hours, I felt as if I didn't have to put on a show, constantly imitating the person I would be if I'd actually wound up well-adjusted.

It was nearly Christmas. Light snow was falling, dusting the rhododendrons and azaleas that lined the driveway. A few minutes after my parents and sister were gone, I put on a peasant skirt and a paisley top. The sad thing was how normal I looked in this. As a boy I looked thin and startled. As a girl I just looked like a hippie.

After a while, I got back into my boy clothes and went downstairs into the kitchen. I saw my distorted reflection in the toaster. I had shoulder-length blond hair and glasses that were shaped like television tubes. I checked the clock. Ten of eight. Onion wasn't expected till late, if she came at all.

The encounter with Onion had been arranged by a guy I knew in my rock band, which was called the Comfortable Chair. I played a Vox Continental, a classic draw-bar organ with the black keys white and the white keys black and the whole business supported by two chrome Z-shaped legs. The Comfortable Chair—which was a name the guitarist had stolen off a television show—didn't actually play anywhere other than people's basements. But it was great fun being in a band, making all that noise. We played songs like "Turn on Your Lovelight," "Hard to Handle," and, occasionally, "Stairway to Heaven," if the extremely cool flute player deigned to join us.

Onion hung out with the band. She went to one of the local public schools, unlike most of the girls I knew, who went to Shipley or Baldwin or Agnes Irwin—the right-wing finishing schools of the Main Line. I was coached, briefly, for my upcoming encounter by my worldly friend Zero, who went to the same private school I did, the all-male Haverford School. Zero and I had been best friends since the seventh grade, when we were both sent to summer school. Each of us had learned the "new math" at our public schools, and now that we were going to Haverford we had to unlearn this and master the old math. My problem, of course, was that I didn't *like* math. The Haverford School decided to solve this problem by making us do five hundred math problems each day—literally, *five hundred*. We started at eight in the morning and kept going until five. I guess their thinking was, *This'll* make 'em like math! They called it *immersion learning.*

Another thing I'd learned at the Haverford School was how to tie a hangman's noose. It was fun; we all loved doing it. The window shades that fell from the blinds were all tied in hangman's nooses, dozens of them across the huge study hall. The master, a sour man named Mr. Deacon, had to come around and untie them all, one by one.

It was like going to high school in a Charles Dickens novel. Haverford's Upper School was a decaying haunted house, with desks from the 1930s and a headmaster from some era even earlier than that. In the corner of each of our desks was a hole for an inkwell. My classmates in the class of 1976 included Mike Mayock, who later played for the New York Giants, and John DiIulio, who went on to direct George W. Bush's Faith-Based Initiative. And then there was Zero, and me, and another guy we just called "Doober."

I didn't know a lot about Onion. She was very blond, and she was missing one finger, the pinkie on her left hand. And she did boys. She had boys the way some people had a paper route.

I got out a tall glass and filled it with ice and Hi-C orange punch. Then I poured in about half a cup of Virginia Gentlemen, which was my father's brand of bourbon. I mixed this around with a swizzle stick my parents had got at some hotel. I raised the glass to my lips and tasted the drink. It was sweet.

The ice cubes clinked in the glass as I carried my drink through the house. Moments later I was in the rec room, which had been decorated by the Hunts in a kind of Wild West motif. It had wagon wheel chandeliers and zebra-striped paneling and red curtains and no heat. I turned on NBC, and for a moment I imagined myself watching the whole Friday night lineup with Onion: *Sanford & Son*, *Chico & the Man*, *The Rockford Files*, *Police Woman*. I took a sip of the Hi-C and whiskey, shivered, and turned off the set. This wasn't the way I imagined myself.

The way I figured, I'd get Onion a drink, maybe one of these Hi-C things I was having, then we'd sit in my room upstairs and talk. I'd try to show her I was not like the other guys she knew.

Once I had sex I wouldn't keep wanting to be someone else all the time; at least that was my newest theory. I hadn't given up on *Love shall cure you*, either. I still believed that.

I walked up the creaking stairs to the beat-up library. Coals from a fire my father had lit were still glowing in the fireplace. Large sheets of stained wallpaper hung down from the ceiling where a pipe had burst. I got out a book my mother owned called *Art Masterpieces of the World*, looked at some of the great paintings. *Starry Night*. *Sunday Afternoon at the Island of La Grande Jatte*. *Nude Descending a Staircase*. *Self-Portrait with Bandaged Ear*. There was this one called *The Turkish Bath* that I liked. Lots of nude women, sitting around. They all looked very clean.

A car pulled in the driveway and sat there idling for a few moments, then drove off. I wasn't surprised. Mrs. DePalma had told us that the Hunts had had an enormous Christmas party every year since 1958. They were the kind of people who went nuts in December, covering the house from roof to shrub with strings of lights. The Friday before Christmas they always had a wild black-tie party. Every year since we'd moved in (in 1972), strangers had showed up at our door this Friday, sometimes in costume, hoping to attend a party given by people who no longer lived there.

I went back out to the living room. A portrait of my grandfather James Owen Boylan hung over the fireplace. I'm named after him, or at least I was then. I was always a little afraid of that painting and frequently suspected that the eyes followed me around. Even now, twenty-five years later, I often see my grandfather's portrait in my dreams, grinning at me.

I lay down on the couch. You weren't supposed to sit on the furniture in the living room, which was kind of odd considering the fact that the ceiling was collapsing. I got out my parents' wedding album and looked for a while at the pictures. It was April 1956, and my grandmother was still with her third husband. My uncle Sean looked pretty sane, too, so you knew it was a while back.

The phone rang. I picked it up.

"Hello?"

"Hello? Is this Jim Boylan?"

"Yes, this is me," I said. I didn't recognize the voice. "Who's this?"

"It is?" the voice said. There were other voices in the background, laughing. "It's Boylan?"

"Yeah," I said.

"You're a fag, man."

He hung up.

I stood there holding the phone. Somebody somewhere was having a big old time.

I put the phone back in the cradle, picked up my orange Hi-C and bourbon. It wasn't the kind of phone call you wanted to get, actually.

Grampa looked at me from the wall. *That kid on the phone,* Grampa said. *He's right.*

I walked across the room and sat at the piano. I put the glass on the windowsill behind me.

"Good evening, everyone," I said. "It's great to be back here in Philadelphia."

I blew into a microphone that wasn't there. "Check, check," I said. "One two. One two. Check."

I looked out into the audience. "Well, all right," I said. "I said, yeah."

The audience said, *Yeah.*

Then I started playing "Mrs. Robinson" in the key of G. I did a long crazy jam before I went into the main riff. When the audience recognized what tune I was playing, they went nuts. People in the front row were standing on their chairs.

We'd like to know a little bit about you for our files. . . . Thank you. Thank you very much.

There was a screeching of tires in the front driveway, a car engine revving, then falling silent. Footsteps came up the stone stairs. The doorbell rang. A moment after that, the knocker that no one used was swinging.

I got up and opened the door. A girl with nine fingers was standing there.

"You're Boylan?" she said. "The piano player?"

"Onion," I said.

"You got it," she said. She fell forward across the threshold. Onion was very drunk. I could see that her car was parked half off the driveway. One of my mother's azaleas lay crushed beneath the tires of her Camaro. Snow had dusted the front porch.

"I'm glad you're here," I said. My heart was pounding in my shirt. "I didn't know if you were going to make it."

"Sure I'm going to make it," Onion said, annoyed. "Why wouldn't I make it?" She took off her orange down coat and dropped it onto a chair in the living room. She sized things up. "Jeez what a place you got here. Gives me the fuckin' creeps."

"It's creepy all right," I said. I was still looking at her. She had long blond hair. Onion was wearing blue jeans and a tight black top. It was definitely something I'd have looked good in.

"Was that you playing?" she said. She was looking at the piano.

"Yeah," I said. The fruit juice and bourbon was sitting on the windowsill.

"Sounded good," she said. "It's good to play something."

Onion walked over to the piano and let her hands fall on the keys with a tremendous clang. The noise was startling, and I was annoyed at her careless disregard for the instrument.

"Ha ha ha," said Onion. "What a hoot."

She banged the keys again, letting her fingers skitter randomly up and down the keyboard.

"Can I get you something?" I said, trying to move her away from the piano. "Are you thirsty?"

"Yeah, sure," Onion said. She got up again. "What do you got?"

We walked into my parents' kitchen. "I'm drinking bourbon," I said.

"Whoa," said Onion. "Hard-core." She looked at me as if for the first time. There was more light in the kitchen. "Hey, you're cute," she said. "You look like my sister."

I thought about this for a while. "Thank you," I said.

"You know how to make a daiquiri?" Onion said. "Here, I'll do it."

A moment later she was getting out bottles of rum and gin and pouring them into the blender. She opened the refrigerator, got out some strawberries and a banana. She got ice out of the freezer. It didn't take her long to set things in motion.

While her drink was grinding away in the blender, Onion got out a package of Newports, stuck one on her lip Jerry Lewis style, and lit it. She did a French inhale. She held the pack toward me and said, "Smoke?"

I took a cigarette from her. After I got it lit she blew smoke in my face, then laughed.

"Hey," I said.

"Well, what do you think, Boylan, you want to do it?"

"I don't know," I said. I couldn't believe she'd just come out and say it. I figured she was talking about something else.

Onion leaned toward me, clamped her mouth down on mine, and injected her tongue into my throat. She sucked on me like a vacuum cleaner. With one hand she reached out and grabbed one of mine and placed it on her breast. It was soft.

"Well, all right," Onion said, leaning back. She took another drag off her cigarette. "*Now* do you want to do it?"

"Okay," I said. "Okay."

She lifted the pitcher off the blender and poured it into one of my mother's Waterford tumblers. "Cool," she said. "Then let's go. Lead on."

We clomped up the back stairs. As we ascended she said, "I heard you're a nice guy, Boylan."

"I guess," I said.

"Nice but shy." She paused, out of breath, dizzy. "Man, you got a lot of stairs in this house."

I couldn't think of anything to say, so I just nodded and blew smoke that I had not inhaled toward her. She smiled at something that seemed to be known only to herself.

We reached the top of the stairs and passed the door of the room that had the fingernail scratches on the other side. Earlier in the evening I'd sat on a chair in that room, wearing a bra and reading *Lord of the Rings*.

"Yeah, I'm shy, I guess," I said finally.

As we walked down the second-floor hallway, she slowed again. Onion was scraping against one wall.

"You okay?" I said.

"Sure I'm okay," she said. "Long day, that's all. You're my last stop." She drank her daiquiri. I started up the steps to the third floor.

"Oh man, not more stairs," Onion said. She looked into my parents' room. "What about in here?"

I thought about it.

"Okay," I said. "This is a better room anyway. Mine doesn't have any wallpaper right now. Just plaster." I stubbed out my cigarette on an ashtray on my mother's bureau.

"Whoo-hoo," Onion said, sitting on the far side of the bed. She put her drink on a table, set her cigarette in an ashtray, and pulled her top off over her head. The straps of her bra traversed her broad, tanned back.

I sat on my side of the bed and took off all my clothes except for my socks because it was cold. I got under the covers. Onion stood to take off her jeans. She took a diaphragm case out of her purse and put it on my parents' bedside table, next to a tube of Ortho jelly—a tube, I noticed, that was rolled neatly from the bottom like a tube of toothpaste.

I saw Onion from the back, looking at her lovely round buttocks, her smooth shoulders, the hair falling down her spine. She picked up her daiquiri and downed the whole thing in a single shot. Then she turned to me and lay down upon the sheets.

On her right shoulder was a blue-and-green bruise the size of a man's fist. I stared at it.

"Jeez," I said. "How'd you get that?"

"Never you mind," Onion said. She looked over at a picture of my father that stood upon my mother's bureau and said, "Some asshole." For a moment I thought she meant my dad.

She took a final drag off her cigarette, then stubbed it out in the ashtray. "Okay," she said then. "It's clobberin' time."

She lowered her face onto my own again. I felt her fingers trace my ribs. Onion was forceful. It was a little scary, being swept along by her, like standing in some very strong gale.

Her fingernails scratched softly down the front of my bony chest. The hand that was missing the pinkie clasped me like a golf club. "Whoo-hoo," she said. "That's the way."

She paused for a moment, looked at me. "So what do you think?" she said. "Am I pretty?"

I was still thinking about the bruise she had, was trying not to look at it. "Yes," I said. "You're pretty."

"Whoo-hoo," she said, and kissed me again. This is great, I thought. So far, sex was turning out to be pretty interesting. I *definitely* wasn't going to keep wanting to be a girl after this!

I guess this too was *immersion learning*.

"Whups," Onion said, pausing.

"You okay?" I said.

"Yeah, just give me a second." She let go of me, sat up in the bed. Her breasts lay there before me, veined and amazing. The nipples were a soft pink. Her hair fell over one shoulder. For a moment I wished that Onion were a mirror instead of a human. It was too bad.

"I could really fall in love with you," I said in a dreamlike voice. Onion wasn't listening. "Are you all right?" I said.

"Yeah, I'm fine. You got a bathroom around here?" she said. "I'm just a little woozy."

"Woozy?" I said. "Yeah. Right in the hallway."

"Okay," Onion said. "I'll be right back, okay?"

I saw the nude girl walk out of my parents' bedroom and heard her going into the bathroom. I lay there alone for a moment, filled with wonder. A moment later I heard the sound of Onion puking.

"Hey," I said. "Are you okay?"

It happened again.

"Onion?"

I waited for what seemed like a while. All was silent. Then, maybe ten minutes after she'd first excused herself, I heard a soft clunk. The sound of a body hitting the floor.

"Onion?" I said. I went into the bathroom and opened the door. She was lying on the floor. There was puke all around her.

"Oh man," I said. "Shit."

I tried shaking her, but all she did was moan once, then nothing. She was breathing heavily. The smell of liquor rose from her like a vapor.

I got some washcloths and got most of the puke off her, then wiped the floor. I tried to wake her up again. "Oh man," she mumbled. "I don't feel good."

She couldn't just stay there on the floor, so I picked her up in my arms and carried her up the stairs to one of the guest rooms. I put her in an old bed that Gammie and Mrs. Watson slept in when they visited and covered her with a quilt. Onion looked very peaceful there.

Then I went back to the bathroom and collected all the washcloths and towels, carried them to the laundry room, and put them in the washer. After this I walked into my parents' bedroom, made the bed, and picked up my clothes off the floor.

I wasn't sure what to do next. About all I could think of was trying to make up a good story for my parents to believe, once they got home. I could say Onion was a friend of a friend, which was the truth. I could say I didn't know her very well, also the truth. I could say she'd had too much to drink. And she had called from some party down the street given by these people I did not know and said she needed a safe place to sleep it off because it was dangerous for her to drive like this. I thought about this story for a while, and it seemed pretty good. Not airtight, but pretty good. As long as Onion didn't wake up suddenly and start talking, they might go for it.

It was at this point that I realized I still had the rest of the night free. My mother's optimism lifted me up. It wasn't too late to make the best of things.

I went back to my parents' bedroom. Onion's bra and T-shirt were lying right there. I sat on the bed and picked up the bra. I held it in my lap for a moment. It was warm, the bra.

I closed my eyes, thinking. If you have breasts, I thought, they go right in here. If you're a girl, you wear one of these and you probably don't even think about it, it's just what you do.

I thought about it for a while. I definitely liked Onion's taste in clothes better than my mother's and sister's. It would have been a great relief to have been a person in life whose body fitted into them. There was no reason I shouldn't put on her stuff—heck, she was passed out upstairs. But I didn't do it. It would be too creepy and, quite frankly, a little bit rude. I owed Onion a certain respect, even if she had passed out naked in her own puke in my parents' bathroom, and it wouldn't be polite to wear her shirt. So I picked up the bra and the T-shirt and carried them up to the room where Onion was lying unconscious and laid them on the bed next to her. I stroked her hair.

"You're going to be okay," I whispered to her, then kissed her lightly on the cheek.

I went back downstairs and sat at the piano bench. The second half of my Hi-C and bourbon was still there, the ice cubes melted. "Good evening," I said. "It's great to be back in Philadelphia."

I started up with "Mrs. Robinson" again, seeing as how I hadn't even got to the chorus last time. I was still in the key of G, back in a crazy jam. I was a sixteen-year-old transsexual, high on fruit juice, and I had a naked girl passed out in my grandmother's bed upstairs. Life is a mysterious thing, was my conclusion.

The doorbell rang, and I stopped playing. "Jesus," I said. "It's like Grand Central Station in here." I finished the bourbon in one gulp, went to the front door, and opened it wide.

A guy in a Santa Claus suit was standing there. He held a bottle of Jack Daniel's in one hand.

"Merry Christmas," he said.

"Merry Christmas," I said.

"Are you St. George?" he asked.

This question wasn't quite as insane as it might sound at first, because St. George was actually the name of one of the Hunt boys. I wasn't him, though.

"Are you Bill?"

Another Hunt sibling. I shook my head.

"Well," Santa said. "Are you Hoops?"

Hoops Hunt was the oldest of the boys. His real name was Al, and Al Hunt later grew up to be a famous journalist with *The Wall Street Journal*. He's also a regular on *Capital Gang*, one of those shows where reporters shout at one another. He's married to Judy Woodruff, the CNN newswoman.

"Well, I don't know," Santa said, annoyed. "Who in hell are you, then?"

"I'm Jim Boylan," I said. "We live here now. The Hunts moved. Dr. Hunt died."

"Oh," Santa said. He felt stupid now. "I been away. Vietnam and all."

I nodded.

"Well, jeez," I said. "You want to come in?"

"Maybe just for a second," Santa said. "It's freezin' out here."

He stomped across the threshold. Cold rain was falling on Onion's car. "You want something?" I said. "A drink, or whatever?"

"Nah," Santa said. "I just figured I'd stop in. They been having this party for twenty-five years."

"I know," I said.

"I thought about this party a lot when I was over in 'Nam and all. Thought about it a lot."

It suddenly seemed very sad to me, this guy in his rented Santa suit, thinking about coming home all those years for the Hunts' party and finding only me.

"So you were in Vietnam?" I said.

"Yeah." Santa sat on a chair by the fire, warmed himself. "Marines. Since Tet." He shook his head as if the words should mean something to me. "After I got back I lived in California for a while. Man, some wild times out *there*!"

A small puddle formed around Santa's boots.

"Should have called first, I guess," he said.

He looked around, examining our furniture, which didn't really fill the place. His eyes fell on the piano.

"Was that you playing before?" he said.

"Yeah."

"What was that? Sounded all right."

"Just like a jam," I said. I thought about it for a second. "You want me to play you something?"

"Whatever," Santa said. He held the bottle of Jack Daniel's toward me. "You want some of this, kid?"

"No thanks," I said. I went back to the piano and sat on the bench. "You want to hear anything in particular?"

"Nah," Santa said.

For the third time that night, my hands fell on the keys. I started playing "Mrs. Robinson," a crazy jam in the key of G. Santa put his feet up on the ottoman and drank some Jack Daniel's. He looked up at the oil painting of my grandfather.

I sang. *Look around you. All you see / Are sympathetic eyes. / Stroll around the grounds until you feel at home. . . .*

It took me about twenty minutes to get done with all three verses and the chorus and three more long jams. Finally I finished.

Santa applauded. *Thank you, Philadelphia. Thank you all very much.*

"Sounds all right, kid," Santa said. He stood up, put the cap back on his whiskey. "Well, I gotta go. Merry Christmas and all."

"Merry Christmas," I said.

Santa went outside into the rain. I stood in the front hallway until I heard his car drive off.

Upstairs, the hallway was full of light. Onion was up. It sounded as if she were in the bathroom.

"Onion?" I said, and opened the door.

She was sitting on a green stool, drying herself with a bluish white towel. She'd been taking a bath, of all things. One hand was raised in the air. I could just see the vague shadow of her pink nipple at the upper perimeter of the towel. An orange robe belonging to my grandmother was draped across the green stool. The room was thick with the steam from her bath, giving everything a shimmering, twinkling quality. The old blue tub stood behind her, still full of water. The crazy wallpaper of the Hunts surrounded her—rippling patterns of pink and purple and white.

Onion's hair was tied up in a bun over her head. She looked perfect, like a painting by Degas. Sitting there, drying herself, one arm raised, she looked immortal, the embodiment of what Goethe called the "feminine eternal." This vision of her filled me with a profound, aching sorrow.

The raised arm dropped to her side, and she looked up at me. "Hey," she said.

"Hey," I said.

"Like, what happened?"

She seemed embarrassed.

"You passed out," I said.

She shook her head. "I don't know what's wrong with me." She turned toward me, and I saw the blue bruise on her upper arm again. "Whoo-hoo. Maybe I'm fuckin' insane."

"You're all right," I said.

"I don't know about that," Onion said. She gathered up her clothes, and I watched her put them on. "Did you, like, carry me up here?"

I nodded. "Whoo-hoo," she said. "Weird."

We stood in the pink-and-purple room for a long time, not saying anything. She was still wet.

Onion looked at her watch and shrugged. "Oughta get going, I guess," she said.

"You have to go?" I said as if I didn't know the answer.

"Yeah," she said. "Listen, I'm sorry, you know? Maybe some other time we could . . ." Her voice trailed off.

"Yeah, that would be good," I said. "Sometime."

I didn't follow her downstairs but stayed in that bathroom, looking out the window at the snow, now turning to rain. I heard the door open downstairs, then I saw her rush out into the night. She got her car off the azaleas, went down the driveway, and turned onto Sugartown Road.

I made the bed in the guest room, hung up the orange robe. Last, I let the water out of the tub. It made a sucking sound.

Then the house was quiet. I walked out into the hallway, wanting to do something, to yell or punch out a wall or weep or smash up the car.

I went up to the door of the locked room where my mother's and sister's dresses hung in their garment bags. I slid back the dead bolt and walked in. There was only one light, and it was way across the room. I had to walk through the dark to get at it, a single lightbulb hanging from a wire in the ceiling.

The swinging light shone on the shunned room, shadows moving across the piles of boxes, a safe, an American flag. I looked at the garment bags full of dresses, but I didn't open them. There was the smell of mothballs.

On one wall, written on the bare plaster, were the words *Al Hunt. I'm sick. Wednesday, October 3, 1956.*

I stood in there for a while. It was funny to be in the place where I usually feared the ghosts would be. Shit, man, I thought. Maybe *I'm* the ghost.

My parents got home an hour later. I was already in bed. They stomped up the creaking stairs.

I should have just let them go to sleep, but my conscience was too guilty about the evening. I had to know if they suspected anything.

"Hi, honey," my mother said as I came down the stairs. I went into my parents' bedroom. My father was already brushing his teeth. "Did you have an all right time?"

"Yeah," I said. "Watched television."

"Good." She sat on her bed and took off her jewelry. "We had a lovely time with the McGatts. You remember John McGatt, honey? He used to bring you Silly Putty when you were little?"

"I remember."

My mother shook her head. "It seems just like yesterday, when you were my baby boy."

"Mom," I said, annoyed.

She took off her watch, put it on her table. There next to the alarm clock was Onion's diaphragm, sitting in its soft brown case. She hadn't seen it yet, but Mom would see a lot of things in the time that was coming.

The Failures of Milk

The phone rang in the Coffin House. "Eleanor, you'll never believe what happened," Aunt Nora said. "I just died."

My mother checked the clock. It was late. "Nora," she said, "what are you talking about?"

"I know what you're thinking," Aunt Nora continued. "But listen. I'm dead now." She paused. "Don't worry. It doesn't hurt. That's what I wanted to tell you."

"Nora," my mother said, "you're not making any sense. Of course you're not dead. You're on the phone."

My aunt made an irritated sound. "You never take me seriously!"

"Nora, are you listening to me? I want you to put the phone down. I want you to go get yourself a glass of milk. Will you do that for me, please?"

"You want I should get some milk?"

"Put the phone down and get yourself a glass of milk. When you have the milk, come back to the phone."

My aunt put the phone down begrudgingly. My mother, alone in her big house, sat on the edge of the bed and listened to the sounds of Nora moving around her apartment. Whatever it was she was doing, it was clear she hadn't traveled in a straight line to the refrigerator. My mother heard furniture moving, a toilet flushing. Aunt Nora was singing something to herself.

About ten minutes later, she came back to the phone.

"I have the milk, Eleanor. I'm still dead."

"Did you drink it?" my mother asked. "Did you drink the milk?"

"I drank it. It tastes like milk." There was a pause. "Being dead doesn't change the way things taste."

"Nora," my mother said, "I want you to stop. I want you to drink the milk and go to sleep. I'll call you tomorrow morning."

"Why should I need sleep?" Aunt Nora said. "I'm dead. I'm not tired. I've got all this energy! Maybe I'll make the children sock puppets."

Aunt Nora was a seamstress. She worked at Lillian's Bridal Salon in Newtown Square, which was just down the street from the place where I took piano lessons in the mid-1960s. After my lesson I would often walk over to the salon and watch her sewing veils.

Aunt Nora was the one person with whom I had thought my secret would be secure. Like me, she seemed to live in a world of her own, although the reasons for her distance from the world were unimaginable to me, at least they were when I was a child.

I would go to her apartment sometimes and sit on the floor in front of her grandmother's clock, eating the cookies she baked (shaped like Scottie dogs, or stars, or running men), and think about telling her. I formed the sentences in my mind.

Aunt Nora, what would you do if I told you I didn't feel like myself, but like someone else? Well, not someone else, exactly, but myself, me as a girl. It's the person everyone thinks I am that isn't real.

What would she have said? Would she have put me on a stool and have me raise my arms into the air and take my soundings with a tape measure? Would she have taught me to sew, how to make darts and pleats? Would she have shown me how to curl my hair, how to make cookies shaped like dogs, how to move through the world as a woman bearing an inconceivable grief? *It's all right, Jennifer. You just try not to think about it.*

But I remained silent. I knew what she'd say.

I sat on the floor and listened to her clock chime.

Sometimes Nora showed me the dances she was learning in her dance class. She'd put on a crazy record from the 1940s called "Old Vienna," which featured an accordion band and a narrator describing a landslide of falling strudel. To this music, Nora did the tango. Sometimes I danced with her.

"By order of zee emperor, zere will be no strudel eating on zee mountain today. . . ."

Nora's life had changed when she married my uncle Francis at age thirty-five. It was as if, after all her long years alone, the sun had finally decided to shine in her life.

There are black-and-white pictures taken of her during that time, in which she stands by the sea with Francis, holding a spotted beach ball. She wears an expression I never saw firsthand—a look of complete contentment and joy, the look of a woman who finally finds that she does exist after a lifetime of believing that she does not.

Uncle Francis died less than a year after they were married, of a brain hemorrhage.

Soon Aunt Nora was working as a seamstress again, sewing together white dresses for other women to wear at other weddings.

When my mother went to her apartment the morning after she'd received the phone call in which Nora explained that she was dead, she opened the door to find the place empty. Aunt Nora had vanished without a trace.

My mother called around, checked a few hospitals. It didn't take long to find her. Apparently Nora had the wherewithal, at some point, to call 911 and explain the situation.

It was midafternoon before my mother finally arrived at Bryn Mawr Hospital. There was Nora, tied to the bed. She broke down in tears when she saw her sister.

"Eleanor, I'm so sorry," she said. "The milk didn't work."

Come Down in Time

(Spring 1979)

I looked up at the top of the piano. The bartender placed another Guinness at the end of the long row of beers that stood there. There were seven pints on top of the piano now, plus the one on the music stand.

Outside, on Oxford Street, rain was hammering down. Everyone in the pub was drenched, and the pub *smelled* like wet English people. It was a Saturday night at Mr. Pitiful's, where I had a job playing piano in the corner. Sometimes my friend Johnny Cooper from Manchester played tenor sax with me, but he wasn't there that night. Johnny was a student at the London School of Economics, which was right across the street from where I lived in Marylebone, just off Fitzroy Square.

I'd been in London for four months now, studying literature. One day, I'd left my flat with an ad in my pocket that I'd torn out of the back pages of *TimeOut* magazine. "British Center for Gender Study," read the ad. "Support and Information Services."

It was a long walk down to Soho, but it was pleasant enough to follow Tottenham Court Road down toward Oxford Street and Piccadilly. The British Center for Gender Study was just off Piccadilly Circus. They had counselors you could talk to.

I got to the British Center for Gender Study, which had no sign on it. I feared it might just be some guy's apartment, some hairy beast in a sleeveless T-shirt who would answer the doorbell and say, *Okay, c'mon in, dude. You can call me Tinky.*

I stood outside the British Center for Gender Study for a long time.

I didn't go in.

The next night, in Mr. Pitiful's, I was playing the blues. It was raining hard. There was something maniacal about the way I was playing. During a break, one fellow came and sat next to me and said, "Are you all right, Yank?" and I said I was fine. Then I played "Bye Bye Blackbird."

Mr. Pitiful's—which was really called the Plough—was a dark cave, with a black tin ceiling and faded red velvet booths and a gas fire that always seemed to be on the edge of flickering out. It was full of old men who sat there not talking to one another, smoking. They liked hearing me play the old songs, though, and when I particularly pleased one old fart or another, he'd buy me a pint and have the bartender place it on top of the piano.

I was pretty good at playing rinky-tink. "Me and My Shadow," "Sugar Blues," "Nobody Loves You When You're Down and Out." Occasionally I'd throw in something cheerful like "Here Comes the Sun," but this was almost never a good idea. The denizens of the Plough didn't come in there to get cheered up.

As I played that night, watching the pints march down the top of the upright, I was thinking about a girl. I'd met her at a party the night before, a few hours after I'd walked toward, and failed to enter, the British Center for Gender Study.

We'd met at a party, locked eyes across the room, and gravitated toward each other. Simultaneously we'd said, "Who *are* you?"

She was Donna Fierenza, a student at Brown, just in London for the weekend to see her brother, Bobby. I liked him. One good thing about Bobby Fierenza was that he had a lot of chest hair. He also had a good laugh and played electric bass.

Donna wanted to be an animator. "I'm not just talking cartoons, Boylan," she said. I told her I was a writer, which was nice. Saying it almost made it true.

She grabbed a bottle of Johnson's baby powder that was sitting on the table. "Yuh ever do this?" She shook it into her hair, then my hair, turning it gray. "This is what we'll look like when we're old," she said.

As it turns out, she was wrong. I don't look anything like that now, although I probably would if I didn't go the salon every couple of months and pay the extra hundred dollars for foil highlights.

Donna was from Massachusetts and had a shocking accent, which was working-class North Shore Italian: "My fatha wuhks in GLAHW-stah." She had curly dark red hair. She had four horizontal creases in her brow that became deeper when she laughed, which was frequently.

"I want to see you again, Boylan. What are you doing tomorrow?"

It was Friday night. She was flying back to America on Sunday.

"You want to meet at the Great Portland Street tube stop at one?"

The hell yes.

Which was where I was at one o'clock the next day, holding a bouquet of roses.

I was still there at one-fifteen.

And one-thirty and one-forty-five.

At two o'clock I threw the flowers in a trash can and walked back toward Fitzroy Square, passing by the London Foot Hospital, singing an Elton John song to myself, an old tearjerker about being stood up called "Come Down in Time": *There are women and women and some hold you tight / While some leave you counting the stars in the night. . . .*

Whatever it was Donna Fierenza had seen in me by night, she had lost sight of it by morning.

That night I played "Come Down in Time" at Mr. Pitiful's. I didn't sing it, though. They didn't like it when I sang in the pub. It was too much like someone talking.

I got paid twenty pounds out of the till when I finished, and I walked in my long dark coat out into the rain.

Then I stopped in the middle of the street and thought. Donna had said that she was going to a concert that night down at the Marquee Club in Soho. That was why we'd made the afternoon date instead of an evening one. If I went to the Marquee Club right now, there might be time to find her. I hadn't waited long enough this afternoon—that was it! Surely she'd showed up after two, crushed that I wasn't there.

I turned around and started walking toward the Bakerloo line. Then I stopped.

I was a woman, or felt like one. What kind of relationship did I expect to have with Donna, even if I found her at the Marquee? Women seemed to detect some sort of inner struggle in me anyway, some sort of feminine streak that kept them from getting too close. Surely Donna had sent me a clear enough signal by standing me up.

I turned around again and started walking home. Then I stopped. The waves crashed against the boardwalk in Surf City. *Maybe you could be cured by love.*

I ran through the rain to the Bakerloo line.

It would have been interesting to watch me, from some high window. A young man in the pouring rain—I *think* that's a man—with a long tattered coat, long blond hair, walking first one direction, then stopping, then walking the other, then turning around again, over and over, spinning like a top. Then, finally, running off in a new direction. I hoped that it was the right one.

The Marquee Club was on Wardour Street. The Stones and the Who and all those bands had played there a long time ago. At the time, I was reading *The Two Towers*, and to me, Wardour sounded like Mordor. I was every bit as scared heading down there as if I'd been heading with Frodo and Sam for the Cracks of Doom. And I was out of *lembas*, the elven way-bread. Actually, *lembas* wasn't the only thing I was out of.

I entered the club at about eleven. It was a punk club now, and a sign on the wall said FUCK HIPPIES. The crowd was breaking up, and the lights were on. People were heading toward the exits. Alone with my long hair and John Lennon glasses, I walked against the tide of pink spikes and blue mohawks. Somebody hit me in the shoulder and said, "Will ye fuck off, ye gay queer?" He pronounced "gay" so that it would rhyme with "hi," at least it would in America.

There, up near the front of the stage, was Donna's brother, Bobby. He was wearing a Hawaiian shirt that was buttoned near his navel. "Hey, man," I said to him. "Is Donna here?"

He looked at me suspiciously. It *was* his sister we were talking about. On stage they were taking apart the drums. A guy in a torn white T-shirt yelled at the crowd: "Everybody get the fuck *out!*"

"I think she left," said Bobby.

I headed toward the exit. Which was when I felt a finger on my shoulder and turned around.

It was Donna.

"I got lost," she said, blushing. "I got to the station at two-fifteen and you weren't there. I bought some peanuts from the *vendah* and went across the street and sat on the steps a some church and ate them. I just sat there, tryin' not to cry."

"Don't cry," I said. "Do you want to get out of here?"

"Yep," she said, and we put our arms around each other and walked out onto the street.

It had stopped raining, and now a warm wind had turned all that rain to mist. The steam was rising up from the cobbles and dissipating around our knees. We began walking through the deserted streets of London. I didn't know where we were going, and neither did she. It didn't matter.

"How was the concert?"

"Uh man, it sucked! Fuckin' noise, and I'm not kidding. Everybody loved it. Me, I just kept thinking how I'd fucked up with you, Boylan. I thought I'd nevah see you again."

After a while we came to a restaurant I knew, the Three Lanterns. We had somehow snaked our way through the mist back to Marylebone and were by now only a few blocks from my apartment, where my bonehead roommates were probably awake and drinking Pepsi.

Donna and I went into the Three Lanterns. The place was deserted. A cat crawled around our legs, then sat in the window. It was incredibly quiet. The waitress, who knew me, came to the table and said, "The usual, sir?"

I nodded. "The usual" was a bottle of retsina. The waitress brought us the bottle with two glasses, and we drank the whole thing as we talked and didn't talk. At one point, Donna leaned over the table and kissed me. We kissed for a long time.

Then we left the Three Lanterns. We walked up the street toward the British Telecom Tower, then up the stairs of my apartment on Maple Street.

Where my bonehead roommates were sitting around drinking Pepsi. There was Frank, who wanted to become a composer of whimsical music, like Leroy Anderson. He played Leroy Anderson music at every hour of the day—"The Syncopated Clock," "The Typewriter," even the one with the mewing cat. And there was Lou Muggins, a computer nerd, who had curved shoulders and a sad little mustache and thick aviator glasses. He liked to make the noise *Haink* in response to things. Like "Lou Muggins, there's a spaceship outside!"

Lou Muggins: "Haink!"

Or "Lou Muggins, there's a man here to give you a check for two million dollars!"

Lou Muggins: "Haink!"

We entered the apartment and I simply said to the guys, "I need the double for a while." At that time, we had a double room and a single. I was in the double with Mr. Syncopated Clock. Frank agreed to stay out in the kitchen for a while. Lou Muggins didn't offer to let me use his single room. He just said, "Haink!"

Donna and I went into the bedroom, and there we talked and we kissed and we made out and did not have sex. I'm not sure if she was expecting for us to have sex then and there, but it didn't really occur to me that that's what was supposed to happen. I was a twenty-year-old virgin—unsure, awkward, stupid, transgender. Still, my life had changed. I didn't want to be a woman so much. I wanted to be in love with Donna Fierenza.

At two in the morning, Frank started making noises outside the door about how he wanted to go to sleep ("I'm tired, Boylan, I mean it!"), so Donna and I left the apartment and walked out into the night again. Now thick fog was everywhere, and the streets were deserted. In the morning of the next day, she was flying back to America.

A taxi's lights stabbed through the fog. The cabbie pulled over and we embraced again and kissed, and she said, "I fell in love in London." I gave the man £10 and said, "Take her to Elephant and Castle," and then she put her hand on her side of the rain-streaked window, and I put my hand on top of hers on my side of the rain-streaked window, and then the cab pulled out into the night, and I stood there on the corner and watched the red taillights disappear into the fog.

I didn't feel like going home yet. I looked around at the dark buildings of London surrounding me. There was the Great Portland Street tube stop. A soft chime came from the bell tower of the church across the street, where earlier in the day Donna said she'd sat on the steps and eaten peanuts.

In the months to come, Donna and I would write dozens of letters to each other. I kept hers in my pocket as I walked across Europe with my ridiculous backpack—through Spain, through France, through Italy and Germany, through Belgium and Holland and Scotland and Ireland. I would lose my virginity—barely—to her in my own teenage bedroom that summer, in the Coffin House. I would travel by Greyhound bus to visit her on the North Shore, where we drank wine and made out on the beach under a full moon. She would talk to me on the phone about her former and then occasional and then "other" boyfriend, Neal, about how Neal didn't understand her, about how Neal didn't believe in her, about how Neal's favorite expression was "and shit," to mean "et cetera," as in, "I really love you, and shit."

In the fall I hitchhiked to Brown from Wesleyan, and there we broke up. I still had slept with her—barely—only the one time. I think Neal began to have a pretty good sense that I was no threat. Still, as Joyce wrote in "The Dead," "I was great with her at that time."

In Providence, Donna showed me the grave of H. P. Lovecraft (with the epitaph I AM PROVIDENCE), and there she said, "I don't think I want to be boyfriend and girlfriend anymore," and I said okay. By then it was all the same to me. I'd already been imagining what I'd look like in her clothes. I left her apartment on a Sunday morning, and I never saw her again. I hitchhiked back to Connecticut and wrote her a poem as I lay in the back of someone's pickup truck, something along the lines of *This is sad but don't forget that night in London, that was really cool.*

As the taillights of her taxi disappeared in the fog that night, I knew I wanted to hold on to the evening just a few moments longer. So I walked toward the church, and as I did, I wondered, had she just made all that up about being an hour and a quarter late this afternoon? Was she ever here at all?

I sat on the steps of the church. It was three in the morning. I was surrounded by fog.

On the steps at my feet were the shells of roasted peanuts.

Monkey Orphanage

(Spring 1982)

I found out about the monkey orphanage while I was doing a story for a magazine about the Skunk Club. Briefly, I was a journalist in my twenties, although not a very good one. I didn't quite grasp the whole concept of accuracy. Whenever I needed a quote, I'd just make one up and attribute it to an "anonymous source." On one occasion, I alleged that something had been stated "according to someone that would know."

Fortunately, *American Bystander* magazine wasn't too concerned with accuracy. Mostly we went for the yuks. The *Bystander*, which was run by former *National Lampoon* editor Brian McConnachie, lasted for a year or two in the early 1980s; it was funded and sustained by a ragtag group of former *Saturday Night Live* performers, some writers from the *Lampoon* and *Second City*, and a handful of cartoonists from *The New Yorker*. The goal was to be "an American *Punch*" or, as we put it then, "a hip *New Yorker*." This was long before Tina Brown and all that.

The other magazine being launched at the time was *Vanity Fair*, which had been defunct for many years and was now being brought back to life by Condé Nast. Over at the *Bystander*, we were skeptical about *Vanity Fair*'s prospects. Oh, sure, like *that'll* last more than a couple of issues.

Being managing editor of the *American Bystander* was my first job out of Wesleyan, and to this day it is the best job I ever had, aside from the fact that I got paid only $600 a month. I rode around on UPS trucks in Manhattan; I had lunch with the *New Yorker* cartoonists; I went bowling with famous comedians. On one particular occasion, I was one of several people who tried to figure out how to float cartoonist Roz Chast across the Gowanus Canal with weather balloons. It would take a lot of balloons, we deduced, but it was doable, at least it was until Roz got wind of the caper and announced, "Listen, I'm *not* doing that."

I lived in a horrific apartment in Spanish Harlem with bad plumbing and bugs and mice. I ate beans. My first roommate was a guy just out of NYU film school named Charlie Kaufman. He was finishing up a movie of his on a giant editing machine he'd rented and kept in a corner of his bedroom. Together Charlie and I put roach poison out for the roaches, mousetraps out for the mice. The mice liked to hang out in our upright piano, one of two pieces of furniture I owned. At night, we could hear their little tails brushing against the strings.

The apartment was on the second floor of an old West Side building, with high ceilings and wood floors. It looked out into the back of the block, where clotheslines were strung from building to building, and German shepherds patrolled the backyards. Downstairs from us was some sort of homosexual dungeon, where in the middle of the night I often awoke to hear the clank of chains from the flat below, one man crying out in orgiastic delight while another sobbed in a voice of almost unimaginable, mortal despair.

Big thick iron bars covered all the windows in the place. One afternoon, I was sitting on the radiator, eating a banana, looking out the window at the dogs and the clotheslines. I put one hand on the bars and with the other held my banana. Now wait, I thought. What do I feel like now?

Later, Charlie Kaufman moved out, and a friend of mine from Wesleyan, John Flyte, moved in. Flyte was a painter, and he sat for hours by the window, painting oils on a canvas.

Toward midnight, sometimes, Flyte and I would walk out into the night and close down various low dives, the two of us sitting at the bar as the tired waitresses put all the other stools in the place upside down on the tables.

Come on, boys, it's closing time.

Occasionally during this period I would go out on dates. Once I asked a girl I met in a bookshop if she'd "like to go and get some pie." She found this hilarious and left the store, still laughing uncontrollably, as I stood there ashamed. I didn't think it was so funny, getting pie. On another occasion I tried asking out the bartender at a nasty bar just down from the Brill Building. I don't know what her real name was, but everyone called her "the Snail." She had a buzz cut and tattoos. I tried the pie business again, and to my surprise, the Snail said sure. "You know, I don't know many guys like you, Boylan," she said.

"Guys like me?" I said.

"Yeah, like non-assholes? You don't see that many."

It was a nice thing for her to say, I had to admit that.

A few nights later, I waited for her as she shut down the bar. When she finally finished, we walked out into the hot New York night to go and get our pie. A man was waiting for her, though, leaning against a brick wall, smoking.

"Where the fuck have *you* been, bitch?" he said to my date.

"Whoops," said the Snail. "Sorry. I gotta run." She walked over to the man and put her arms around him. "It's okay," she said to him softly. "I been busy."

"Who's this guy?" I said, and the Snail looked over at me as if unsure whether or not I existed.

"I'm her boyfriend, fuckwad," the man explained helpfully. "And maybe you'd like a bullet in your ass?"

"Ah," I said.

I took the number one train home.

Then, as throughout my life, I found myself attracted exclusively to women. I never even thought about men romantically; it never even crossed my mind. Still, my relationships with women were decidedly odd. "What's it *like* to have breasts?" I'd ask. "How does it *feel*?" It was a question women found baffling.

"It doesn't feel like anything," one girl told me. "It feels like having an elbow, a nose, a toe. It just is." I couldn't believe she expected me to believe this. Of all the things that I thought being female would feel like, *nothing* wasn't an answer I'd considered.

On another occasion I went out with a woman named Casey. She was tall and beautiful and worked as a fashion photographer. One Saturday we rode the Circle Line around Manhattan, and she took pictures of me, standing by the railing, looking at the Little Red Lighthouse beneath the George Washington Bridge. Casey's long blond hair was held in place with a New York Yankees cap, which she wore backward, catcher style. From underneath, I thought the George Washington Bridge was frightening, the distant roar of traffic high over our heads. I felt as if I'd never been that close to something so large before.

Afterward, Casey and I walked up through Riverside Park, looking at the Hudson. I reached out for her hand and held it. We paused at one place where a large number of people were fishing. A large culvert emptied gray water into the river.

"Who are those people?" I asked Casey. "What are they doing?"

"Those are people fishing," she said, "for the fish that live on shit."

"Ah," I said.

We had dinner at a Chinese restaurant on the West Side. One of our dishes was entitled Two Kinds Meat. It was pretty clear to both of us by then that I wasn't quite in Casey's league. She knew lots of other people in the restaurant, many of them photographers or agents or models. Some of them looked at me, then her, then smiled.

"Listen, Jim," she said finally. "You're sweet. But what's up with you? I mean, really? What's your story?"

"I don't know," I said.

"Liar," she replied.

Once a week I walked up to see Dr. Smegala, my psychiatrist. "Well, it sounds to me," he suggested at the end of one session, "like you're a transsexual."

"Don't say that," I told him. "Please don't say that."

My mother helped me pay for the shrink, which was embarrassing, since I didn't want to tell her why I needed one. I just told her I was sad. "That's okay, honey," said Mom. "You'll cheer up." Still, she gave me the money to see Dr. Smegala. I wasn't sure she'd keep paying for it if I told her what the problem was.

My mother's whole life seemed to be a lesson in the transformative powers of optimism and faith, and this lesson had not been lost on me. Even then, as I stepped over dead junkies en route to Dr. Smegala's, as I killed mice by dropping the *Columbia Encyclopedia* on their heads, as I interviewed the incomprehensibly bitter director of the Skunk Club, I still believed that somehow, everything would work out for the best. I wasn't depressed, most of the time. Instead I felt lucky and blessed, ridiculously grateful to be having such an *adventure*.

The Skunk Club was a support group for people in Manhattan who had skunks as pets. The woman who directed it had black hair, tied back in a tight bun.

"Listen," she said, infuriated by the mere suspicion that I seemed to think the Skunk Club was funny. "People shouldn't *have* skunks! They don't *make* good pets!"

Toward the end of the interview, she mentioned that skunks weren't the only pets that made their owners' lives unpleasant. There was a couple in Pennsylvania, she said, who had a monkey orphanage. They had about a score of monkeys down there, all of whom had been abandoned by their owners.

Turned out, monkeys didn't make good pets, either.

I got the phone number for the monkey orphanage, which was run by a couple whose name was D'Angelo. The husband answered. "Monkeys, sure we got monkeys," he said. "Come down for a visit, we'll show you around." To my surprise, they didn't live all that far from my parents' house. All the time I'd spent growing up in the Philadelphia suburbs, and I didn't know a monkey orphanage was just around the corner. It's possible to live in the same town as a monkey house, I thought, and never even know it.

A week later, I went down to Philly on the Amtrak train, stayed the night in the Coffin House, and drove off the next morning to see the destitute monkeys. Prior to leaving, I'd confirmed all the arrangements with the D'Angelos by phone. Just before I hung up, however, the husband said something peculiar. "Listen. Do you know about me? I've . . ." His voice faltered. "Well, you'll see when you get here."

Whatever it was that had happened to Mr. D'Angelo, it sounded scary. I imagined that he had third-degree burns all over his body. Either that or bite marks from the chimps.

I got to the D'Angelo house just before noon, and a large woman ushered me in. Her name was Samantha. Something about her suggested that she was a professional nurse, the nurse of the husband, I assumed. A woman hired to rub salve into his scars.

Samantha talked about monkeys while I wrote in my notebook. "You know what people think?" Samantha said. "They think they can give a monkey to the zoo." She shook her head sadly. "You know what happens to domesticated monkeys in the zoo? They get *beaten*. They *starve*."

At that moment another woman came in. Her name was Maria, and she had a thick eastern European accent. Maria and Samantha talked about monkeys for quite a while. As it turned out, the orphanage was limited to monkeys—no chimps allowed. "Ve had *vun* cheempanzee," Maria said. "Zen eet suffocate in eets pajamas!" She shook her head sadly. "No more cheemps!"

I was sitting there wondering where Mr. D'Angelo was when

suddenly it hit me. The big woman, Samantha. With the deep voice. And the huge hands. *That* was Mr. D'Angelo.

Okay, I thought. Focus. You're working for the *American Bystander.* You're doing a story about a monkey orphanage. One of the owners of the monkey house has had a sex change, just like you want to have. That shouldn't affect the story. Not much, anyway.

I tried to focus on the questions I'd written down, although these were now not the ones I wanted to ask. What do they eat? *Purina Monkey Chow.* Where do they sleep? *They all sleep in the shed in the backyard, except for Marbles, the vicious one, who sleeps in a cage in the kitchen.* Can they do tricks? *No, mostly they try to get near your face and bite you.*

After a while the D'Angelos took me to a shed out back. There was a fair amount of screaming and swinging from trapezes. Other monkeys sat motionlessly, looking through the bars of their cage, their hands thrust through the bars and folded quietly in front of them. Some of those hands held bananas.

We went back inside and the D'Angelos asked me if I wanted a drink. "Yes," I said very quickly. Samantha opened a bottle of red wine. "You know who I am?" she said after a while.

I nodded. "Sure," I said nonchalantly.

"I wasn't sure if you'd be able to tell."

Oh, I could tell all right.

I talked with Samantha and Maria for a while. It was the first conversation I'd ever had with another transsexual. "It's hard for people to understand," Samantha said, drinking her wine. "But in the end, you are what you are. You fight it for your whole life. Eventually you accept yourself. That's really all there is to it."

I nodded. The longer we talked, the more I began to recognize a certain bravery and dignity in Samantha. Still, she filled me with melancholy. Was this what the future held for me?

Maria seemed to accept everything about her husband with a certain sad grace. She just said, "Crazy vurld," and shook her head. "Crazy, crazy vurld."

Before I left the D'Angelos', I used their bathroom. There on top of the commode was a bottle of prescription pills. *Samantha D'Angelo*, read the label. *Premarin 2.5 mg/day. Conjugated Estrogen*.

I opened the canister and shook a Premarin into my hand. For a moment I thought about swallowing it, just to see what it would feel like. I didn't, though. It would be eighteen years before I held another one in my hand. That time I *did* swallow it.

Twenty years later, the phone rang on a Saturday afternoon. I had spent the morning raking snow off my roof.

"Hello? Jennifer? This is Casey. From New York?"

It took me a moment to recall my date with the woman who had observed the people fishing for the fish that lived on shit. But I remembered her.

"Hi, Casey," I said. "How are you?"

"I was doing a Web search for all the people I used to know? And I found your Web site and read about your transition and saw your photograph. And all I could think was, *whoa*."

"Whoa. Yeah, well, that's what I thought about it myself, actually."

"Anyway, the reason I'm calling? I don't know if you know this, but—did you know, back when we went on those dates, twenty years ago—did you know I was a transsexual, too?"

I held the phone, not saying anything for a while. I saw the Little Red Lighthouse, fallen under the shadow of the great gray bridge.

No, I told her. I hadn't known.

The silence that trans people cloak themselves with had hidden us then, even from each other.

I met Casey again in the spring of 2002. I was in New York visiting some film people, and Casey and I made plans to meet in a bar in midtown. I sat there waiting for her to come through the door. I wondered how she had changed over twenty years. There weren't many other people in the bistro, just some tourists, a woman at the bar, the bartender.

After a long time, the woman at the bar and I looked at each other closely, then smiled. She picked up her drink and came over to my table.

"Hello, Jenny," she said.

"Hello, Casey," I said.

Casey had gained some weight. Her blond hair was now mostly gray.

"You look good," she said. "Whoa."

"So do you," I said.

"Liar," said Casey.

Casey was drinking single-malt Scotch. She finished the Scotch she was drinking and ordered another. I told her the story of the D'Angelos, of my roommate John Flyte, of my encounter with the Snail.

"Tin Pan Alley," Casey said. "I remember that place. They tore it down, though. They razed everything on that block to build the Marriott Marquis."

"Why didn't you tell me?" I asked her. "When we went out on those dates. When I was your friend? Why didn't you tell me you were trans?"

"I knew what you'd do," said Casey, withdrawing into herself. "You'd do what guys always do, you'd run away in horror. You'd tell everyone." She sipped her drink, and tears filled her eyes. "You know how people are."

I didn't say anything for a while. I thought about how beautiful she'd been in her early twenties, how we'd walked into that Chinese restaurant and all the beautiful people had seemed to recognize her. Two Kinds Meat.

The bar we were in was nearly empty now. Outside, in the late afternoon, people were streaming through the streets of midtown.

"Yeah," I said. "I know how people are."

Casey's eyes dripped big fat tears, and she wiped her cheeks with the table napkin. Then she lifted her water glass to her face, and the water poured down either side of her chin. In exhaustion, she put both elbows on the table and flopped her face into her palms. The pressure of her head in her hands knocked over the table, and a moment later, her Scotch was on the floor.

I righted the table, then looked at my watch. "Listen, Casey," I said. "I have to go."

"Listen, Jenny," said Casey. "I want to tell you something. Things are very new for you. You have a lot to learn. It's going to get bad— terrible things are going to happen to you, in the years to come. And when they do—*you're going to need me.*"

I let this sink in. I got to my feet and put on my coat. "Okay," I said. "Thanks, Casey." We hugged. I remembered sitting in the D'Angelos' house, asking myself, Is this what I'm going to become? Is this what the future holds for me?

"Remember," Casey whispered again. *"You're going to need me."*

I walked out into the bright sunlight of the spring day and rode the number one train up to 110th Street. Then I walked over to Amsterdam to look at the facade of my old apartment building. I looked at the roster of tenants in the foyer next to the doorbells, but my name wasn't there anymore.

It all seemed like a long time ago.

A few years after we were roommates, John Flyte killed himself with a shotgun, walked up into the mountains and pulled the trigger with his toe.

I thought about the time we'd lived together, about those dark early days of trying to be a writer, of sitting on the radiator eating a banana and holding the bars on the window with one hand.

Crazy vurld.

House of Mystery

(Summer 1987)

Graduate school turned out to be a lot like *The Man Who Shot Liberty Valance*, with me in the Jimmy Stewart role. A short-story writer from Texas, Glenn Blake, played the part of John Wayne. Liberty Valance, in the black hat, was Don DeWilde, a brilliant magic-realist who'd grown up not far from my mother's house in Narberth, Pennsylvania.

I had expected that Johns Hopkins would be a lot like Wesleyan—doing bongs with your professor, everyone giving each other back rubs, the university chartering schoolbuses to take everyone to the Dead concert. Instead it was this cowboy movie, poets hiding behind rocks and firing off pistols, and crazy drunken people burning down the saloon, and constantly meeting people in the street at sundown with your guns drawn.

Glenn Blake and I met in a bar every night and talked about the skills one needed as a writer: *Ya don't jerk the trigger, pilgrim. Ya squeeze it.*

I don't know why graduate school was like this. Don never did a single unkind thing to me, and neither did any of the other people in his gang of henchmen. But we all just hated one another. People tell me grad school is always like this. You put a bunch of smarty-pants together and the next thing you know you're living in the Wild West. It creeped me out, though. I had never had enemies before.

Partly it was the atmosphere of Johns Hopkins, a place that was famous for taking itself too seriously, and partly it was because I was psychotic. I was sitting on top of a mountain of secrets so high that it was almost impossible to see the earth anymore. For one thing, now that I lived alone, I was living as a woman about half the time. I'd come home and *go female* and pay the bills and write and watch television, and then I'd go back to boy mode and teach my classes. I didn't venture out into the world much *en femme*, although I did get out now and then. It was unbelievably frightening. The first time I ever went outside wearing a skirt and a knit top, I thought I was going to perish from fear. The world felt raw and intimidating; the cold wind howled on my bare legs.

I got as far as an Esso station, where I filled up my tank at the self-serve pump. I waited in line to pay for the gas, and no one looked at me twice. "Thank you, ma'am," said the attendant.

Then I drove home.

I lived in constant fear of detection and kept waiting for the chair of the program to call me up and say, *Boylan, we've heard stories. I hope you understand the consequences.*

I knew what the consequences would be. If word got out I was trans, I'd disappoint everyone who had put their faith in me.

My father was dying of cancer all that year. In addition to switching back and forth from male to female, I was also constantly taking the train up to Philly to check on him. He had a brain seizure the day after the *Challenger* accident. I rode up to Philly on the night train, and there in the Coffin House was my father, bald from the chemo, emaciated, his kind eyes still shining as he lay in his bed. "Dad, what can I do?"

"You can get me a cigarette," he whispered. I got him one, and lit it, and stuck it in his mouth.

"What else do you need?" I asked.

He smiled grimly. "How about a blindfold," he said.

In January I traveled up to Wesleyan to attend a memorial concert for a friend of mine who had died of lymphoma. Tim Alcock, a gentle, funny man, had also been a brilliant guitarist and African drummer. There was a big reunion of friends who had gone to Wesleyan in the late seventies and early eighties, and there was a performance of a composition written in memory of Tim. The lyrics to the piece were a single phrase that Tim, in his final days, had written in a notebook, again and again, over a hundred times: *I, Tim, am now a channel for the music which comes through the light.*

I was supposed to go on stage at one point and play "Beautiful Dreamer" on the Autoharp, but I was too sad to do it.

After the concert, there was a reception at a Mexican restaurant in downtown Middletown, and there at the table next to mine was a woman named Grace Finney. She'd gone out with a couple of my friends, years ago. I'd thought about her since college, wondering what had become of her. She wasn't the kind of woman you forgot. The first time I'd ever laid eyes on her, she was on stage in Mamet's *Sexual Perversity in Chicago*, and all I could think about for days afterward was, *Whoa*. Who was *that*?

Grace had moved back to Washington, her hometown, after working in a theater she'd helped found in New Haven. Now she was working at the Studio Theatre in D.C., which was only an hour's drive from Baltimore. We talked about getting together sometime and exchanged phone numbers. Maybe we could go to an Orioles game, she suggested. Old Memorial Stadium was not far from my house.

I left the party early and headed down to New Haven to catch the sleeper train back to Tombstone. I called Grace once I got back, but we never quite connected. After a while I lost her number.

Aside from being psychotic, the worst problem facing me at Johns Hopkins was the fact that the chair of my department liked me. I had been in John T. Irwin's class on Poe and Borges in the fall, and I had loved it. Irwin was a genuine eccentric and something of a genius. His speculative readings of Faulkner had produced a classic in American scholarship: *Doubling and Incest/Repetition and Revenge.* I had the fortune—which later became my misfortune—to discover, wholly by accident, a key missing work that would help Irwin complete his Borges book, which was entitled *The Mystery to a Solution.*

I had to do an oral report for the class on the *Astronomicon* and its influence on the Egyptians, which would in turn further shine light on the *mutually constitutive bipolar opposition of spectral doubles which inhabits Poe's work and which is then recapitulated in the analytic detective tales of Borges.* It was that kind of class, people talking like that. One night I was researching the *Astronomicon* in the very lowest level of the Hopkins library, a frightening building that was built down into the ground like the world's largest military bunker. On the lowest, darkest, most oppressive floor of the library—literally on the bottom shelf (where I'd been looking for something else entirely)—I put my hand on a collection of fifteenth-century lithographs of what Talmudic scholars imagined the universe to look like. One of them was a quincunx-shaped diamond, divided in half so as to form two triangles, each one reflecting the other. In the middle was the name of JHVH written in Hebraic script. The *tetragrammaton.*

To me these etchings looked about as crazy as the seal with the Pyramid and the eye on back of the dollar bill, but I recognized the tetragrammaton from a story by Borges. The two triangles represented the mind of God, which is perfect (triangle number one), and the universe, which is an imperfect reflection of that mind (triangle number two).

When I used this symbol (as well as a lot of other highly entertaining argle-bargle) in my report the next day, John Irwin practically fell off his chair. By the time I got home, there was a message on my answering machine from the department secretary: *The chair would like to see you, first thing tomorrow morning. And bring that book you used in your report!*

Irwin and I hit it off. I liked his brilliance and his unpredictable imagination. I also liked the fact that he had a sense of humor—he too saw critical theory as something of an exercise of the imagination, and that didn't preclude thinking the whole business was entertaining. Irwin offered me a teaching position at Hopkins on the spot, right then and there, before I'd even finished my degree.

I stammered. I didn't think my fellow writers in the workshop were going to like this very much. Most of them were scared of Professor Irwin. They thought he was demented.

"I don't know, John," I said. "Do you think John Barth is going to be okay with this?"

"Sure he'll be okay," he said. "You want me to call him?"

"Okay," I said. His secretary got John Barth on the phone. Irwin told him he wanted to give me a lectureship. He nodded and hung up.

"Jack's fine with it," he said. "You know Jack. He's pretty mellow about things."

Actually, Jack Barth (it took me forever to get used to calling him "Jack") was an incredible teacher. He was the most articulate man I had ever met and performed stunts with words that were the literary equivalent of what the Harlem Globetrotters did with a basketball. To make matters worse, he was also one of the gentlest souls I'd ever met. Rick Barthelme once described him as "equal parts brilliance and kindness." He was a lot of things, and mellow was only one of them.

My fellow workshoppers would not be mellow about this, though, as Irwin knew, and he asked me not to breathe a word of the lectureship he'd just given me. "Things could get ugly if this gets out," he said.

Things were *already* ugly, and since everyone there was pretty smart, they figured out rather quickly that something was up with me. They'd ask me if Irwin had promised me any particular goodies, and I had to lie to them and say, *Oh, heavens, no,* for the whole year, and of course everyone knew that this was a pathetic lie since I had a face that apparently betrayed every secret about me except one.

So now I had a secret in my academic life, a secret in my personal, sexual life, and my father was dying. Still, we had a pretty good time. Glenn Blake and I used to go to this little bar and drink Anchor Steam Beer and eat Mrs. Irvin's Red Hot Potato Chips. They really were hot, too. Glenn would say Texas things like "Well, god*damn!*" and sometimes he'd say, "Well, *god*damn!" and once in a while he said, "*Well!* Goddamn!" He had all kinds of Galvestonian slang. One time he said to me, "Boylan, you're slipperier than owl shit on a sycamore branch." Another time he described the work of one of my fellow workshoppers as "farts in the bathtub," which wasn't exactly a compliment.

I spent less and less time at school as my father got sicker. In mid-March I withdrew from Hopkins, unsure if I was ever going back. John Irwin was unbelievably generous to me. "You take care of your family," he said. "We'll sort out everything else later."

My father died on Easter Sunday 1986. When he died, Beethoven's Ninth Symphony was on the radio. After he died I sat next to him for a long time, just holding his hand. *I'm going to make you proud, Dad,* I told him. *You wait and see.* I wasn't quite sure how I was going to do this, but I intended to keep my word.

I started therapy again. This time I saw a gender specialist who lived down near Fell's Point. She was a smart, vigorous, hugely fat woman named Carol. I'd turn into a woman and drive down to the Point in my Volkswagen, and we'd talk. At the end of that year, she said to me, "Well, listen. You're a transsexual. The condition isn't going to go away over time. It's going to get worse. What you need to do is learn to conquer your fear. If you choose, you can live a perfectly normal life as a woman. You're lucky—you have feminine features, you have good hair, you're not married, and you're young. You have a lot going for you, if only you find the courage to move ahead with your life."

That was the last time I saw Carol. I didn't want to be told I had to be a woman. What I wanted from her was *the mystery to a solution.*

I wanted to learn how to accept who I wasn't.

What I felt was, being a man might be the second best life I can live, but the *best* life I can live will mean only loss and grief. So what I wanted was to learn how to be happy with this second best life. My mother's boundless optimism still buoyed me. In spite of my father's death, in spite of spending a year in Tombstone, in spite of the constant, private grief that I felt, I still believed that it was a life full of blessings. People can't have everything they want, I thought. It is your fate to accept a life being someone other than yourself.

I don't think this is so crazy, even now. If I could have pulled this off, I would have.

In March I ran into Grace Finney again at a party in Boston, up at Moynihan's house. We traded numbers again, and this time I did connect with her. We went out on a few dates, sometimes in Washington, sometimes in Baltimore. We didn't see the Orioles, though.

One hot spring night, Grace Finney and I went out to dinner at a place called Niçoise, in Washington. It was upscale French cuisine, served by waiters in black tuxes and roller skates.

Grace was that rarest of creatures, the native-born Washingtonian. Her father, Tom Finney, had been true Democratic Party royalty. He'd come east from Oklahoma in the 1950s to work for Senator Mike Monroney, then he'd worked on the Adlai Stevenson campaign; he was one of the key players who helped draft the compromise that seated the Mississippi delegation at the national convention in 1956. Later, he advised JFK on trade legislation and went into private law practice with Clark Clifford and Paul Warnke. In 1968 he was national campaign chairman for Eugene McCarthy; in 1972 he held the same position for Edmund Muskie.

"He was there in the trailer in Manchester," Grace said proudly, "when Muskie cried in the snow."

In short, the Finneys had a long tradition of championing noble, lost causes. Grace's father had died in 1978 of Lou Gehrig's disease. Her mother, Sally, had died in 1984 of emphysema.

Tom Finney had liked to smoke cigarettes and tell stories after dinner, just like my own father. They would have got along well, our fathers, even though my dad had been a Republican delegate to the national convention in 1952 for Robert Taft and had voted for Nixon three times.

"How do you get over missing your father?" I asked Grace as we ate our salades niçoises. "What's the secret?"

Grace looked at me with her large green eyes. "There's no secret, Jim," she said. "It just hurts. After a while, it hurts a little less."

I could tell from the way she said this that she didn't especially like the fact that bereavement was something we shared. It wasn't the thing she wanted me to find interesting about her. But she shouldn't have had to worry about that.

Grace was half Dutch, half Irish, equal measures elegance and salt. She drank Jameson's Irish whiskey and could whistle with two fingers in her mouth. She liked Little Feat, the Nighthawks, the Seldom Scene, and Bruce Springsteen. When her car broke down she could open the hood and fix the engine by herself. At black-tie theater galas, she wore elegant gowns and pearl earrings; she moved through a room with a poise and style that made people turn their heads and blink. She had shoulder-length blond hair, an infectious laugh, and freckles.

After dinner, we went to see the final performance of *As Is* at the Studio Theatre, where she was the production manager. I sat in the house afterward and watched the crew, including Grace, tear down the set. They were a tight group, the Studio crowd, and I felt a little like an outsider, in spite of the fact that Grace very nicely introduced me to everyone. From the lighting booth, during the show, I had seen the manager of the theater, and the director, and the light board operator, all eyeing me with suspicion. They weren't in the mood to start sharing Grace with anyone.

At the end of the night, a large crowd of people from the production had burgers and beers in a local diner called Trios, which was run by three elderly women who called you "hon." By my count there were at least two other guys there auditioning for the part of Grace's boyfriend. Her *real* boyfriend was now in the Peace Corps, serving out the year in Africa. She thus viewed all her suitors with tender suspicion.

Toward two A.M., Grace remembered that she'd neglected to throw a large bag of trash from the theater into the Dumpster. So we all—the other boyfriends and I—climbed back into a car and drove to the Studio and waited in the parking lot as Grace hauled a large bag of trash out of the theater and toward a giant Dumpster. We all offered to do this for her, but she just looked at us as if we were crazy. "I got it, I got it," she said.

The Dumpster was so large that she had to climb a small wooden ladder to get the trash bag in it. Up the rungs she went, as we watched from the Honda. Grace reached the top of the ladder, threw back the lid of the Dumpster, and teetered.

The driver of the car, aka Auditioning Boyfriend #1, said, "She isn't going to—"

"No, don't worry," interrupted Auditioning Boyfriend #2 with authority. "I've seen her do this before, lots of times."

Grace windmilled her arms around.

"*Lots* of times," said AB #2 again, to make sure we got the point.

"I don't know," I said. "It doesn't look good."

Alone among these gentlemen, I had imagined the future correctly. Grace teetered off to one side, then disappeared completely into the Dumpster. The last we saw of her was a pair of feet sticking straight up. Then these too vanished.

Interestingly, the men stayed in the car. No one leaped to his feet to rescue her. I think we all knew Grace well enough to understand that she would prefer to rescue herself from this predicament, and we were right.

After a few moments, Grace's head appeared out of the top of the Dumpster. There was a banana peel on one of her shoulders. Her face was lit by an enormous, proud smile. She looked as graceful as a flamenco dancer, as if she were sitting there with a rose between her teeth.

Grace climbed down the ladder and got back into the front passenger seat.

"Don't. Say. Anything," she suggested.

We didn't. We drove up 16th Street, toward our homes. As the out-of-town guest, I was sleeping on Grace's couch that night. Halfway there, AB #1 very gently rolled down all the windows in the car, to provide us with some badly needed fresh air.

"Sorry," Grace said with unquashed charm.

I sat in the backseat, hopelessly in love.

That summer, my friend Curly got engaged to the heiress to a whiskey fortune, a wild debutante named Mary Catherine. The wedding was going to be in Charlotte, North Carolina, about as high society a wedding as one could imagine. Curly asked me if I'd be his best man. It would involve lots of toasting. I asked Grace if she'd accompany me to Charlotte, and she said she'd think it over. She wasn't sure if she was busy or not.

I called her in the weeks following the Dumpster incident, but I didn't get through. She didn't call me back, either. I left messages, then stopped. I figured that by not returning my calls, she was letting me know how things stood.

I sat in my father's black leather chair in my apartment in Baltimore one night, after I'd left Grace a message asking her to call. The loudest sound I'd ever heard was the sound of that phone not ringing.

On the one-year anniversary of my father's death, I loaded all my things into the Volkswagen and started driving north. I wasn't sure where I was going, but I knew I wanted to get away from the Maryland spring, with its cherry blossoms and its bursting tulips and all that bullshit. I figured I'd keep driving farther and farther north until there weren't any people. I wasn't sure what I was going to do then, but I was certain something would occur to me that would end this business once and for all.

My first stop was New York City, where my mother and my sister and I had dinner at what had been my father's favorite restaurant, the Leopard, on the East Side. It was one of those restaurants where there weren't any menus. This very large Frenchman simply came over and told you what he was going to bring you. The three of us sat there like pilots flying in the missing man formation. I had a steak.

The next morning I drove up to Maine. I'd set my sights on Nova Scotia. The only ferry was the one out of Bar Harbor. As I drove farther north, the spring receded. It felt better that way. In the afternoon I drove onto the SS *Bluenose* and stood on the deck and watched America drift away behind me.

There was someone walking around in a rabbit costume on the ship. He'd pose with you and they'd snap your picture and an hour or so later you could purchase the photo of yourself with the rabbit as a memento of your trip to Nova Scotia. I purchased mine. It showed a sad-looking young man with long hair reading Coffin and Roelofs's *The Major Poets* as a moth-eaten rabbit bends over him.

In Nova Scotia I drove the car east and north. When dusk came, I'd eat in a diner, and then I'd sleep either in the car or in a small tent that I had in the back. There were scattered patches of snow up there, even in May. I kept going north until I got to Cape Breton.

In Cape Breton I hiked around the cliffs, looked at the ocean. At night I lay in my sleeping bag by the sea as breezes shook the tent. I wrote in my journal, or read *The Major Poets*, or grazed around in the Modern Library's *Great Tales of Horror and the Supernatural*. I read one up there called "Oh, Whistle and I'll Come to You, My Lad."

In the car I listened to the Warlocks sing "In the Early Morning Rain" on the tape deck. I thought about my father asking for a blindfold. I thought about Grace Finney falling into the trash. I thought about Onion drying herself off with that towel, one arm raised. I thought about the clear, inescapable fact that I was female in spirit and how, in order to be whole, I would have to give up on every dream I'd had, save one.

I stayed in a motel one night that was officially closed for the season, but which the operator let me stay in for half price. I opened my suitcase and put on my bra and some jeans and a blue knit top. I combed out my hair and looked in the mirror and saw a perfectly normal-looking young woman. This is so wrong? I asked myself in the mirror. This is the cause of all the trouble?

I thought about settling in one of the little villages around here, just starting life over as a woman. I'd tell everyone I was Canadian.

Then I lay on my back and sobbed. Nobody would ever believe I was Canadian.

The next morning I climbed a mountain at the far northern edge of Cape Breton Island. I climbed up to the top, trying to clear my head, but it wouldn't clear. I kept going up and up, past the tree line, past the shrub line, until at last there was just moss.

There I stood, looking out at the cold ocean a thousand miles below me, totally cut off from the world.

A fierce wind blew in from the Atlantic. I leaned into it. I saw the waves crashing against the cliff below. I stood right at the edge. My heart pounded.

I leaned over the edge of the precipice, but the gale blowing into my body kept me from falling. When the wind died down, I'd start to fall, then it would blow me back up again and I didn't. I played a little game with the wind, leaning a little farther over the edge each time.

Then I leaned off the edge of the cliff at a sharp angle, my arms held outward like wings, my body sustained only by the fierce wind, and I thought, *Well, all right. Is this what you came here to do?*

Let's do it, then.

Then a huge blast of wind blew me backward, and I landed on the moss. It was soft. I stared straight up at the blue sky, and I felt a presence. *Son? Are you all right, son?*

This time it wasn't a cop, though.

I headed down the mountain and got into the car and started driving home. There wasn't a rabbit on the ferry this time.

I had a big party for Curly in New York a month or so later. It was a kind of anti–bachelor party featuring performances by all the musicians and writers and actors we knew. I played "Good Lovin'" on the Autoharp: *I said doctor (doctor) / Mr. M.D. / Now can you tell me (doctor) / What's ailing me?* . . . I hired a set of twins who played trumpets to perform a duet. I also hired something called the Mini-Circus, which consisted of a clown named Winky who had performing monkeys. Her boss, a domineering woman with a wig, demanded that we turn on all the lights when Winky was performing. "We don't work in the dark!" she shouted. Winky made us all join a parade, and then everybody on the groom's side marched behind Winky and the performing monkeys, one of whom was named Zippy.

All of the people on the bride's side remained in their seats, not joining the parade. They were deeply frightened. At one point a monkey jumped off Winky's shoulder and landed in the maid of honor's hair.

There was a party after the party at the home of a journalist down in TriBeCa. Everyone except me got drunk and danced. I went into an empty bedroom and sat on the radiator and looked out at the dark streets of the city.

"Hey," said a woman's voice. "Where did you go?"

It was Grace Finney. I hadn't known she was there.

"I just came in here to sort of catch my breath, I guess," I said.

"I don't mean just now. I mean this last month. You were around, and then you weren't. How come?"

"I went up to Nova Scotia," I said.

"What was that like?"

"Kind of depressing," I said. "I thought I was going to get away from everything, just kind of groove on the ocean and the trees and everything, but all I felt was sad."

"I had a trip like that last summer," Grace said. "I was climbing Mt. Rainier with my boyfriend, before he went to Africa. I told myself I was doing it for my mother. I kept saying, 'Do it for Sally. You've got to do it for Sally.' Then I stopped halfway up the mountain and realized, Sally doesn't care if I climb the mountain. Sally could care less. Sally would want me to come down and sit at the table and eat lobsters and corn."

"Are you still seeing him—the boyfriend?"

Grace smiled at me. "That depends," she said.

I stayed the night at my sister's apartment down on Hanover Square. Grace slept on the foldout couch. The next day we went to the Statue of Liberty on the ferry. We noticed that on the ferry all the tourists stood in the front of the boat, taking pictures of the Statue of Liberty. The New Yorkers stood in the back, looking back at Manhattan.

Later that summer I brought Grace home to Pennsylvania to meet my mother. "Your mother is the nicest person I've ever met," Grace said. "It's almost scary how kind and cheerful she is. She's like a balloon filled with helium."

"You got it," I said.

Grace came as my date to Curly's wedding in Charlotte. The groom's friends were all emaciated Caucasians from the East Coast. One guy, pale as a sheet of typewriter paper, cut himself shaving and bled and bled and bled all over his tuxedo shirt. The bride's friends, meanwhile, were all tanned and southern and poised. The wedding went on for days. There was a bridesmaid's party and a rehearsal and a rehearsal dinner and a barbecue given by the grandmother and a special play that Curly wrote in honor of the occasion and the wedding itself and the reception afterward and then a party the next day, after the reception, at Uncle Rochester's house.

In the receiving line, Mary Catherine's mother took me aside and had me sign the family Bible. Then she started crying. "What's wrong?" I asked.

"Oh," said Mary Catherine's mother. "I am just so concerned about this marriage. You see, it's your friend Curluhee. He's a—a—well, you know. I suppose the word is *heathen*."

I nodded. She had that right.

Curly and Mary Catherine started arguing about money on their honeymoon and were divorced within the year.

The day after the wedding, after Uncle Rochester's party, Grace and I got in the Volkswagen and started heading north. We took small back roads through Virginia, and at one point, in some small hamlet, we passed a rickety-looking log cabin that had exactly half of a Ford Mustang embedded in its outer wall. In big neon lights there was a sign that read, HOUSE OF MYSTERY. And in smaller lights: "Now Open."

We turned to each other and said, simultaneously, "Do you want to stop?"

Then we each shrugged and said, "No. Let's just keep going."

So we didn't stop at the House of Mystery. I don't know what it was. In the years since, though, I've often wondered about what we would have found inside. A whole different life, perhaps.

I dropped Grace off at her apartment, then returned to Baltimore. I was twenty-nine years old and felt, for the first time, as if my life were finally beginning.

My apartment felt like an Egyptian tomb when I got home, a place where incomprehensible strangers lived unfathomable lives, thousands of years ago. There were statues of Anubis in the kitchen, funerary urns by the bed.

I went to the closet with an enormous garbage bag. Into this I put my skirts, my hose, the blue knit top, some underwear, my makeup, some bobby pins, everything. Then I tied up the trash bag and walked out to the curb and left it there.

We will never speak of this again, I thought. Here at last we shall leave all of this and move onward with this new life, finally, miraculously, *healed*.

There I was, standing beneath the Baltimore sky, but as I stood there I remembered waves crashing against a jetty in Surf City, a child praying to be transformed by love. I looked inside myself, searching for the woman I had always felt myself to be. But she's not there.

Sssh. She thinks it's classical.

Part 2

Florence, Italy, 1999.
Then we passed across the Bridge of Sighs.

Bright Star
(1988–1999)

Grace and I had an Alaskan honeymoon. We spent a week on land, in Denali National Park, in Nome and Kotzebue and Fairbanks and Anchorage. Then we took a cruise ship down the Inside Passage past Juneau and Ketchikan to Vancouver. It was daytime, all night long.

On the cruise ship we were seated at dinner with another couple named the McHenrys, from Ohio, as well as the ship's radiotelegraph operator, a Scotsman named Freddy. We were the only newlyweds on the ship. The captain sent us a bottle of champagne. During dinner one night, Lois McHenry explained that during *her* wedding twenty-eight years ago, she had left her body, had floated above the ceremony like an angel.

"You never told me that story," said her husband. He didn't sound glad to hear about it now.

"I know," said Lois. She sounded sad.

" 'Tis streenge," said Freddy, drinking champagne, resplendent in his epaulets. "Iddin' it?"

We nodded. It was streenge all right. "Ah, but 'tis a good life," he added. "The life at sea."

On the *Royal Princess* we drank blender drinks and sat on the deck playing Scrabble and watched giant chunks of ice calve off glaciers. In Denali we rented a small plane and flew around Mt. McKinley, which was shrouded in clouds. We saw a grizzly bear chasing a baby moose.

At the table next to ours in the galley was a couple celebrating their fiftieth wedding anniversary. As a result of two different strains of cancer, the husband couldn't talk and the wife couldn't hear. They looked happy.

" 'Tis a good life," said Grace. "The life at sea."

———————

We rented a giant U-Haul and moved to Maine, where I'd landed a teaching job at Colby College, in Waterville. I drove the truck, and Grace drove her Prelude, and Zero drove my Volkswagen. Each of us took on an alias for the road. Grace became Sweet-Pea. Zero became Bluto. And I became Little Sal. It took three days to drive to Maine, and the U-Haul died, literally, in the driveway of our new house.

In the morning we woke up in our new bedroom, boxes piled up to the ceiling. We opened the windows. Our house stood in the middle of a green field; at the edges of the field was a pine forest. We heard the chirping of crickets in the field, peepers in the woods.

———————

One of our wedding presents was a cardboard box full of Thai ingredients and a Thai cookbook. There weren't any Thai restaurants in Waterville, so Grace started cooking. Suddenly my meals contained things like coconut milk and *galangal*.

We had a fireplace and a wood-burning furnace. The snow began to fall just before Thanksgiving, and that was the last we saw of the lawn until April. We loved the intense Maine winter—icicles three feet long hanging off the rain gutters, snow thigh deep, our breath gathering around us in cold clouds.

We took up cross-country skiing. We traveled through farmers' fields and down fire roads that cut through forest. One of the trails led to a barn where a fellow ran a spa. There we would sit, steaming in a wood-fired sauna. Then we'd run through the snow into another barn where there was a cedar hot tub. Grace and I drank champagne in the tub and listened to Coleman Hawkins on the stereo, then ran naked through the snow again and sat in the sauna. I had never spent so much time naked outside before. After all this, we'd head home and watch Alfred Hitchcock movies on the VCR as a fire blazed in the fireplace.

One time we watched *Vertigo*, which I found kind of sad. I felt bad for Jimmy Stewart. He seemed to have lost perspective.

———————

In our second year in Maine, we planted a garden—tomatoes and pumpkins and squash and Brussels sprouts and corn. To our shock, it all grew. The garden made a lot of demands on us, though—weeding and tilling and watering; it was worse than having a dog.

So in July of 1989 we abandoned the garden and went on a bicycle trip through Burgundy. We spent our days cycling past vineyards and castles. We stood in the ruins of Cluny. We rode downhill through Beaune. Grace bought cheese and baguettes and chocolate from grocers, and we ate them in hay fields. One day, we ate lunch at the edge of the field in which were the grapes for Gevrey-Chambertin. That afternoon we paused at Château Charlemagne.

In the château was a grumpy old woman who showed tourists around. At one point, she said, "Some people think"—she paused for breath—"time is money." Pause again. "But time is not money. Time is—a gift from God."

———————

Grace was accepted at the Smith School for Social Work and began the MSW program in the summer of 1990. Smith requires three summers of residency in Northampton and two internships in the years in between the residencies. As she drove off for the first residency, in Boston, in her blue Prelude, she cried. I stayed behind, working in the garden.

A few days later I got a phone call from my friend Walt Bode, an editor at Grove Press. I'd sent him my novel, *The Planets*, which was based on a symphony by Holst, sort of. Walt wasn't sure he could publish it at Grove, but he'd given the manuscript to Gordon Kato, who was an assistant to an agent at International Creative Management. A few days later, Kris Dahl at ICM called me. "Listen," she said. "I think we can close a deal on this book."

"Who are you again?" I said.

"I sent it out to editors at Norton, Simon and Schuster, and Random House. We've got offers from Norton and Poseidon—that's the imprint at Simon and Schuster. I'm gonna let 'em stew until Monday. But it's looking good. I'm hoping we can make this a two-book deal, with a film option."

"Who are you again?" I said.

The Planets came out the following year, 1991. It got good reviews. *The New Yorker* said I was "wacky." Kris closed five foreign rights deals, and soon *Die Planeten* and *Planety* and so on were coming out in Germany, Poland, Japan, Holland, not to mention the United Kingdom and Ireland and Australia. *The Times* of London said it was a "book of the year." The *Independent* said, "This is the great success of American literature in this country. *The Planets* is glorious and brilliant."

The New York Times thought it was stupid.

Still, *Planets* established me, for a little while, anyway, as a writer on the national scene, and a year or two later it had a pleasant life as a paperback in the Vintage Contemporaries series. The film rights were sold to a man named Mark Rosenberg, who had made *Dry White Season*, *The White Hotel*, and most significantly, the touching

King Ralph. A few months after optioning *Planets* he dropped totally dead of a heart attack, which was of course not my fault.

In 1991 we moved into a bigger house in Belgrade Lakes. I bought a dog from a pig farmer, who claimed Lucy was a golden retriever. She looked more like a short-haired yellow Lab, though. Her tongue was bright purple.

————————

We had a hot tub on the back porch of our new house. We'd sit out there under the stars, drinking. One July Fourth, Grace got out of the tub and lit a sparkler. Then she ran around the backyard naked, her body illuminated softly as the sparks flew all around. She ran to the garden and back.

"What was that?" I asked.

"Naked woman fireworks," she said.

She wasn't kidding, either.

————————

Grace started working as a social worker at a local mental health agency. Soon she was seeing a caseload of clients, most of them suffering from the traditional vices and agonies of rural life: spousal abuse, incest, ignorance, alcoholism, drug abuse, child abuse, abandonment, and so on. I used to ask her, "Listen, you have these clients who are two hundred pounds overweight, they're married to their brother, they can't read or write, they're alcoholics, and they're only fifteen years old. Don't you ever want to say, 'Hey, man, your problem is, your life sucks'?"

Grace smiled, but then she answered. "No," she said. "I never want to say that."

One day she came home and mentioned one of her new clients. "You know anything about transsexuality?" she asked.

I nodded. I knew something about it.

"I've got this woman who wants to be a man," she said.

"Uh-huh," I said. "Well, all I know is that life must be very hard

for transsexuals. I think it's a condition most people don't understand."

"You got that right," said Grace.

Colby decided, after about five years, not to fire me, and somehow I
passed almost seamlessly from *the guy who was probably just about to get
canned* to *campus legend. The Insider's Guide to American Colleges* came
out one year and said that I was the one Colby professor whose course
you had to take before you graduated. The course they had in mind
was Literature and Imagination, whose reading list included *The Cat
in the Hat Comes Back*, "The Love Song of J. Alfred Prufrock," *Four
Quartets*, *A Streetcar Named Desire*, *Henry IV, Part I*, *Giovanni's Room*,
Going After Cacciato, *Love in the Time of Cholera*, "Ode to a Nightingale,"
"The Dead," "Uncle Wiggily in Connecticut," *Frankenstein*, and *The
Yellow Wallpaper*. I used to give the students two papers to do—and the
assignment was the same for each one: "Write a seven- to ten-page
paper related to class affairs. The paper may be as scholarly or as per-
sonal as you wish." *That* kept 'em busy.

A lot of the books on the list concerned characters using their
imaginations to find solace from the sorrows of the world.

In the spring, Grace and I always attended the annual faculty-trustee
cocktail party and dinner, which frequently failed to be electrifying.
Trustees would always ask me if I was a senior. One year, just before
the dinner started, Grace turned to me and whispered, "What do you
say we blow this joint?" and I said, "I'm with you," and the two of
us jumped in the Volkswagen (I had a Passat by now) and drove to a
fancy restaurant in Litchfield, almost an hour away.

We'd been married for five years. They had been, without question, the five happiest years of my life.

"So do we want to have kids?" Grace asked me.

"I don't know, do we?"

For the next two hours, over the appetizers and the salad and the
main course, we talked about all the reasons not to have children.

How we feared the unknowns of pregnancy and child rearing. How we feared that the world was an unstable place. How we feared that we would not be good parents. How we feared a loss of intimacy, that the arrival of children would take us away from the sweet years we had shared and into a new and unknown place.

The dessert came, a thick chocolate torte. We drank Cognac.

"So I guess that it's not a good time to have kids," Grace said.

"I guess that's what we're saying."

"But we do want to have them someday, right?"

"Yup."

"Do you think there will ever be a good time?"

I shrugged. "Nope."

"So then," Grace said. She raised her Cognac glass. I raised mine.

That night we discontinued the use of birth control. Exactly nine months later, on a freezing cold Maine February day, a child was born.

It is some testimony to Grace's steadfastness that she had the baby *exactly* on the due date. When our second child was born, *he* arrived exactly on the due date as well.

When I got home from the hospital the night of Luke's birth, I went outside into the falling snow to walk the dog. The baby book had said to bring a soiled diaper home with you from the hospital, so the dog could sniff it and get used to the idea of the baby's smell. I put a tiny diaper on the floor of the kitchen. Lucy sniffed it, then looked at me. *Yeah, so? You guys went and had a baby. What do you want me to do, throw a parade?*

I walked in the snow with the dog on a leash and a glass of Hennessey and a cigar. It was hard to hold all of these things at once, but I did.

———————

The college hired a new creative writer named Richard Russo. I didn't know anything about him when he arrived except that he'd published a quirky novel called *Mohawk* and another less quirky one called *The*

Risk Pool. Like mine, his paperbacks were Vintage Contemporaries. We were going to share an office in the fall, which I wasn't crazy about. I went over to meet him at a summer place he'd rented, and there he was—short, eloquent, and hilarious. His wife, Barb, had beautiful laughing eyes, which didn't surprise me a bit. After an afternoon of Russo, I could see that anyone who spent much time around him would have laugh lines.

I now think of the time that Russo and I shared an office as best of all the years I've spent teaching at Colby. I used to come back to the office and find no one in the department, the place apparently evacuated—but one professor's door would be closed and I'd hear Russo's voice, and I'd open the door, and there would be the whole department, maybe fifteen professors, all jammed into one room, listening to Russo tell dirty jokes. I particularly remember one story, the punch line of which was, *"And the bear says to the guy, 'Say, you don't really come up here for the huntin', do you?' "* As this line was delivered, scholars fled from the office with tears running down their faces, their pants wet.

Russo's presence was a definite plus.

One day I bought an inflatable pterodactyl with an eight-foot wingspan, blew it up, and hung it from the high ceiling of our office. I threaded strings through the wings, through pulleys, and attached them to the doorknob, so that when Russo opened the door, not only would the pterodactyl dive toward him, it would also flap its wings.

He didn't notice it.

———

Luke and I were alone in the house, and the lights were out. This wasn't that unusual. In rural Maine the power goes out all the time, at least once a week.

I lit candles and fed the baby. Luke, sitting in his high chair, looked at me with an odd grin. Suddenly I said, "Luke, can you talk?"

He smiled and looked around. Then he said, "Hi, Daddy."

———

I woke up from a nightmare, covered in sweat. Moonlight shone down on the snow outside.

I asked myself, in the softest of voices, You don't *still* want to be a woman, do you?

And I said, *Shut up, shut up, shut up.*

You do.

I got back into bed. The baby lay asleep in the bed between Grace and me. I put my arm around them, mother and child, protecting them. They were warm.

———

The Russos and the Boylans went to Disneyland together. Grace sat on a wall outside of It's a Small World breast-feeding Luke while the two famous authors rode screaming down Splash Mountain. *I didn't say it was your laughin' place, Br'er Fox, I said it was* my *laughin' place.*

In the evening we went out to dinner at a seafood restaurant. I ordered Chesapeake Bay crabs, which were served Baltimore style, a big heap of peppered crabs just poured onto some newspaper on the table. Everyone else had a demure and proper dinner; the Russo daughters had fish, Barb and Grace had chicken, Rick had a steak. Baby Luke had milk. Long after the time everyone else was drinking coffee and settling into a postdinner quiet, I was still hacking the crabs apart, biting down on their peppery guts. My cheeks were shiny with crabmeat and butter. I had cut my hand on one of the crabs, and blood trickled slowly down my arm.

With some embarrassment, I suddenly realized everyone was observing me in horror and disgust.

"What can I tell you, Boylan," Russo said. "You're losin' blood."

———

The magazine *Granta* came out with a list of the "Thirty Best American Writers Under Forty." I wasn't on it. Russo wasn't on it, either, which was some consolation, but then on the other hand, he wasn't under forty. A few weeks later, the *New York Observer* came out with an article slamming the *Granta* list as "literary beefcake" and put out their own list. I made that one, along with a few other comic novelists.

I called up my mother and explained the situation. "Well, isn't that nice," she said. "Now what's this *Granta* again?"

"It's a magazine, Mom."

"Would I see it at the hairdresser's?"

"Probably not."

"Well, anyway, it's still nice. You might as well enjoy it while you can. A few years from now, any list of people under forty is a list you aren't going to be on."

She had me there.

In our little office, Russo and I used to put our feet up on the desk at the end of each day and complain to each other about the fate of comic writers in America.

"You know what pisses me off, Boylan?"

"What?"

"Well, on the back jacket of your book here there's this quote from *Entertainment Weekly* about how the best part about your prose is how it sounds like you're just making it up as you go along."

"Yeah?"

"Well, let me ask you, were you just making it up as you went along?"

"No, of course not."

"How many years of work on that book did it take you to make it feel as if you were 'just making it up as you went along'?"

"Two or three."

"See, this is the worst thing about being a supposedly comic writer. In order for the prose to work it has to feel effortless, almost weightless. And yet, if you do your job right, everyone's going to think that you didn't work hard enough. That's the thing about effortless prose—it feels as though you didn't put any effort into it."

"Exactly," I said. "Sucks for us, doesn't it."

Russo shrugged. "Sucks for *you*, Boylan."

In spite of his artistic handicap, Russo hit it big with *Nobody's Fool*, got hired by Scott Rudin and Robert Benton to consult on the screenplay, then co-wrote the script for their next movie, *Twilight*. One day at the gym, he told me he was quitting Colby and moving out to Camden on the coast. It wasn't a surprise, but it was sad. I had a feeling I was never going to have as much fun at work again in my life.

A year later, Russo published his fourth novel, *Straight Man*, a wicked satire of academic life in general and English Departments in particular. My friend Murphy, a colleague at Colby, read it before I did. One evening I ran into Murphy at a party at the department chair's house, and he said, "How about Russo, naming that character after you?"

Rick hadn't said anything about this to me. I felt my heart quicken. "Which character?" I said.

"You know, the cross-dresser." Murphy laughed. "He must know something about you that the rest of us don't, ha ha ha!"

A number of my colleagues, standing nearby, laughed along with Murphy. There I was, in the elegant house of my boss, looking at the faces of the men and women I worked with, all of them doubled over in hysteria. It was really funny, I guess.

I stood there mortified, wondering what on earth Russo knew, how much he had told others. Why wouldn't he talk to me about it first, before outing me in a novel? It seemed a cruel, terrible thing to do to someone you liked as much as Russo supposedly liked me.

Eventually, I read a copy of *Straight Man*, and sure enough, there was a character named Phineas—nicknamed Finney—who had a cross-dressing fetish. He played the role of the villain in the book. It was even worse that it was my middle name he was using, because it was, after all, Grace's name. I'd taken it for my own when we got married, as a gesture of love.

When I finally confronted Russo about this a few weeks later, he kind of turned pale for a moment, then laughed.

"Holy shit, Boylan," he said. "That *is* your name. It never even occurred to me!" He laughed as though it were funny, which, since he assumed I wasn't a transsexual, it ought to have been. "Oh well!"

Years later, after I became a woman, a lot of people told me they assumed Rick had known all along. Why *else* would he name that cross-dresser after me?

Why indeed. Looking back on it now, Russo's a little chagrined about the whole business, at least he *says* he is. It was just a weird coincidence, that's all. Probably lots of transsexuals are named Finney.

Oh well.

One October, when Grace was three months pregnant with science project number two, we drove down to Freeport to a pumpkin patch. A farmer pulled us around in a hay wagon and let us off in the middle of the patch, which was miles and miles wide. In every direction were brown vines, the huge orange globes of the pumpkins. A red barn stood at the top of the hill.

Luke picked out a pumpkin, but it was too heavy for him, and a moment after standing up with it he fell over. He thought this was funny. We got back in the hay wagon and the farmer pulled us up to the barn, and we drank hot mulled cider and bought apples and chrysanthemums. Then we drove home and carved the pumpkin. Luke couldn't believe all the gunk inside.

After he went to sleep, Grace and I ate dinner. She made my favorite dinner, which was Thai shrimp with cracked black pepper, and string beans with spicy pork. The food was so hot that tears streamed down my face. Like Walter Cronkite after the moon landing, I lost the ability to speak for a while.

Later we sat by the fire and played Scrabble and listened to Maine

Public Radio—*Prairie Home Companion, The Thistle and Shamrock, World Café, Music from the Hearts of Space.*

" 'Tis a good life," I said to her. "The life at sea."

———————

Grace had a cesarean when she had Patrick, same as with Luke. She didn't mind. By that point it was all the same to her. I watched the whole thing. It was a surprise that I was not squeamish. I held my wife's hand and tried to be reassuring. The doctor squished around for a while, then announced, "I'm going for the baby." A moment later a small human looked around, sizing up the situation. He cried.

After that they started piecing Grace back together again. I asked the doctor what that pink thing was. "Oh, this?" she said. "This is the uterus."

That's what I thought, I said.

Dr. Gross decided it was time for an anatomy lesson. "And these here are the fallopian tubes," she said, pulling back the incision to display my wife's guts. The fallopian tubes looked like a drawing from science class, little hands clasping the ovaries.

Man, look at that, I thought. Ovaries.

"Hey," said the anesthesiologist. "You know that little girl, the one who was flying the plane by herself across the country?"

Yeah, I said, I knew about it.

"She crashed," he said, and shook his head. "Died."

Aw jeez, I said. That's too bad.

"Yeah, well," said the anesthesiologist. "Some parents, you gotta wonder."

———————

Patrick's birth ushered in a fortnight of catastrophes. The baby was born with supraventricular tachycardia, which meant that his pulse raced up to 250 beats a minute and stayed there. The morning after he was born, he was taken from his mother and rushed away in an ambulance. They wired him up to a dozen machines. I went to visit him in the Portland hospital, nearly two hours away, just as my father had visited me when I was a newborn in danger.

Russo was waiting for me at the hospital when I got there. I hadn't even told him that Patrick was ill. He'd been out of town, had heard that we were in trouble, flown home, and driven to the ICU. The tiny child was there behind glass, covered in wires and tubes.

"Jesus Christ, Boylan," Russo said.

Grace got a spinal headache from the epidural, which had fallen out in the middle of the cesarean. This meant that she spent a week with a jackhammer in her head. The only cure was caffeine, which Grace wasn't allowed to have, because it might wind up in her breast milk and overstimulate Patrick's heart.

We stayed in the Ronald McDonald House, and I was humiliated to be the benefit of the burger conglomerate's charity. Every few hours I'd push Grace's wheelchair up the hill to the hospital and she'd nurse the baby. Afterward I'd hold him and sob, saying, "Paddy, am I *never* not going to worry about you?"

The children's ICU was kind of like a prison. "What's yours in for?" other parents would ask us. There were all sorts of cases, all of them heartbreaking. One child, Drano Baby, had swallowed Drano at five months, which burned out his entire digestive system as well as his larynx. They were building him a new esophagus out of his small intestine. Then there was Traction Baby, whose pelvis and femurs were unfused; the baby had to lie on his back with both legs in casts and elevated, as if he had had the world's smallest skiing accident. Then there was Small Pale Baby. No one knew what the deal was with Small Pale Baby. Sometimes she was accompanied by Small Pale Mommy, who sat by the child's crib each night and cried.

They eventually got Patrick's heart rate stabilized using digitalis, and we were allowed to go home. The other parents were glad for us, but not really. There was a sense we'd been pardoned by the governor, perhaps unfairly.

The disasters continued when we got home, nearly a week after going into the hospital. Grace got mastitis, an infection of the breast.

Then Patrick got a clogged tear duct, so that gunk gathered in his eye. We called him Little Gunky Eye, affectionately, for a while. Then he got a cold, and Grace got a cold, and Luke got a cold, and I got a cold.

Two weeks after he'd been born, we took Patrick back to the hospital to see if we should put him on drugs for the flu. We were seen in the very same ward where Grace had been in labor—were seated, in fact, in a room exactly across the hall from the place where two weeks earlier Patrick had been delivered by C-section.

Another couple was now in that same room. We heard the husband shouting, "I can see the head, darling! I can see the head! It's coming! It's coming!" The wife screamed. "It's a boy! Honey, it's a boy!" Then the tiny cry echoed in the space. Everyone was crying and hugging.

Grace and I looked at each other. We hadn't slept in two weeks. We'd been through a cesarean, supraventricular tachycardia, a spinal headache, a failed epidural, mastitis, a gunky eye, and four head colds.

I wanted to go across the hall, where Perfect Mommy and Perfect Daddy were having their Perfect Newborn Baby moment, and say to them, "Do you people *mind*? Do you think it would be possible if, just for a moment, you could all *shut up*?"

The doctor came into our room. "Ah, the Boylans," she said. "And how are we doing?"

———————

I made a lot of pizza. Luke liked watching the hook on the Mixmaster punch the dough around. Often he'd ask if he could have a small piece of dough to walk around with. Even at age three, he was aware that dough contained yeast, which made it a living organism.

One night Luke formed a particular attachment to a baseball-size glob, which he named My Friend Dough. He tried to take My Friend Dough into the bathtub with him, but I drew the line at bathing with it. My Friend Dough sat in the soap dish and watched as Luke scrubbed up. At bedtime, it sat in a glob next to the bed, watching over Luke while he slept.

In the morning I was awakened by bitter, heartbroken sobbing. Luke was standing by the side of my bed, the glob of dough in his hand. During the night the dough had fallen and a hard crust had formed where the moisture had escaped.

"My Friend Dough," Luke sobbed. "He got hard and *died*."

I often woke up and lay there in the dark. Usually this was about a quarter to four. I'm the wrong person, I thought. I'm living the wrong life, in the wrong body.

To which I would respond: You're a maniac. An idiot. You have a life a lot of other people dream about, a life so full of blessings that your heart hurts.

To which I would respond: I know. Still.

To which I would respond: Well, what do you think you're going to do about this now? Have a sex change, at age forty? Abandon all the love that has made your life whole, so that you can enter into a new life, about which you know nothing? What kind of woman do you think you'd be now, having never had a girlhood? What kind of person do you think you'd be, leaving your children without a father, your wife without a husband?

To which I would respond: *I know. Still.*

To which I would respond: Well, you go on and have a sex change, then. Just leave me out of it. I'll just say my prayers so I can appreciate the things I have and not launch off like an imbecile into a life of lurid marginality.

To which I would respond: You know, don't you, that no amount of wishing that this were not the case can *make* it not the case. No amount of praying that you are not transgender will make you something other than what you are. No amount of love from anyone will make you fit inside a body that does not match your spirit.

To which I would respond: Well, I'll be goddamned if I'm going to break anybody's heart. I'll be goddamned if I'm going to let my family down. I'll be goddamned if I'm going to give up everything I've always wanted just so I can *fit*.

To which I would respond: I know. Still.

To which I would respond: Well, all right, then. You'll be goddamned.

———————

Some nights, Luke and Patrick lay in our bed, their eyes all sleepy. Grace sang a song to them that I did not know, but which she remembered from her own childhood, called "Two Little Boys":

> *Do you think I could leave you crying?*
> *When there's room on my horse for two?*
> *Climb up here, Jack, quit your crying,*
> *We'll mend up your horse with glue.*
> *When we grow up we'll both be soldiers*
> *And our horses will not be toys.*
> *Maybe then we'll remember*
> *When we were two little boys.*

———————

One fall day the phone rang. "Hi, it's Charlie Kaufman," said a voice long-distance. My old roommate from 108th Street had seen the review of *The Planets* in *The New Yorker*, and he'd called up to congratulate me. Charlie had moved out to Los Angeles since last we talked and was now one of the writers for a new Chris Elliott TV show called *Get a Life*.

I thought about our room on 108th Street, the bars on the windows, the little pieces of film all over the floor. Working at the *American Bystander*, all that time dreaming big dreams that had, in the end, come to nothing. Still, Charlie and I had been friends. It made me feel a little better about that lost time.

"Let's stay in touch," he said.

———————

One night Russo and I went out drinking in Camden, and after dinner, decided to work off the weight we had presumably gained by taking a long walk through the town.

It was unimaginably dark. We heard the roar of the ocean through the trees, the sound of bells on buoys.

"I just hope I know where I'm going," Russo said as we left town.

"It would be a first," I said.

"Shut up, Boylan," Russo suggested.

We turned down a street at the edge of town that wound through woods. As we walked it got even darker, something that didn't seem possible. "This is one of my favorite walks," Russo said. "You have to trust me, when the sun's out, it's really beautiful."

"Since when have I trusted you?"

I had never known the world to be as dark as it was that night, as Russo and I walked down that road through the woods. I could literally not see my hand in front of my face. There were no stars, no moon, and the black sky was covered with invisible clouds. We stumbled through the dark like blind men, aware that we had strayed from the pavement only when our shoes touched soft earth. We reached out for each other and walked with our arms on each other's shoulders, lurching drunkenly through the void.

"You know, it would be good for Grace to see you getting us lost for a change," I said to Rick. "She admires you so much. It would be good for her to know the real you."

"What are you saying, Boylan, that if she knew the real me, we wouldn't be lost in the dark?"

"No, we'd still be lost, she'd just be able to hold you responsible for it."

"I'm going to get us home just fine," said Russo. "I know exactly where we are."

"Where are we?" I said.

Russo's voice came through the darkness.

"Up shit's creek," he said.

"Well," I said. "That's reassuring." I squeezed his shoulder. It was good knowing he was there.

"You know, come to think of it, if Barbara were here, she could see the real you, Boylan."

"Which is what?"

"A pathetic coward."

Rick did finally get us home, but it took hours. We weren't on the road he'd thought we were on, either. Somehow we'd taken a wrong turn and walked miles out of our way. Rick now claims he knew this at the time but didn't want to tell me. The other thing he didn't tell me was that on one side of the road, as we walked through that haunted darkness, was a huge, creepy graveyard, its headstones bearing skulls and angels crumbling into dust.

I started playing rock and roll again. I hadn't been in a band since the Comfortable Chair. My new group, put together by a guy in the Geology Department, was called Diminished Faculties. We broke up when he didn't get tenure.

Then I met some other musicians who didn't have anything to do with Colby. Pretty soon I was playing with the Smelts, and then the Roy Hudson Band, and then Blue Stranger. I spent my days teaching the poetry of Keats, the afternoons playing Candyland, and the nights performing "Brown-Eyed Girl" for millworkers.

Sometimes, when I played in bars, people would buy me a pint. Occasionally the beers would stand in a row on top of the sound module.

I thought about Mr. Pitiful's, and the night I met Donna Fierenza, the rain hammering down in the streets of London. *There are women and women and some hold you tight / While some leave you counting the stars in the night. . . .*

One day I autographed a copy of *The Planets* "To Donna and

Neal, with love" and sent it off to the last address I'd had for Donna and her husband, a studio in Boston. I defaced the picture of myself on the back flap, so she couldn't see what I looked like now.

She didn't write back.

———————

There was a large tract of forestland across the street from our house, and I used to take long walks there on the fire road. Sometimes I'd follow the stream into the forest as far as I could go. Frequently I'd run into moose. They'd give me a dirty look, then lumber off.

As I walked through the woods, sometimes, I worked on the "being alive" problem. I'm still transgender, I thought. Even though my life has been transformed by love. I still feel like a woman inside. At every waking moment now, I was plagued by the thought that I was living a lie. It was there on the tip of my tongue as I taught my classes; it was there as I made meatballs for the woman I loved; it was there as I took the car through the car wash and shoveled the snow and built the fires and played piano and flipped pancakes. It was fair to say I was *never* not thinking about it.

Now I had two problems. One was being trans, which was stupid enough. But worse than this was the problem of having a secret, of having something so vital about myself that I had withheld from Grace. How am I going to tell her? I wondered as I walked among the pine and maples. This would destroy her, would destroy us, would destroy all the gifts we have been given.

Sometimes I'd think, *Say, are you insane?*

I'd get back to the house and Grace would say, How was your walk?

Good, I'd say. It was good. My children would come over and wrap their arms around my knees. *Daddy's back.*

———————

One fall a friend of the family stopped by with his grandson. They were doing the college tour of New England. We all went out to dinner. I remembered visiting colleges with my own father in the summer of 1975, drinking beer with him in Oberlin, Ohio, him treating me like a grown-up for the first time. The next day I started writing a short bit about taking the college tour with a dysfunctional family.

In less than a year I'd finished the book, which I called *A Guide to the Colleges of New England: A Novel*, which follows a high school senior named Dylan as he and his father visit, in order, Yale, Harvard, Bowdoin, Colby, Middlebury, Dartmouth, Williams, Amherst, and Wesleyan.

Each of the main characters in the family is keeping a very important secret from the people he or she loves the most.

My agent got the book on a Friday. The following week she'd closed a film deal with Geena Davis and Renny Harlin. A few weeks later, she sold the manuscript to Warner Books, and a month or so after that, New Line Cinema had hired me to write the screenplay. It was a hilarious and lucky time, money just raining down out of the sky.

The publisher didn't like the title, though. Could I think of a new one? Grace said, "How about *Getting In*?"

Great idea, I said. It's just disgusting enough to work.

———

With the money from the film deal, we bought a summer house by Long Pond, which doubled in the wintertime as my writer's office.

I spent all of my days there when I wasn't teaching. It was a beautiful post-and-beam house, built entirely out of pine and pegs. There wasn't a nail in the thing. From a second-floor balcony I could see all of Long Pond twinkling before me. I set up my desk in an atrium next to the porch and started work on a new novel.

Sometimes while I worked I put on a skirt and a knit top, just so I could work without being distracted. Then I'd think, *Why am I doing this?*

And the response came, the same one as when I was fourteen: *Because I can't not.*

I was chosen to direct Colby's program in Cork, Ireland, from 1998 to 1999. It was a great gig. The college would pay to move the whole family over to Cork for the year and provide us with a house to live in and a car to drive. As an exchange professor, I would teach at University College, Cork; I'd do a course in the fall for graduate students and a course in the spring for undergrads. And I would shepherd several dozen American students through the UCC system, take them on field trips to Dublin and Connemara and the Aran Isles.

Colby and University College, Cork, swap one faculty member each year. The year I was in Ireland, Colby got a zoologist, which most of my colleagues thought was a fair trade.

Several months before we left for our year in Ireland, I took a long walk through the woods.

I thought about Grace and the life we shared. I thought about how much I loved her. I thought about the two of us driving back from Charlotte and passing by the House of Mystery, stopping to kiss at every red light from North Carolina to Washington. How my eyes filled with tears when she made Thai shrimp with black peppercorns. The expression on her face as she'd walked down the aisle in the National Cathedral. I'd slipped a ring on her finger; inside the ring were the engraved words *Bright Star*, from the sonnet by Keats.

Her voice, soft and hushed as Luke cried for the first time in the delivery room. "That's amazing," she'd whispered.

I came back inside, my face ashen. "What is it?" she said. "What's wrong?"

I sat at the dining room table. Grace was looking at me with a worried expression.

"What is it, Jim?" she said. "It's okay. Whatever it is, it's better you talk about it."

Is it? I thought. Is it really better if I talk about it? Isn't keeping this hidden the only way I can protect you, can protect this family?

Isn't that my job, taking care of us? Sometimes you can do that better with silence than with words.

Wouldn't it be better, after all, to be like the couple we saw on our honeymoon, the husband who couldn't talk and the wife who couldn't hear?

"Okay, listen," I said to the person I loved more than anyone in the world. "There's something I have to tell you."

The Troubles

(Cork, Ireland, 1998–1999)

I fell off my bicycle on the way home from An Spailpin Fanach and lay there in the streets of Cork, looking up at the clouds. Soft rain fell on my cheeks. I felt completely contented lying there, the wheels of my bike spinning somewhere nearby.

Son? Are you all right, son?

I rode my bike to the pub only on those nights when I knew that, as they said in Ireland, "drink would be taken." On this particular evening, I fell off the bike because a car in front of me had stopped quite suddenly. I jammed on the brakes and was, moments later, launched skyward.

It was an evening on which I had sung "Fooba Wooba John" in public. In the mornings, in the office of the chair of the English Department at UCC, I would often be able to tell just how drunk I'd been by the songs I'd sung.

"I didn't sing 'The Dog Crapped on the Whiskey,' did I?" I'd ask my friend Eoin, whose name, by the way, is not the name of one of the dwarves from *The Hobbit* but is, in fact, a perfectly respectable Irish one pronounced the same as the English "Owen."

"Ah, sure you did," Eoin said with immeasurable delight.

"I didn't sing 'That's the Way You Spell Chicken,' did I?"

Eoin nodded again. "Ah, but a *carse* ye did!" he said.

I sighed. "Just tell me I didn't sing 'Fooba Wooba John,' please," I said. "That's all I ask."

"Ah, James," he said. "You *sang* it."

"Jesus," I said. "Was there anything I didn't sing?"

"No," said Eoin, "I can't say as there was."

So there, drunk in the street, lay the emergent transsexual. Before we left America, Grace and I had gone shopping together. I'd assembled a small wardrobe of women's things that looked all right on me. I had a couple of skirts from Coldwater Creek, a knit top from Territory Ahead. Some nights at home in the Colby flat, after the children were asleep, I would put this stuff on, and Grace and I would sit by the peat fire reading books together or playing Boggle.

Grace was strangely tolerant of all this. She thought of it as a hobby, like playing in the rock-and-roll band. For all that, though, it wasn't a hobby she particularly wanted to share. There didn't seem to be a place for her in it.

When I came out to her, I had not told her I was transsexual. I told her what I hoped could be true, which was that expressing just this much of myself would be enough. I didn't want it to threaten our marriage or our lives.

Still, for much of that year I felt like a chalk painting dissolving in rain.

I stood and picked up my bicycle off the sidewalk. The horizon swayed, as if I were on board a ship on the high seas. Interestingly, the car that had stopped in front of me was still sitting there. I was annoyed with the driver for having pulled up so suddenly. I might have been hurt. For a moment I considered having words with the man behind the wheel.

Then I noticed that the car was unoccupied. The car that had surprised me by stopping so suddenly was *parked* there.

———————

I spent that year in the traditional Irish manner—drinking heavily, singing songs, and wearing sheer-to-waist panty hose.

By mid-September I had fallen in with a crowd of people who followed several bands around Cork. There was Nomos, a traditional group that included both a sixty-year-old ex-policeman on fiddle and a nineteen-year-old teen idol on guitar. There was North Cregg, which included the teen idol's older brother on silent movie–style piano and a man named Christy Leahy on the box. Christy physically resembled a short Herman Munster, but his features were transformed by the music into something delicate and serene. The best place to hear these bands was the upstairs of the Lobby Bar, which was across the street from the Cork City Hall, on whose steps John F. Kennedy had stood early in 1963.

Another good venue was the Gables pub on Douglas Street, where Christy, along with North Cregg's guitarist, Johnny Neville, sat in a corner on Thursday nights and played their brains out. Frequently all sorts of their friends showed up as well, and there in the corner would be Christy on the box, Johnny on guitar, a piper, a banjo player, a mandolinist, and six fiddlers, their bows waving through the air in unison. I usually sat at a table about three feet away from this menagerie and just listened, transfixed. Every now and then Johnny would look over at me and say, "You liked that one all right, then, Boylan?"

On the surface of things, I was simply enjoying what I felt was the finest music in the world—traditional Irish—in the finest of venues— old pubs where Murphy's and Beamish were slowly poured by barmaids who knew my name. Beneath this, though, there was a sense of urgency and desperation in my heart. Slowly I was becoming aware of how little time might be left to me as a man. I feared that our return to America, in July, would begin a period of transformation and loss.

One night I was taken to a ceili where North Cregg was playing. There were about three hundred people all packed into a dance hall, and everyone was drinking pints of Murphy's and shots of Jameson's and Paddy's and Tullamore Dew. The band started playing well after midnight. For a few moments there was elegant set dancing, an elaborate kind of square dance that everyone had clearly learned in grade school. After a few moments of this, however, the whole business fell to pieces, and drunken madmen crashed through the lines like asteroids. Everyone else dove in, transforming the scene into a hilarious melee, a seething mass of arms and legs and women being lifted in the air and spun.

Riverdance, it wasn't.

At one point, North Cregg's banjo player busted a string, and without pause he just threw his banjo aside like it was a piece of junk and dove into the crowd, where he was properly fielded, then passed around on everyone's shoulders.

A girl asked me to dance late in the night, and I said, "I don't know how to dance to this music."

She beckoned toward the crowd, where punches were being thrown and giant rugby players were doing back flips in the air, and she just said, "Ah now, I'm sure somethin'll come to ye."

On the whole, I liked ballads and songs better than the jigs and the reels, because the lyrics seemed to speak to me. In the ballads I heard the constant theme of emigration. Surely they had me in mind when they sang about having to leave the land of one's birth because of the Great Hunger. Standing on the deck of a coffin ship, waving farewell to one's sweetheart. Making a difficult ocean crossing. Arriving at last in a new world, the land of promise, the land of freedom. But never quite fitting in, in the new land, always speaking with a trace of a foreign accent.

Sometimes I think the best way to understand gender shift is to sing a song of diaspora.

Our ship at the present lies in Derry Harbor
To bear us away—o'er the wide swelling sea.
May heaven be our pilot, and grant us fine breezes
Till we reach the green fields of Amerikey.
Oh, come to the land where we shall be happy.
Don't be afraid of the storm, or the sea.
And when we cross o'er, we shall surely discover,
That place is the land of Sweet Liberty.

One night I sat in the Four Corners, listening to a boy I did not know sing this song, tears coursing down my cheeks. *Don't be afraid of the storm, or the sea,* he says. How could I *not* fear the storm, or the sea? Surely, before I reached the green fields, I would perish in the briny ocean. Or, even if I did successfully *cross o'er,* how could I live without the love of the girl I'd left behind?

The people are saying that these two were wed,
But one had a sorrow that never was said.
He moved away from me, with his goods and his gear.
And that was the last that I saw of my dear.

———————

On New Year's Eve, our children went to bed early, and Grace and I were able to say good-bye to 1998 like adults. I made Peking duck for dinner. After we'd finished the last of the plum sauce, we snuck off into the bedroom and made love. We lay there in the warmth of each other's bodies for a while and then heard, far off, muffled in the Irish rain, the sounds of midnight as it was celebrated throughout the city.

"Happy New Year," we said to each other.

"You know what this year feels like, 1999?" I said.

"What?"

"It feels like a sneeze coming on."

Grace laughed and then rolled over and went to sleep.

The boys went to a Montessori school that year, where they learned to sweep the floor and put sponges in cans. Grace had an early morning workout at the gym, which she often followed with a trip to the English market in Cork's downtown. That left me at home in the Colby flat, where I would frequently put on the Coldwater Creek skirt and a black top and sit in the office and work on a screenplay. Occasionally Grace would come home to find me *en femme*, and she'd just shake her head and laugh. "No pearls before five," she'd say nervously before heading out again.

More often than not, though, I was alone in the house as a neo-female. I'd pay the bills for the program or I'd sit at the upright piano and sing "I Wanna Be Like You" from *The Jungle Book*.

Sometimes I would put on my pumps and my coat, and I'd stand there in the front hallway, thinking about going out into the world. I looked in the mirror. I thought I looked fine, if you didn't look too close. Still, I stayed indoors. I did not want to jeopardize the program or my own professional integrity by risking intrigue. Instead I waited on this side of the door, the Irish rain coming down outside, wondering when, and if, I would ever be able—as a woman—to feel that rain upon my face.

In March, we went to the Canary Islands, just off the coast of Morocco, with our children. There we played on purple black sand volcanic beaches. One afternoon I lay by the pool with a family of German tourists. All of the women took off their tops, even the grandmother, and I pretended not to look on amazed. Later that afternoon, over the loudspeakers at the resort, I heard the theme from *Shaft* in Spanish:

"*¿Quién es el detectivo negro?*"

"*Shaft!*"

"*¡Sí!*"

(This is merely an approximation.)

We returned home for several weeks, then left our children with a friend for several days while Grace and I went to Venice, then Florence. Venice, in particular, was haunting. Grace and I rode in a gondola, drank Chianti at a table in the Piazza San Marco, viewed the rising Venus. Then we passed across the Bridge of Sighs.

Grace's sister arrived from Oklahoma, and the two of them went off to London for a few days. I felt unbelievably mournful in Grace's absence, though. I spent the days in Cork in an absolute dark purple despair, playing the illean pipes in our apartment while the children were at school, or drinking at the Gables in the evening when I had a sitter, listening to Christy and Johnny play "Arthur MacBride and the Recruiting Sergeant." Songs of forced conscription also touched me deeply and seemed to speak to my condition.

> But says Arthur, ye needn't be proud of your clothes,
> For you've only the lend of them as I suppose,
> And you dare not change them one night, for you know
> If you do you'll be flogged in the morning.

Forced conscription, I thought as I drank yet another pint. You've got it, lads.

One afternoon, I walked around the city in a mournful private fog, eventually winding up on top of the spire of St. Ann's Cathedral, and there I stood above the city as the church bells began to ring, deafening me. On every side was the great city of Cork, the Beamish brewery and the college and the English market and the river Lee, rolling down to the sea. *What am I going to do?* I asked myself as German tourists below me banged out "You Are My Sunshine" on the carillon. *What am I going to do?*

When Grace and her sister returned from London, we took a ferry to the Aran Isles and were shown an ancient fort on Inishmore by a man we called Seamus O'Twotimes because he said things like "The population here is nine hundred. Nine hundred." He was like a Celtic-fried version of a character from *Goodfellas*.

The highlight of this tour was climbing a path to a mountain fort high above the sea, overlooking vast cliffs. Seamus O'Twotimes glee-fully explained how several years earlier a Danish student had gone off the edge. "He just walked right out into space. Into space."

I said to him, "Excuse me, but I have a question. This is a re-markable fort. But I was wondering, who was it the people who lived here were defending themselves against? I mean, who'd want to take over—*this* place? Wouldn't most warriors look at this cliff a half a mile in the air at the top of an island in the middle of nowhere and just say, 'Okay, you guys can *have* it!' Who was it they were being attacked by?"

Seamus O'Twotimes thought long and hard about this question. Then he said, "Persons such as themselves."

———————

At Reidy's Wine Vaults, Grace and my friend Eoin and I celebrated my birthday in June. Eoin noted that forty-one is the "age of a villain." And, further, "If you wanted to make someone a villain in a work of fiction, all you would have to do would be to tell the reader that he or she is forty-one and the reader will guess the rest."

A week later, I went to Amsterdam by myself for a few days to clear my head. I brought all of my girl things and stayed in a fine hotel and spent four days as a woman. On this occasion I decided to leave the confines of my hotel room, and so it was that in June of 1999, for the first time since my Baltimore days, I went out in the world wearing a skirt.

I spent about two hours getting ready, making sure I'd covered every nuance, shaving my arms, my legs, my face. I made sure my makeup was perfect. I looked in the mirror. I looked like a very nervous American tourist, like a mom from Connecticut who walks around with her passport in a money belt.

Then I stood by the door, trying to muster the courage to go outside.

Suddenly there was a knock on the door, and a moment later, it swung open.

"Oh," said the bell captain, "pardon me, madam. I thought you were the chambermaid."

Then he left, and I thought, *I'm not the chambermaid.*

I walked down the hallway and pushed the down button.

I stood in the elevator and watched the numbers descend. In a matter of moments, the doors were going to open in a crowded lobby. There I'd be, standing as a woman in a room full of people.

The door opened. I walked forward. No one looked at me twice.

I walked out into the streets of Amsterdam. I had forgotten what it felt like to wear a skirt outside and was frightened and chilled by the feeling of the breeze on my bare legs. I walked through the city, did some shopping. I walked over to Vondel Park and sat on a bench and watched the swans.

At the end of the day, I walked over to the Stedelijk Museum and there found the *Violinist* of Chagall, the green man who stands with his violin atop the rooftops of a city.

I stood there for a long time, looking at that man hovering, weightless, levitated by music above the sorrows of the world.

The Ice Storm

(*Winter 2000*)

Back in Maine again, our family stood on the banks of Great Pond, watching fireworks, as the millennium came to a close. In the house behind us were the voices of our friends, the music of Jimmy Durante: *Don't you know that it's worth, / Every treasure on earth, / To be young at heart. . . .* Corks popped off of champagne bottles. Couples slow-danced, their arms wrapped around each other.

Our children looked up at the night, their breath coming out in frozen clouds. Rockets exploded in the sky above us. Fiery blue streamers fell toward earth.

A few days later, I dropped Patrick off at day care and drove back through the snow toward home. I passed through the Colby campus, where a woman was doing a figure eight on the ice of Johnson Pond. Across the street, the Colby Woodsmen's Team was throwing hatchets at a large wooden bull's-eye. An ax struck the center of the circle as I drove past. *Thunk.*

I drove down the icy hill on Rices Rips Road and crossed the

Messalonskee Stream, its small waterfalls frozen into cascading stalac-
tites. As I approached the railroad tracks, the lights began to flash at
the crossing. A long freight train lumbered past, and I stopped and
looked and listened. The boxcars were covered with various legends:
*Bangor and Aroostook, Georgia Pacific, Chessie System, Southern Serves
the South.*

I reached for the radio and turned it on. From Blue Hill came the
sounds of the Zombies on WERU, "She's Not There."

I turned off the radio. There were all sorts of sounds already—the
squeaking of the wheels of the freight train, the idling of my engine,
the caboose rolling into the distance. The soft dinging of the crossing
bell ceased. Horns honked from behind me, engines gunned angrily.
People shouted as they drove around the Audi: *Hey, what's the matter
with you? Why are you just sitting there?* Snow fell on my windshield.
The wind howled.

I pulled the emergency brake. I stayed in the car, motionless, for
a long time.

Okay, I said. Okay, okay, okay. *Enough.*

———————

That night I said to Grace, "Listen, would you mind if I got back into
therapy again?"

She looked perplexed. "How could I mind it if you went into
therapy?"

"I know," I said. "It's just that I feel like I'm being crushed, with
the whole gender thing. I'm beginning to wonder if maybe what I
need is to be a woman full-time. But even just thinking about that
makes me crazy, all the losses it would mean for us. All I know is, I
can't do this alone anymore. I need to talk to someone."

Grace looked pale. "If you need therapy," she said softly, "you
should get it."

———————

I saw a therapist not far from my home who claimed to specialize in gender issues. He had an office in a building that more than anything else resembled the Island of Misfit Toys. Beneath a single roof was a massage therapist, an aromatherapist, a polarity therapist, and a numerologist. And then there was my advocate, a concerned-looking man I called Dr. Strange.

Strange listened to my story for six weeks, twice a week, two hours a shot. He took a lot of notes, talked about Greek mythology, lectured me on the nature of the soul, and asked me how I felt about my penis.

At the end of our sessions, I got a hug.

He gave me dozens of diagnostic tests. Some of them were relatively straightforward, others seemed completely obscure. Later, he asked me to find archetypal images of masculinity and femininity and to bring them in and talk about them. I brought in prints of twenty Impressionist paintings, including *After the Bath* by Degas.

"Very interesting," said Dr. Strange.

He asked me to talk about the differences between male and female and how I imagined that these were distinct from the differences between masculine and feminine. He asked me to trace my entire history as a trans person, from my earliest memory to the moment when I froze at the railroad crossing. We talked about sexuality, about marginality, about culture and archetype, about the difference between reality and fantasy. He researched my medical history, inquired about any history of abuse or neglect, searched my life in vain for symptoms of pathology.

I tried to comply with all of this and told him the truth, as best I knew it. He seemed startled by how well-adjusted I was. There didn't seem to be any explanation for it.

At the beginning of March he sat me down and said, "All right, look. We've been talking for a while now, and I think I have a pretty good sense of where you fall along the scale." He looked out the window. "You want to know what I think?"

"Okay," I said.

"First of all, let's agree on what you're *not*. You aren't a cross-dresser, or gay, or intersexed, or suffering from any other condition, like multiple personality disorder, or dissociative disorder. You operate at a strangely high level of functionality, actually, considering what you've been dealing with."

Dr. Strange cleared his throat.

"I would consider you a strong, positive candidate," he said, "for gender shift."

It was snowing outside, and the flakes ticked against the windowpanes. The radiator pipes clanked and hissed.

"Are you surprised?" he asked.

"No," I said.

"You're familiar with the Benjamin Standards of Care?"

"Yes, I know about them." The winter wind shook the windows.

"Well, the standards provide you with a safe and cautious manner of proceeding, if proceeding is what you want to do."

"If proceeding is what I want to do," I said. I felt like punching him. "How can I know if *proceeding is what I want to do?*"

"Do you doubt that this is what you want?"

"Of course it's what I want. But that's not the point. If I do this, I'm going to lose everything, don't you understand that? *Everything.*"

Dr. Strange reached forward and squeezed my hand. I snapped it back from him. I didn't want to be squeezed.

"Listen, Jim. You can start by doing what the standards suggest, which is talking the situation over in a therapeutic setting. You need to understand what you need to do, and the consequences. You can, if you so decide, start taking bigger and bigger steps out into the world as female, monitoring your reaction to that experience, and observing whether being female in the world is what you expect it to be. You don't have to do everything at once."

"Doing everything at once isn't the problem," I said. "The problem is doing anything at all."

"You need to talk this over with Grace," he said.

"You're telling me."

"It seems, from everything you've said, that you want to stay with Grace. And yet, you should know that most couples don't survive this. The ones that do aren't exactly *couples* after transition. They're more like friends, or sisters."

"I don't want to be sisters with her."

"Well, that's not a choice that's necessarily yours to make." He looked sad. "You also should be prepared for this to be the thing that others most misunderstand about transsexuality. People generally have a hard time distinguishing between sexual orientation and gender identity. But as it turns out, gay and lesbian people don't necessarily have that much in common with transsexuals."

"Yeah," I said. "Except for the fact that we get beaten up by the same people."

"You should be ready for people who don't get this to say, 'Oh, well, he was really just gay and couldn't deal with it.' "

"I know."

"Let me ask you. If you weren't married to Grace—if you didn't know her—and you were female . . . whom would you be attracted to, men or women?"

"I can't imagine not knowing her."

"Humor me."

"I don't know. I mean, my world has always revolved around women. I've never thought about men that way. I mean, it's never even crossed my mind."

"Well, be prepared for it to cross your mind. Once you start on hormones, it's likely you'll see the world in a different way. Of the previously heterosexual male-to-female transsexuals I've known, about a third of them remain attracted to women after transition, another third make the leap to men, and another third become kind of asexual. The best thing you can do is to just keep an open mind."

"I'm not sure I want an open mind," I said, "if it means destroying my relationship with Grace."

"Well. The very first thing you have to do, as far as I can see, is to begin including Grace in your transition. From the little work I have done with you already, I can tell you with absolute certainty that if you and Grace split up, the results will be *atomic.*"

"Atomic," I said. "Yeah, that's a pretty good word for it."

"And you should start thinking about talking to a larger circle of people about your being transgender. Not everyone has to know at first, and the people you tell first need not be the most important people in your life. But slowly, you need to start bringing this thing that has always been secret into the light of day, and sharing it with the people you love."

I nodded. "Uh-huh."

"After a few months, we can start to prescribe hormones for you, if that's what you want. Most people going from male to female start out on Premarin, usually a low dosage, increased gradually over time. You might also want to start in on an antiandrogen, to bring your testosterone down. I have an endocrinologist I work with I can recommend; or you can consult your own family doctor. In any case, hormones are dangerous, and you should make sure that you take them in consultation with someone who knows what they're talking about. You know what hormones will do, don't you?"

"I have a pretty good sense of it."

"Well, I'm going to say this anyway, just so I know you heard it. Your skin will soften. Your hair will get thicker and fluffier. The hair on your arms and legs and chest will grow finer. Your breasts will start to grow, gradually reverting you to the genetic shape you've inherited from your mother and grandmother. A general rule of thumb is that you'll be about a cup smaller than your female relatives."

I nodded again. I came from a family of large-busted, slim-hipped women.

Dr. Strange continued. "You'll experience something called 'fat migration.' The fat in your body right now is centered in the male places—on your cheeks, in your neck, and on your belly. Over time it will move away from those places toward the female places—your bust, your buttocks, and especially your hips. Your overall weight will probably remain the same, but people will think you're losing weight since your features, and your face in particular, will change.

"People who have taken hormones report that the most dramatic effect of all that estrogen is on your brain. There is said to be a distinctly different way that your brain will function, and in which you experience the world. I don't know if this is true or not, but you will probably want to keep a journal and monitor those changes."

"I'm going to be writing," I said quietly.

"Your voice may soften over time, more from culture than biology, but you might want to talk to a voice specialist. There is a woman at Bates College who works with transsexuals. Here's her card."

I took it. "Tania Vaclava," I said.

"She's Hungarian," he explained.

"Great," I said. "So I'll talk like a Hungarian woman."

He smiled. "When you've been on hormones for a year, the standards require you to seek a second opinion from another mental health care professional. You are specifically required to see someone with a medical degree, either an M.D. or a Ph.D. When you have two letters of recommendation from your therapists, you can schedule surgery, which usually takes place a year or two after that. People in Maine tend to go to Drs. Menard and Bressard in Montreal, but other top surgeons include Schrang in Wisconsin, Meltzer in Oregon, Biber in Colorado, and Alter in Los Angeles. There are others, too. You should research each of the available doctors and see whom you're most comfortable with. Maybe you'd like to go to Thailand. There are a lot of good surgeons in Bangkok."

I shook my head. "Bangkok," I said.

"Anyway, before you can have the gender reassignment surgery—or GRS—you are required to live full-time as a woman for a minimum of one year. During that period you may not go back to being a man at any time. You are expected to be psychologically preparing for your new gender. If you have any reservations or second thoughts, the time of your real-life experience, or RLE, is the time to learn of them, not after surgery, which is permanent and irreversible."

"I know," I said.

"Okay," said Dr. Strange. "Now the first thing you want to do is sit down with Grace tonight and talk this over with her. You are going to need her every step of the way. My own opinion is, you cannot get to where you need to go without her support and her love."

"But, doc, how can I expect her to participate in a process that by its very definition will take the man she loves away from her? That will destroy the life we have lived?"

"You can't expect it," Dr. Strange said. "But you can ask for it."

"I can't do this to her," I said to him.

"Listen," he said. "You aren't 'doing' anything. You are a transsexual. Amazingly, you have managed to carry this burden all these years. It is time for you to get help. You need to turn to the people you love to help you. You can't keep carrying this burden alone."

"I'd rather keep carrying it alone," I said, "than cause all this grief to the people I love."

"Well," Dr. Strange said, "that's your choice, I guess. Do you really think you can keep on the way you've been going? How much further do you think you can go?"

"I can't go any further at all," I said to him.

"Then what you have to do is clear," he said.

"No, what I have to do is completely *unclear*," I said. "Just because I can't go any further as a man doesn't mean I can just pick up and start on the road to being female. I don't know how to do that. I *can't* do that."

"Maybe Grace will help you," he said.

"Maybe Grace will want to suffocate me with a pillow."

"Jim," Dr. Strange said, "do you really think that's what's going to happen?"

"No," I said, "probably not. Actually, she'll probably want to suffocate *herself* with a pillow."

"Jim, Grace is a social worker. These aren't new issues to her. I'll bet she has more of a sense of how this works than you think. She does love you, no matter what else is true. She is going to want you to be happy."

"You really do live on your own little planet," I said, "don't you."

Dr. Strange stood up and spread his arms. "Have a hug," he said.

That evening just before sundown, Grace was in tears, her heart broken in two.

———————

The burden that had been mine alone for all these years was now Grace's, and in the weeks that followed she walked through her days broken and crushed.

I had spent most of my life hearing the refrain of our culture, which says that truth is always better than lies, that we shouldn't have secrets, that the truth will set us free.

Now that I had told the truth, I felt anything but free. Every time I looked at my family, I thought, *Remind me again what's so terrible about mendacity.*

Of course, our lives continued, in spite of the atom bomb that had gone off in our midst. Luke continued to board the bus for first grade each day, and Patrick was taken over to day care several mornings a week. We would all get home at the end of the day, and the boys would eat macaroni and cheese and get their baths, and Grace or I would make dinner and we'd sit down and eat it while the children watched *Rugrats* on television.

I made salmon on the grill, marinated in jerk sauce. Actually, *jerk sauce* began to feel like the house brand.

"So how are you doing?" The children were watching television in the sunroom.

"Oh, I'm terrific," Grace said. She drank her Chardonnay. "Never better."

"Have you been thinking any more about . . . you know, the *issues*?"

Something in the next room broke into hundreds of pieces.

"What was that?" Grace shouted.

"Nothing," Luke and Patrick said in unison.

"I mean," I continued, "I'm trying to think about the issues. . . ."

Grace's eyes filled with tears. "Jim, what do you want me to say?"

"I don't know," I said. "I just want to know if you're, like—"

"Stop it," said Luke. "Mommy! Patrick's annoying me!"

"Luke," I shouted. "Patrick. If you can't play nice together, I'm going to have to separate you."

Grace looked down at her salmon. "I feel like you're on a runaway train," she said.

"What do you mean?"

"I mean, you see this Dr. Strange, this maniac, for like six weeks, and all of a sudden it's like, that's it, you're going to—"

"Luuuuke," Patrick said angrily. "I'm warning you! Don't make me BITE you!"

"THERE'S NO BITING!" I shouted.

Grace sipped her wine.

"I'm not on a runaway train," I said. "I've been thinking about this stuff for years, for decades. I've tried negotiating with it every way I can think of. I have to do something now, or I'm going to go crazy."

"Well, I haven't been thinking about it for decades. I've been thinking about it for what seems like five minutes."

"Ow!" Luke yelled. He came running to the table. "Daddy, Patrick bit me!"

"I'm sorry, Luke. But did you do anything to make him bite you?"

"He said he was going to bite you," Grace said.

"He was annoying me!"

Patrick came into the room. "Paddy," Grace said, "we don't bite people in our family." She looked at me. "No matter how much we want to."

"That's right," I said. "That's not how we express ourselves. Not if we can help it."

"I want a cheese stick," said Patrick.

"Okay," Grace said.

"I'll get it," I said, and went to the refrigerator.

Grace finished her wine. Luke went back into the sunroom. Patrick grabbed the cheese stick as if it were the Olympic torch and ran as fast as he could toward the television.

"What do you think we should do, Grace?" I said.

"We?" she said. "What do you mean, we?"

"I want to include you in this," I said. "I want for this to be something that we do together."

"Together? How is it going to be something we do together?"

"I don't know. By sharing what we're going through—or . . ."

Grace didn't say anything. "Can I get you anything?" I said. "While I'm up?"

Grace wiped her eyes. "I want what I had," she said.

———

In mid-March I drove over to Russo's house. His family was out. He knew something was up; he'd seen the looks on our faces that winter, and I'd warned him by phone I needed to talk.

"Sounds ominous," he said.

"It is."

On the drive over to Camden, I listened to Bob Dylan in the car, "Visions of Joanna": *We sit here stranded, though we all do our best to deny it. . . .*

I didn't know how Rick was going to take the news. I knew I could count on his loyalty, but for that matter he was loyal to Grace, too. He had always put his own family first, and I couldn't imagine him condoning anything that would place my family at risk.

It was possible, I thought as I drove toward Russo's house, that he wasn't going to want to know me anymore.

He opened a bottle of wine. We sat in his living room for a while as I tried to muster the courage to say the words I needed to say. It was terrible. I sat there in mortal anguish, trying to gather the necessary momentum.

I talked about Colby, about my latest novel, about some friends of ours, each of us knowing I was only trying to warm myself up to say something impossible.

"Okay, Russo," I said at last. "Listen. You know that you are just about the best friend I've ever had, right?"

"Boylan," he said, "can I just tell you, don't worry. Whatever it is, I'm with you, all right?"

I shrugged. "Maybe you should let me say what I need to say first."

"You didn't murder anyone, did you?" said Russo.

"No."

"I mean, it's okay if you did. I just want to know what I'm in for."

"Russo?" I said. "Shut up."

He nodded. "All right."

"Rick, I'm closer to you than anyone, except for Grace. And over the years, we've shared all kinds of great adventures."

He nodded. "We have."

"Except that there is one thing about me that you don't know. Because I've kept it secret from you." I paused. I could hear the clock in the next room ticking.

"It's hard for me to tell you *now* because I fear I'll lose your friendship, you'll think I'm just some circus freak."

I felt as if I were pulling back the string of a bow.

"But the thing that you don't know about me is that I'm transgender. I'm a transsexual. I've identified as female since I was a child. My sense of having a woman's spirit has almost never left me. The only time it ever vanished was when I fell in love with Grace, and when that happened I felt that what I had always hoped for was true, that I'd at last been cured by love."

I paused to catch my breath. Rick was absolutely motionless.

"Except that I haven't been cured. And now I'm faced with the impossible task of trying to balance my own need to be female with my desire to protect and support the woman that I love."

I paused.

Very quietly Rick said, "Jesus, Jim."

"Wait, let me finish," I said. "There's a lot of things I need to explain, so just let me get this all out, okay?"

"Okay, but before you say anything else, let me just say this, all right? You're my best friend, Boylan, and as it turns out, I don't make that many friends." He leaned forward. "What you need to know is, you will *always* be my friend. If you're going to be a woman, well, Jesus. You'll be my friend as a woman."

Tears came to my eyes.

Russo shook his head. "Jesus, Jim," he said.

"I know."

I told him the rest of the story. It took a long time.

Russo opened another bottle of wine. We drank it.

"You know what, Jim," he said after a while. "The thing is, if you were living a life on your own, it would be different. I mean, I think I'd still be pretty much taken aback, but I still think I'd be all right with this. But your life is not only your own, and it seems that while you are going to get a chance to be happy—I must say you always *seemed* happy before—Grace isn't going to get that chance. I'll be all right, I guess, with the idea of your decision. But I think I'm going to have a hard time with the consequences of that decision."

"It's not a decision," I said. "It's just something that is. It's more like an erosion than a decision."

Rick shrugged. "I'm not sure I understand that."

"I'm not sure I understand it, either."

"I'll tell you what, Boylan. You know I'll follow you wherever you need me to go. But I'll tell you one thing. You're asking me to accept a fundamental change in the one person in the world of whom I could honestly say, 'I wish he would change nothing.' "

"I guess that's a compliment," I said.

Russo shrugged. "It used to be."

A few weeks later, Grace and I drove down to Portland for the weekend, with me as Jenny. I wore a floral skirt, a linen top, and an eggshell cardigan. We had a baby-sitter for the night, and the plan was that we'd drive down to Freeport, do some shopping, then stay at a hotel in the city and go out to dinner. We'd come home the next day. The theory was that it would do us both good to spend some extended time together—for Grace to get used to being with me as a woman, and for me to get used to being with her, and for both of us to see what it was like to be out in the world as a couple in this new form.

As we arrived in a crowded restaurant for lunch and waited for our table, Grace was stricken by the fear that someone was going to come up and punch me in the nose.

My fear, of course, was that the person punching my nose would be Grace.

After lunch, we walked around the Old Port of Portland and went shopping at some stores, including a children's clothing outlet, where Grace called to me across the store, "Jim! Jim!" The sales clerk looked at me and smiled with pained politeness.

Being unveiled thus did not diminish my awe at being out in the world at last. My heart pounded and my head felt light. Everything struck me with total amazement, as if I were walking on the earth for the first time.

When we got back to the hotel there was a message on the answering machine. It was the baby-sitter.

"Jim, Grace? Listen, we're at the emergency room. Patrick's had a fall. He was running around the house naked after he got out of the bathtub, and he fell on a heat register and cut his chin. He's going to be all right, but he needs to get stitches. It's, uh—midnight now, and they say they'll be able to get to us around one-thirty, maybe two A.M. We're all fine, but I just wanted you to know what was going on. Don't worry, we're all okay!"

Grace sighed, looked over at her husband, who was wearing a Coldwater Creek skirt and a twin set, and began to cry. "I want you back," she said softly. "Oh God, Jim, I just want you *back*."

I came over to the bed and embraced her. It felt strange, though. After all these years together, I was becoming something unfamiliar.

Wibbly Wobbly

(Summer 2000)

Dr. Peabody, the endocrinologist, wasn't what I was expecting. I don't know what I was expecting, except perhaps the talking dog from *The Rocky and Bullwinkle Show.* "Greetings, everyone, Peabody here."

Instead he was a sharp, tired man with a bald head and a bristly mustache. He wore a bow tie.

"James," he said, "have a seat."

His desk was piled high with papers. It was hard to see him behind the mountains of stacked-up books, medical charts, and faxes.

"Tell me about yourself," he said.

So I did. I talked about growing up, about my experiences as a transgender person, about teaching at Colby, about my marriage with Grace and my children.

"Have you resolved the issues around your marriage?" he asked.

"We're working on it."

"And your job, at Colby? Do you expect you'll be able to keep it?"

"I don't know," I said. "I think it will be a big shock at work but that eventually people will get over it. I think a college is a pretty good place for transition, though. We do talk a lot about issues of diversity and inclusion there."

"Mm-hm," he said. He fingered his mustache. "Okay, let's take a look at you."

We went into his examination room, where he examined things I wasn't even sure you could examine, with instruments I did not know existed. He weighed me: 150 pounds. He measured my height: five feet eleven inches. He felt my chest and squeezed my nipples. He dug around in my gut to consider the topography of my liver and kidneys and bladder.

"Okay," he said. "Put your clothes back on and come back to my office."

I got dressed and then sat down again.

"You're in very good health," he said. "I'm going to want to take a new set of metabolic panels on you, though—a chem twelve, lipid levels, and an endocrine workup. But I don't see that there will be any problems."

He thumped the eraser end of a pencil on his desk.

"So, do you want to get started, then?" he said.

Everything seemed very quiet. His voice echoed in my heart.

"Okay," I said in a small voice.

He wrote out a prescription: "Let's begin with .3 milligrams of Premarin, for three weeks. Then we'll increase it to .625, for four weeks. Then up to .9, for a month, then 1.25 for a month, and finally to 2.5 a month after that. We'll stay with the 2.5, and then we'll do another round of levels and see what kinds of results you're getting."

"Okay," I said.

"You should know that estrogens work very slowly, over a period of years. But basically, at age forty-two, you're going to go through female adolescence." He shook his head.

"What?"

"I'm just glad it's you and not me," he said.

"What will the hormones do?" I asked.

"Well, everyone reacts differently. Even genetic women experience them differently. As a rule of thumb, we know that most people like you come to resemble the body shape of their mothers and sisters. But of course, even within one family, women are all shapes and sizes. So in the end, we don't really have any idea what kinds of results you're going to get.

"But hormones are powerful, and any changes in your endocrine system are going to have to be done slowly and with care. You know that you have an increased risk now of breast cancer, and of pulmonary thrombosis. I want you to get good exercise and do breast self-exams. You know how to do a breast exam?"

I said I'd learn.

He looked out the window. "You need to know that this is all kind of unknown territory to me," he said. "I've had other transgender patients. But it's not the reason you go into endocrine science. I'm sorry if I'm not an expert. If you want an expert, you should probably go down to Boston." He shrugged. "Or New York."

"I'm comfortable with you as my doctor," I said.

"Okay," he said. He wrote out all the prescriptions. "Here you go," he said. "Good luck."

I shook his hand. "Come back in six months," he said. "And we'll see what we've got."

I got in the car and drove south. The prescriptions sat on the car seat next to me. *So, do you want to get started, then?*

I drove home in silence, my heart pounding. I stopped at True's Pharmacy on the way to the lake, and they put together the prescription and said, "Here you go, Mr. Boylan." The pills were green.

I went to the lake and sat on the dock with a Bass Ale and watched the sunset on the water. I felt frightened and alone, and I missed Grace.

I drank the beer and listened to the loons calling on the lake.

Grace pulled up in the Jeep, and I ran up to the house to be with her. She came in the house bearing gifts. It was my birthday.

"What do you have there?" she asked me. I was still carrying the pills.

"The hormones," I said. "He just wrote me out a prescription."

Grace nodded as if this were no surprise, then said, "Open the card."

The birthday card had a rainbow on the front. Inside she had written these words: "Here's to forty-two years of joy and struggle, conflict and resolution, dreams and possibilities. And with love for all that's yet to come. Happy Birthday, Grace."

I read these words and began to weep. Grace held me in her arms.

The next present was a group of "meditation stones." Although in general I was much too sarcastic to be taken in by something as new age as this, once again I was reduced to tears.

The stones were each engraved with a different word. The five words Grace had chosen were *CLARITY, GRACE, SERENITY, HARMONY,* and *ACCEPTANCE.*

Then she said, "I was going to get you earrings, but our favorite hippie store was closed."

She gave me a fine bottle of champagne, and together we walked through the woods down to the water and sat on Adirondack chairs on the dock. I told her about my meeting with Dr. Peabody. She was a little surprised I seemed so blown away. "After all," she said, the bitterness and loss clear in her voice, "you're just following the script you came up with back in January."

We ate salsa and chips and listened to loons and watched a hawk circling high above the water.

Then I opened the bottle of Premarin and shook out one oblong green pill, put it in my mouth, clinked glasses with Grace, and swallowed it with a mouthful of champagne.

Estrogen tasted bittersweet.

We finished the bottle of champagne between the two of us, then went out to dinner by the Kennebec River. I had a spicy gumbo. Grace had sea bass. We ate pie for dessert.

In the morning I woke up with my head pounding. I got out of bed and took another pill and let Grace sleep and made the children breakfast.

Within a few days I began to feel a strange buzz. My skin was sensitive. I imagined that I could feel the ridges on my fingertips. A sense of warmth pulsed inside me.

The line between male and female turns out to be rather fine. Although we imagine our genders as firm and fixed, in fact they are as malleable as a sand castle.

That July, a maintenance man in the Philadelphia airport called me "ma'am," even though I was "presenting" as a man at the time. I wore a flannel shirt and blue jeans. I wondered if this was an isolated occurrence and went over to a woman selling peanuts in the concourse, directly opposite the ladies' room. I asked her, "Excuse me, where is the rest room?"

She looked at me as if I were blind. She pointed across the concourse. "Turn around, honey," she said.

I did.

"You see that sign *right there* that says 'Ladies'?"

I nodded.

"Well, honey. *That's* the rest room!" She laughed.

"Thanks," I said.

So I walked across the concourse and into the room that said "Ladies," and there were half a dozen women doing what women do, and no one looked at me with any surprise whatsoever. I went into a stall, then came out of one. I looked in the mirror. A tall, thin person with long blond hair looked back.

The fat migration that Dr. Strange predicted was the first and most dramatic effect of the estrogen. Like my father, I had carried much of my male weight in my chin and cheeks and belly. As the estrogen coursed slowly through my body, all that weight melted off my face and took up new residence on my hips and buttocks.

The strength in my upper body was another early casualty of hormones. Within a few months I found it hard to open jars or even lift up my children. In August, when Grace and I made our annual climb up Mt. Katahdin, I was amazed how hard it was to carry a backpack and ascend even an average mountain trail.

One afternoon I was playing a board game with Luke, and I rolled a pair of dice. As I did so, he started laughing, and I said, "What?" and he pointed to my upper arms and said, "Wibbly wobbly." I shook my arm again, and there it was—the loose flab of the middle-aged female triceps. I remembered how my sixth-grade orchestra conductor, Mrs. Liesel, had flab on her arm that swung so freely, we feared the first violinist was going to get struck by it.

My breasts, too, changed fairly quickly. The nipples evolved first, expanding in diameter and changing in texture. The veins around them grew heavier and thicker. My chest ached.

When I began hormones, my measurements were 35–30–36. A year later, they were 37–30–38. When all was said and done, I was a C cup. And I still weighed exactly the same.

Estrogen and antiandrogens profoundly affected my libido. I certainly thought about sex a lot less often and with a different sensibility. As a man, my sex drive frequently resembled a monologue by a comic book hero succumbing to an evil spell. "Must—have! *Must!* Trying—to—*resist!* Getting harder to— *Must have! Can't—resist!*"

I'd been driven to such delirium not only by the sight of breasts, but by the *suggestion* of breasts, even by the *theory* of breasts.

Now, when I looked at my own breasts, I had a simple sensation of, *Well—there they are.* My friend Curly, early in the process, asked me, "What's it like? What's it like to have boobs after all this time?"

"It's not *like* anything," I simply said. "They're just *there.*"

Curly shook his head. "Man, Boylan, you *are* turning into a woman. One thing about women, they have no idea how interesting their tits are. They don't think they're all that remarkable at all. I mean, when I'm with girls sometimes I just want to say, How can you concentrate on *anything*, looking like that?"

"Sorry," I said. "They're great, but you know. The world doesn't revolve around breasts."

"Listen to you!" Curly shouted. "Of *course* the world revolves around breasts! What *else* would it revolve around?"

I shrugged. "I don't know," I said. "Like maybe the *sun?*"

Curly looked at me as if I were a stranger. "The sun, yeah, right." He sighed. "I wish you could hear yourself."

"Sorry, dude," I said. "There are more important things in the world than breasts."

My friend looked regretful.

"What?" I said.

"I'm trying to think of something more important than breasts."

"How about family? Children? Relationships? Good health?"

"Traitor," he said.

That fall, at Colby, as my body morphed, people knew something was up. Yet, perhaps understandably, *imminent sex change* was not the primary deduction. What they thought was that I was sick, fighting some disease I did not want to discuss.

When people asked me about my "weight loss," I came up with a cockamamie story about how I had lost the pounds I'd picked up drinking Murphy's in Cork. This seemed to satisfy people; at the very least, it ended the conversation. Privately, though, all of my colleagues at work were worried about me. At least now they *say* they were.

After six months of Premarin, I had another round of levels taken. I was found to have 59 nanograms of estrogen in my system. The average for an adult male is 6. The mean for females is 26.

Dr. Peabody nodded and said, "You're doing fine." In the fall he added an antiandrogen, which made my testosterone level go down. When people asked me, later, what the effects of the pills were, I cleverly said, "Well, the one pill makes you want to talk about relationships and eat salad. The other pill makes you *dislike* the Three Stooges."

I noticed that I was more sensitive to stimuli now. I was much more aware of changes in heat and cold, and I was much more likely to complain that a car I was riding in was too hot or too cool, and I was frequently taking off sweaters or putting them back on again.

My skin grew softer. The hair on my arms and chest grew fine until it virtually melted away. The hair on my head grew fluffier, and I could feel it as it moved softly around my shoulders and neck. I shaved my legs, an activity that gave me exactly zero pleasure.

My moods began to shift capriciously. A friend sent me a "list of twenty-five reasons why it's great to be a guy"; one of them was "one damn mood, all the damn time." I used to cry at things like Pepsi commercials and *It's a Wonderful Life.* Now I was less likely to cry at these things and was more likely to tear up when a dinner I had cooked didn't turn out right, or when someone said something cruel, or when Luke put his arms around me and told me he loved me. I would sing an Irish song to a friend and suddenly become completely choked up, unable to finish. And when I cried, it wasn't just the stoic silent leaking I was accustomed to. These were big, sobbing tears, and my body shook as they poured out. It felt great.

I liked the freedom of tears. But it was unnerving how close they were to the surface.

Above all, I was aware of a change in the way I occupied my body. I felt raw and vulnerable, exposed to the world. One day I was walking in a skirt through Lewiston, Maine, as rain fell and the wind howled around me, and I thought, There is nothing in a man's experience that is like this, and I didn't mean just the physical sense of cold wind on my legs.

The thing that I felt testosterone had given me more than anything else was a sense of protection, of invulnerability. I had never imagined myself to be particularly invulnerable when testosterone had free rein in my system, but this new world I was approaching seemed to have no buffers. Things that used to just bounce off me now got under my skin. There were a number of occasions when I wished I still had that male shield standing between me and the harshness of the world.

I began electrolysis of my beard that summer. Electro is a process by which one kills off hair follicles by placing a burning hot electric needle deep into one's pores and basically deep-frying the roots of each individual hair like an onion ring. It was unbelievably painful, like being shocked and jabbed and barbecued all at the same time. It left my face looking like a Quarter Pounder, without cheese. I'd endure two and a half hours of this a week, for a year and a half, then I did it for an hour a week for another year. My electrologist estimated that I had about forty thousand follicles on my face. Each one had to be char-grilled four or five times. All told, I probably spent about 250 hours, over two and a half years, in the fryer.

I also tried, on three occasions, the new "laser electrolysis," which was performed by a plastic surgeon who scorched my face with something that looked like a Jedi light saber. It felt as if I were placing my face into one of those giant steel cauldrons one sees in foundries, a gargantuan bucket filled with white-hot molten lava. This left me beardless for a few months, then it all grew back again. I asked the plastic surgeon about this, and he said, "Yeah, that's the problem." Apparently you had to keep getting smelted, again and again.

I tried to explain the horrors of this process to a few people who knew what I was going through, but they weren't particularly moved. Their attitude seemed to be, "Well, sorry you're in such agony, but if you don't want to be in such agony, stop having your beard burned off like an imbecile."

Their attitude, toward electro as well as toward the entire condition of transsexuality, resembled the spirit behind an ancient Henny Youngman joke:

Guy goes in to see a doctor, he says, "Doc, you gotta help me, I get a terrible pain every time I go like *this.* What should I do?"

Doctor says, "Don't go like *that.*"

I began to play regularly with a rhythm-and-blues band called Blue Stranger. The brains behind the band were a couple named Nick and Shell. Nick was the bass player, and his wife, Shell, beautiful and fearless, was the lead singer. She regularly charged out into the audience with her remote mike and danced on top of the bar.

It was a great band to be in; everyone was an adult with a job and a family, and we played only for the sake of having fun. For all that, they were excellent musicians. Playing music with Blue Stranger was more fun than almost anything else I could imagine, and best of all, we played only covers—no annoying original material whatsoever. We played "Brown-Eyed Girl" in seedy Maine bars for drunken working people. What could be better than that?

Shell, who could swear like a sailor when she was in the mood, was one of the first people to ask me directly about the changes in my appearance. "You look weird," she said. "What are you on, the AIDS diet plan?"

"I've been losing some of the weight I picked up in Ireland," I said.

"You're not dying, are you?"

"I'm not dying."

" 'Cause if you are, and you're not telling your friends about it, all I can say is *Fuck you*."

"I'll let you know if I'm dying," I said.

"You'd better," Shell said. "Or I'll fucking kill you."

Grace, of course, was also acutely aware of the changes in me, and they frightened her. The rapidity of my body's response to estrogen, which was not entirely typical, further reinforced her sense that I was on a "runaway train." It was true that I'd begun hormones, begun electrolysis, begun this transition, all with a sense of experimentation, to see, as Dr. Strange had suggested, whether being increasingly female in the world was what I had expected it would be. I still had the sense that I could suspend or reverse this journey at any moment, if I found that the world I was coming to inhabit was one in which I did not wish to live. Yet Grace didn't see that, and if I said as much—that all of this was still on a trial basis—she did not believe it.

She, too, saw me as increasingly female, and as a result, she began to react to me as she might react to another woman, which is to say, as a close friend or relative rather than a lover. Her eyes no longer sparkled when I entered a room, and the embraces and kisses I gave her she endured rather than enjoyed. By the end of that summer, we were quickly becoming like sisters—sharing a home, a family, shepherding children, but without a physical relationship.

The last time we slept together we were at the lake house, in autumn. The dock had been pulled out of the water, the canoes were overturned in the boat rack, and the loons had headed south. The red leaves of the maples and the soft brown needles of the pines were fallen on the lawn.

We lay in bed after making love, lying back on our pillows, the sheet covering us at the waist. Grace was curled onto me, but her head was resting on a female breast.

I felt something liquid on my ribs, and I leaned forward to see the tears, flowing quietly from her face and rolling down my body.

"Grace," I said. "It's okay."

She didn't say anything for a long time.

"It's just . . . ," she said at last. "Each time we make love now, I'm afraid—it's going to be the last time."

"I'm not going anywhere, honey," I said. "Don't worry. I will always love you."

But my words to her only made clear how little I understood what she meant. I *had* gone somewhere, whether I loved her or not. And the fear she spoke of, that each time together would be the last—was not the fear that I would lose my affection for *her*. It was the fear that she would lose hers for me.

Someone who did not know us, who might have looked through

the window at us lying there, might have seen two women, curled in each other's arms, one of them in tears. *What a shame,* such a stranger might have thought. *I wonder what's come to make those women so sad.*

———————

I saw a review in *The New York Times* of a film that had been the highlight of the New York Film Festival, *Being John Malkovich.* The screenwriter and co-producer was one Charlie Kaufman.

I thought of my old roommate on 108th Street, remembered us trying to catch the mice that lived inside the upright piano. The sound those little feet made as they sprang across the strings.

I gave Charlie a call at the last number I had for him in Los Angeles, and I got his answering machine. "Hey, Charlie," I said. "I saw the review of your film in the *Times,* and I just wanted to say congratulations. Give me a call sometime if you want to be in touch." I thought about explaining the whole sex change business, but it didn't seem like the right thing to stick on an answering machine. I'll tell him the story if he calls back, I thought.

He didn't.

———————

One day the doorbell rang unexpectedly when I was at the lake, and I looked out the window with apprehension. The unannounced visitor was what I always feared when I was there "as" Jennifer. Out in the driveway was a car I did not recognize, a boat on its trailer. A woman sat in the passenger seat.

A voice called from downstairs. "Hello? Anybody home?"

I decided, *Well, here goes nothing,* and went downstairs. I was wearing a green skirt and a T-shirt and a minimum of makeup.

"Hi," said the visitor. "It's me, Italo Calvino [not his real name]. I'm your neighbor?"

Italo had the house in back of us—he lived in New Jersey and always came up to Maine for a few weeks each summer.

"I'm Jenny Boylan," I said.

"Hello. Are you Jim's sister?"

I nodded. Okay, that was a good idea. "Yeah," I said. "I'm Jim's sister, Jenny."

"Well, listen, I just needed some help getting my boat in the water. Is Jim going to be back later?" he said.

"I don't think so."

"You're his sister?" He looked at my breasts. "You ever read his books? They're funny."

"I've read them," I said.

He reached forward to shake my hand. "I live up the street. We live in Jersey, come up here every summer."

He looked out at his wife, sitting there in the car. "You married?"

"Yes," I said.

He thought this over. "Well, you see Jim, you tell him I said hi. Maybe the four of us could do something sometime." I tried to figure out which four he meant. Was he counting my husband? His wife? Of the four he had in mind, was I two of them?

"I'll tell him."

He shook my hand again and held it for a little too long, then he headed down the steps. As he did, I suddenly realized he hadn't asked *me* to help with his boat. I guess the way he figured, being a woman, I'd only screw it up.

As he got to his car, I heard his wife say something. Italo responded to her with a phrase that seemed to seethe with diminution. "Naaah," he said to her. "It was only his *sister*."

And the way he said this showed me exactly how little a person of importance he considered me to be. It hurt my feelings. I'm *only* my sister? I thought, What am I, chopped liver? I went to the bathroom and looked in the mirror. An average-looking woman in her early forties stared back at me. I held up one finger and wiggled it like the possessed child in *The Shining*.

"Jimmy isn't here anymore, Mrs. Boylan," I said.

It was a sentiment that Grace increasingly shared, as the months went by and she watched her husband slowly disappear from sight.

Boygirl
(Winter 2000–2001)

The Coffin House hadn't changed much in twenty-five years. The steps up to the third floor still creaked, and most of the posters I'd hung on the wall in tenth grade were still there. The dog door still led into the kennel, although the dog had been dead twenty years. Everywhere there were framed pictures of the family—of my parents in their youth; of my grandfather, still sternly standing watch above the fireplace; of me wearing a mortarboard at Wesleyan graduation. The keyboard cover on the Cable Nelson in the living room still bore the scratches made by my fingers a long time ago. A low C still had a small chip in the ivory. That was where my tooth had hit the keyboard one night in eleventh grade, when I'd tried to play the low notes with my nose.

In the morning I would tell my buoyant mother that I was a transsexual.

I slept in the bed in which I had lost my virginity to Donna

Fierenza in 1979, the same bed in which Grace and I had conceived Patrick. The bathtub where Onion had bathed was still there, although the walls of the bathroom had been painted a cream color. On a bookshelf was still the thick volume *Art Masterpieces of the World*. The pages still fell open to *The Turkish Bath*.

The house was just as haunted as ever. At night it groaned and creaked; soft footsteps padded through the attic above my head. The wind rushing through the drafty windows suggested the soft voices of whispering children.

I am not sure what time it was when I felt my father standing next to my bed, but when I opened my eyes, there he was, just as he had been in life.

Dad had always been a shy, polite man, and for a moment he looked almost embarrassed to be materializing, as if it were such a tacky and clichéd form of behavior for the dead.

He raised one hand as if to tell me not to worry. I could smell the Alberto VO5 he used to use on his hair. He glowed.

"Jenny," he said.

I wanted to respond to him, but I could not find my voice. Still, for all that, his presence wasn't frightening. As in life, my father seemed incredibly gentle in spirit. Being dead didn't seem to have particularly embittered him.

"I want you to know," he said, "I've been looking out for you, protecting you, for these last fifteen years. Being your guardian. I know a lot of things now I didn't used to know."

He looked sad.

"I know that you have to become a woman, Jenny. It is going to be all right. Your mother will always love you, and so will I."

He stood there floating for a while.

Then he said, "But you need to know this. If you become a woman, as I know you must, I'm not going to be looking out for you anymore. You will be on your own."

Then he looked at me coldly, harshly, and faded.

I sat bolt upright in bed, terrified. I turned on the light. The room was full of the smell of his hair gel.

————————

Russo and I went out drinking at our usual place, the Seadog in Camden. I wore a white T-shirt and jeans. We occupied a booth near the bar. The Red Sox were on television. We drank something called Old Gollywobbler.

Russo was finishing up the novel he then called *Nantucket*, later to be renamed *Empire Falls*. He'd asked me to take a look at one chapter in it, a scene in which the hero, Miles, goes in to visit Mrs. Whiting, who wields all sorts of power over him. Her daughter, who hobbles around on crutches, is desperately in love with Miles; in that particular scene, among other events, her cat scratches Miles until he bleeds.

"So I need to know if you think this is too cruel," he said. "It's supposed to be funny, but I don't know. My work seems like it's getting darker and darker."

"What, now *that's* my fault, too?"

He laughed. "I don't think it's your fault," Russo said. "Although . . ." He paused, happily, to consider what might, after all, not be his fault.

"I don't know if the cruelty issue is the right question," I said, and sipped the beer. "I think the issues are whether it's funny, and whether it's real."

"Okay. So is it funny?"

"Yeah, Russo," I said. "It's a riot."

He laughed again. "Good. I'm glad you think so. I'm crazy about it."

"Well, that's probably a pretty good sign right there. But, see, the reason it's funny is because it's serious. And that makes it feel real, too. I think the reason you can get away with the comedy is that you've got that terrible cruelty of Mrs. Whiting simmering underneath the scene. It acts like ballast, to keep the silliness of the business with the cat from getting out of hand."

"Well, I wanted to know what you thought, Boylan, because that's what your fiction does, too, when it works."

"Right," I said. "On those rare occasions."

"Yeah, on those incredibly rare occasions." He laughed. "You love that place between what's funny and what's terribly sad."

I nodded. "It's a great place for a story to be," I said. "Keeping a reader unsure whether to laugh or cry."

He drank his pint, looked at me. "I guess there's a reason you write that way, huh."

I nodded.

He said, "You know, of all the writers I know, it's always seemed to me that there's the least of you, personally, in your fiction. I mean, some authors I know, all they really do is change the names of the characters in their own lives, and that's it, that's the novel. But you, Boylan, whenever we have dinner together, you always tell these amazing stories about your own life, that just have everyone on the floor. But those stories never wind up in your novels. Your stories are always about people a million miles away, acting like maniacs. I mean, your friends would recognize a certain entertaining *voice* in your work, but the actual events and the characters seem to come from someplace very far away from you."

I finished my beer.

"I used to wonder why it was you didn't write about your own life, examine your own emotional center. But now I know why." He shook his head. "Jesus Christ, do I know why."

The waitress came by. "Would you like another one, miss?" she asked.

I smiled. "Please."

She took my glass and walked back toward the bar.

"Jesus, Boylan," Russo said. He turned deep red and looked around the Seadog. All this time he'd presumed we'd just been two guys sitting at a booth drinking. Suddenly it occurred to him that people thought he was sitting with some girl, getting drunk. Did people think I was his date?

"I gotta go to the men's room," he said, and stood up.

"I gotta pee, too," I said, and followed him. As we walked toward the bathrooms, he seemed to take another hard look at me. "Which one are you going to use?" he said. "Will you at least do me that favor, and tell me before we get there?"

"Which would make you more uncomfortable?" I said. "I'll use that one."

"Tell you what, Boylan," Russo said. "If you get back to the table first, you leave a mark. If I get there first, I'll rub it out."

Our children ran around the house, pursued by their friends Carrie and Sam, carrying water guns. There was a squirting sound, then a scream. Luke and Patrick came running back in the other direction, soaked to the skin. Grace and I sat on the porch, watching the sun reflect off the lake.

Sam came running up on the porch, holding his Super Soaker. He paused when he saw me.

"Why are you wearing those earrings?" he said to me.

"Don't you like them?" I said.

Patrick and Luke came up on the porch behind him, out of breath.

"They make you look like a girl," said Sam. "You look like a girl!"

"Our daddy's a boygirl," said Patrick, smiling. It didn't sound like a bad thing, the way he put it.

"But we love him anyway," said Luke. He came over and gave me a big hug.

Then the kids ran inside to fill up their water guns again.

Grace looked over at me. "We're going to have to tell them something," she said.

"I know," I said. "But what can we tell them?"

"Well . . . ," said Grace. She sounded more confident and clear than she'd seemed the previous winter. "I've tried to do some research on what families do when someone changes genders. I checked with some other therapists."

"And?"

"There's no research whatsoever."

I shrugged. "I'm not surprised," I said.

"I tell you what," she said. "When all else fails? Use common sense."

From inside came the sound of a terra-cotta planter smashing into a thousand pieces.

"Oops," said a voice.

"What was that?" Grace called inside.

"Nothing," said Luke.

They all ran out the door, soaking one another with the squirt guns.

"What do you mean, common sense?" I said.

"Well," said Grace, "first off, they should know that they're loved. They shouldn't question whether any changes in you mean that your love for them is different. I think that's probably the most important thing."

"That sounds good."

"And they should know that this won't happen to them, that it's rare. They should know they didn't cause it. They should know they can talk about it whenever they want, and that it's all right to find the whole thing pretty weird."

I nodded.

"And most of all, I guess they should know you aren't going anywhere." The sound of our children's voices grew distant as they ran toward a neighbor's.

"I'm not?"

"Well, of course not."

"Does that mean we're not getting divorced?"

Grace sighed. "I don't know what the future is, Jenny. But we're all going to be together for the foreseeable future. That isn't going to change. I mean, who knows, one day it probably will. But not for now."

"Is that what you decided?" I said.

She shrugged. "It's not a decision. It's the only choice we've got. I mean, I don't want to be apart from you, and I don't want the children to lose you. And you don't want to leave. So what can we do? We have to figure out a way of making this work as a family."

I reached out and took her hand. "It sounds like you're coming to terms with things."

She squeezed it and let it go. "I don't know what I'm doing. I am so totally pissed off at you, I don't know what to say. Except I can't be pissed off at you, because it's not your fault. So I just sit and steam at everything. I feel totally gypped, like I've been cheated out of my husband. It's not fair!"

"I'm sorry," I said.

"I know you're sorry," she said. "But your being sorry doesn't help. There aren't any good choices for me. Every choice I have *sucks*."

The children came running back. Patrick had somehow lost all of his clothes. Water dripped down from his hair. "Can we go to the toy store?" he asked.

Patrick's phrase *boygirl* became the personal shorthand that I used to describe the place I was in during 2000–2001. I made up a little joke during this boygirl period, namely: What are the three phases of male-to-female transition? Step one: *Hey, that guy looks a little weird.* Step two: *Hey, that person looks* really *weird.* Step three: *Whoa, that chick is ugly!*

By now I was hovering, it appeared, between steps two and three.

I seemed to pass from being perceived as male to female at a moment's notice, depending on whom I was with, where I was, whether my hair was tied back or loose, how I crossed my legs. During the boygirl period, I gradually increased the amount of time I spent "presenting" as a woman. By the end of that year, the only places

I was consistently male were on the Colby campus and around my children.

My voice had always been somewhat androgynous, and after two or three sessions with Tania Vaclava, the voice coach at Bates College, I became relatively content with the way I sounded. I managed to perfect, with the coach's help, a spectacularly convincing female voice; my coach said it was because I was a musician and a writer. My pianist's ear helped me hear the appropriate female pitch and modulation; my author's sensibilities showed me inflection and phrasing. For a while, it was like learning a whole new language.

Yet after a few months I gave up on this new voice. It sounded convincing, but it didn't feel authentic, I suppose. My voice dropped back into a more androgynous place, and although its resonance and inflection became more feminine, as a matter of course I no longer gave my voice any thought. This was much to the relief of my friends, who'd found that the "Jennifer voice" sounded like the voice of a stranger.

Above all, I wanted my friends and family to know that Jenny was not a stranger, that she was someone they already knew. It was a puzzle, though—if Jenny was so very much like James, didn't that mean she was not really female? And if she really was female, didn't that mean that she was someone unknown? That I could be both un-ambiguously female and, at the same time, the person they had always known seemed impossible. Yet it was an impossibility that was largely true.

I was aware, during the time of boygirl, that I had been given a rare and precious gift, to see into the worlds of both men and women for a time and to be able to travel almost effortlessly between them. I taught my classes at Colby with my baggy, button-down shirts hiding my figure, I wore a tweed coat and my hair tied back in a ponytail. In the parking lot, after class, I would take off the coat and the shirt (leaving on my undershirt), slip in a pair of earrings, and shake my hair loose, and I would then be seen as female, at least by people who did not know me. It was like being Clark Kent and Superman, in a way. I really did have that sense of "Into a nearby phone booth ..." and could move from one world to another with an ease I found uncanny.

I undertook, during this period, the writing of a supposedly amusing magazine piece making use of my superpowers. What I had in mind was to perform certain gender-pungent rituals in society, several weeks apart, first as James and then as Jenny, and to then compare the experiences. I wanted to apply for a job, for instance, first as man and then as a woman, and see which one of me would get the offer and whether the starting salary would be different. I thought of spending an evening sitting at a bar with Russo and going in the following night as Jenny with Grace. I considered going to a formal shop, getting fitted for a bridal gown, then a week later being measured for a tux. I was full of ideas.

I actually got as far as three of these exercises—buying a car, shopping for a handgun, and purchasing a pair of blue jeans at the Gap. I wrote the story and showed it to a few editors, all of whom loved it and wanted to know when it would be available. I said I wanted to wait until I officially "came out" and became Jenny full-time, probably in the summer of 2001. (By that time, however, I put the article in a drawer; it seemed by then too playful and sarcastic, as if being a woman were all just a clever game for me. The piece didn't seem to reflect the sorrow of the journey, and its joys seemed superficial.)

My experiences in writing the piece were perhaps predictable, but I found them amazing, at least I did at the time. For instance, when I went to the Nissan dealer as Jenny, the salesman showed me the most expensive car on the lot, the Maxima, and talked up the cup holders and the illuminated speedometer. A week later, he tried to sell James a midrange car, the Altima, and his focus now was on the platinum-tipped spark plugs. The punch line, although inevitable, was still remarkable, I thought: The deal they offered me as a man was a thousand dollars better than the one they'd offered Jenny.

The gun shop part of the article didn't really work, since I didn't know anything about guns and couldn't bring myself to go back there a second time as a man. The owner of the store, though, a nice man in Winslow, Maine, tried to sell me something called the "Chief's Special." He said the two good things about the gun were 1) that it had no safety, and 2) that it was "double-acting." This didn't make much of an impression on me, though; the only thing I knew that was double-acting was baking powder.

Buying the jeans at the Gap was more sobering to me as a soon-to-be-former man than it was to my female editors. What I found in the Gap was what most women know already—that buying clothes is complicated. As a man, of course, you simply made the choice between regular or relaxed fit, told the salesman the measure of your inseam and waist, and were then led to a huge wall of pants in your size, all of which you knew would fit just fine, even if you never tried them on. As a woman, I found that there were six different styles of jean, from "boot cut" to "reverse," and that the sizes bore no relation to any known system of measure.

The jean that fit me best at the Gap was the "reverse," which I thought was appropriate. I was right between a ten and a twelve and spent some time neurotically trying to tell myself I could get by in the tens. They're perfectly comfortable if I don't sit down, I thought. How much time do I actually spend sitting, anyway? If I buy the tens, it will be an incentive to lose weight.

I recognized the insanity of this kind of talk, recognized it from the lives of the women I knew, and as I moved into this territory I realized, not for the first time, that all of the cruel expectations that society puts upon women—and that so many women put upon themselves—were now falling on my shoulders. I had seen so many transsexuals who felt that being a woman was the same as being a *girl*, and the lives they lived post-transition seemed to be those of completely unapologetic prefeminists. So many "former" transsexuals, although now ostensibly female, spoke in odd falsettos, teetered around on heels, and demanded that doors be held open for them. Again and again, I told myself, *You're going to incredible effort to become a woman, Jenny; don't surrender your common sense in the bargain.*

No issue was as hard to resolve as the issues around food. My weight was stable, and at five feet eleven, I was healthy, tall, and slender. Yet whenever I went out for lunch, I would hear myself ordering diet soda or asking for the spinach salad. I bought a scale and started weighing myself constantly. I'd say, *If only I could lose five pounds.* I bought Slim-Fast and had thick, gloopy milkshakes for lunch instead of food.

It was madness, and it was exactly the kind of madness that I found least appealing in the lives of the women I knew. Yet the culture had its hooks in me, like it or not. In no time at all I'd internalized many of the things I'd spent years imploring my students to fight against. I worried that I was too fat. I apologized when someone else stepped on my foot, as if it were my fault. My sentences often ended with a question, as if I were unsure of myself. All of these changes transpired without any conscious thought, and if I became aware of them, I felt ashamed.

Partially, I think what I wanted was to *belong.* If being female— to others, at any rate—seemed to include self-doubt, insecurity, and anorexia, then some part of me felt, *Okay, well, let's do all that, then.*

Later, when I tried to let some of this go, there were some who saw me as "less female"—like when I ordered the barbecued baby back ribs for lunch instead of a salad and a diet soda. Why shouldn't a woman eat real food for lunch, I wondered, instead of the pretend kind?

I realized, as Jimmy Durante used to say, that "them's the conditions what prevails," but it didn't sit well with me. There were times when it was as if I were trying to prove I was truly female by oppressing *myself.*

Luke and I were reading a book about Eskimos. "What would you do, Mommy," asked the Inuit child, "if I turned into a walrus?"

"I would be afraid," said the mother. "But I would still love you."

"What would you do, Mommy," asked the child, "if I turned into a polar bear?"

"Then I would be really afraid," said the mother. "But I would still love you."

It was kind of a cross between *Nanook of the North* and *The Velveteen Rabbit*. When we finished reading the book, I asked Luke, "Okay, let me ask you this one. What would you do, Lukey, if I turned into a woman?"

He looked unsure. "I would . . . still love you?"

"Would you?" I said.

He thought it over. "Sure," he said. "You'd still be you, wouldn't you?"

"Uh-huh." We sat together on the couch for a while.

"Have you noticed that I've been looking more and more like a girl over the last year?" I said.

"Some of my friends think you *are* a girl," he said.

"That must be hard for you," I said.

"Not really. I just tell them, 'That's my daddy.' "

"Lukey, I need to talk to you about something. I have a condition, it's like when a person's sick, that makes me feel like a girl on the inside, even though I'm a boy on the outside. Does that make any sense to you, that a person's insides and outsides wouldn't match?"

"Sure," he said. "I know what that's like."

"So I'm taking some medicine that is slowly making my outsides more and more like a girl. After a while, I'm going to totally be a girl. I know that might make you sad, but it's what I need to do."

Luke gave me a big hug. "I won't be sad," he said. "You said you'd still be you."

I hugged him back. "It's a very complicated thing, this condition I have. You probably don't want to know everything about it now.

But you should know I'm not going away, and that you didn't cause this. And that I will always love you. That's never going to change."

"I know," he said. He picked up another book off the table. "Can you read me another story now?"

"How about if I sing you a song, one of my old songs, from Ireland?"

He crinkled up his nose. "How about another story?"

———————

I kept a low profile at Colby that year—which was odd, because at the college I had always been one of the most visible and vocal members of the faculty. Many of my colleagues were still certain that I was fatally ill or bearing some kind of terrible secret sorrow. Later, another teacher told me, "You looked as if you were being slowly crushed in a vise."

The president of the senior class called me up one night and said, "Congratulations, Professor Boylan. You've been chosen as the Professor of the Year."

Terrific, I thought. Turns out the best way to get Professor of the Year was to have a sex change. I hoped it wouldn't start a trend.

I had to give a speech as Professor of the Year, a big lecture in the student union, filled with students and faculty and the president of the college. I began my lecture by showing Groucho Marx playing Professor Wagstaff, president of Huxley College, in the movie *Horse Feathers*. As I spoke to the school, I got all choked up. It was an incredible honor, and I feared that when they learned the truth, they would feel I had let them down. As I stood before the audience, my breasts ached beneath my shirt.

"Whatever it is," Groucho sang to the trustees, *"I'm against it! / And even when you've changed it or condensed it, / I'm against it!"*

———————

One day Luke said, "We need to come up with a better name for you than Daddy, if you're going to be a girl."

"Okay," I said. "Well, what name do you think would work? You know, I use the name Jenny when I'm a girl."

"Jenny!" Luke said, bursting into laughter. "That sounds like the name of a little old lady!"

Trying not to be hurt, I said, "Okay, well, what else can you think of?"

Luke thought about it for a moment, then said, "How about Maddy? You know, like half Mommy and half Daddy?"

I just sat there amazed at the versatility and ingeniousness of children. Patrick, at this point, chimed in, "Or Dommy."

The name Dommy made them all laugh some more. And I said, "You can call me Maddy if you want to."

They started calling me Maddy then and there and within a month or two had changed pronouns as well.

I shifted genders so slowly and so gently around my children that when I finally appeared before them for the first time wearing a skirt and makeup, they hardly noticed the difference. On this occasion I had spent the day at the lake working, then went down to Freeport to do some shopping. I came home late in the afternoon to find that the baby-sitter (who had also been briefed on the situation) already had them in the tub. I walked into the bathroom to say hi to my children, and Luke looked up at me and said, "Hey."

And I said, "Hey what?"

And he said, "You're not wearing your glasses."

I said, "Hi, Paddy," waiting for him to give me his reaction.

"Maddy!" said Patrick, annoyed. He was holding a little plastic submarine.

"What?" I said.

"We're *trying* to play a *game* here?"

"Oh," I said. "Sorry."

———

In the spring, Grace and I went out to breakfast one morning, with me as Jenny. It was a rough, up-north kind of place with truckers in flannel making up most of the population. Grace and I didn't feel very comfortable, and guys kept stealing looks at us, and at me. Was I being read as male? Was I just being checked out? Did they think the two of us were lesbians? It was impossible to tell what was going on, but it gave us the willies.

The next morning, we went out to a different place. This time I went as a male. We both felt a lot more comfortable this time. It was a relief to be a normal, heterosexual couple again.

At the end of the meal, the waitress came over. "Hi," she said. "Can I get you ladies any more coffee?"

It was as good a sign as any that the period of boygirl was coming to a close.

———————

The following weekend, Grace went to visit her sister and brought the boys with her. I went over to the Russos in Camden for dinner, and we sat out on their deck drinking wine. I was over there "as" Jenny, which by that time simply meant that I was wearing a skirt instead of jeans. We did what we always did, told stories and drank wine, but something in the air seemed melancholy. It felt as if we were working harder at something that used to seem effortless.

At one point Rick told me that some of the friends we had in common were relieved that Grace's spirits seemed to have improved.

"She seems good," Rick said. "She seems better than she's seemed all year. I mean, last year at this time, it was like she was carrying a load of bricks. But now she's laughing again. She's engaged, she seems like her old self."

"Yeah, she's kind of come back to life," I said. "I think around Christmas, maybe, she realized she was just going to have to take control over what was happening to her, and to the family. Since then it's like she's back from the dead. She's talked to the boys, she's talked to a lot of our friends, she even explains and defends me in some conversations with people."

"That's amazing, when you think about it," Russo said. "Considering how much she hates what's happening."

"It is amazing," I said.

"She is a strong woman," said Rick.

Barbara Russo, who was sitting beside Rick, said quietly, "I think she's the strongest woman I know."

"After you, Barb," I said. "I don't envy the woman who has to put up with Russo twenty-four hours a day."

Barb nodded. "It's made me tough," she said, smiling.

Rick filled my wineglass. "Maybe you knew how strong Grace was when you got married, Boylan. Maybe you chose her because you knew you'd need someone strong."

"No, that's not it," I said. "When I got engaged to Grace, I really thought that the whole gender thing was behind me. It was like, finally, after years and years of struggling with it, I was cured. I threw out all the gear that I had, all the women's clothes and makeup and all of it, and I felt like, from now on, I get to just be one person. I never will have to decide to be a man again."

"What does that mean, decide to be a man?" Barb said. "How do you do that?"

"Well, when I was a man, it was something I decided I'd do. It was something that I woke up every morning and convinced myself I could do, that it was something that I *had* to do. When I first fell in love with Grace, it was the only time I felt like I didn't have to think about it. It was like, her love made my life possible."

I was drunk now, and I wasn't sure I was making any sense.

"But how can a person choose to be who they are?" said Barbara. "I mean, I don't understand that."

"Oh, I think a lot of people do that," said Rick. "I think *I* did that. I know when I was a teenager, there was a time when I went out with a whole bunch of tough guys, and we busted up people's mailboxes with a baseball bat and did things like that. One night we broke a plate-glass window at somebody's house, and we all drove off laughing, and when I finally got home, I remember seeing my grandparents, and thinking how incredibly ashamed they'd be if they knew what I'd done."

"But you didn't wind up like that," I said. "How come you escaped Gloversville, New York, and wound up a novelist and an English professor? Did you choose to be who you are, or did it just happen?"

"I chose it," Russo said. "I mean, odds were, I should have stayed in Gloversville and kept breaking people's windows and I'd have wound up like most of the guys I grew up with, playing the lottery and working in a mill. But instead, I decided to be someone else."

Barbara looked alarmed. "You mean you could have decided to be *anybody*?"

"Not anybody, but the person I became. I think we are who we are because consciously, or unconsciously, we choose ourselves."

"Yeah, well, that's what I've been struggling with," I said. "Because I felt like I always had to *choose* to be James. Being Jenny, though, isn't like that. I just am."

Russo's expression darkened. "Then why doesn't it feel like that?"

"Feel like what?"

"Why doesn't it feel like it's natural?"

"It doesn't seem natural?"

Rick looked at Barb. She looked away. "I don't know, Boylan," he said. "It doesn't feel like you, though. Not to me."

"But—this is me. I'm here. This is it."

He nodded. "Okay." His eyes shone. "If you say so," he said.

We sat on the deck for a long time, not talking. In the distance I heard the sound of the buoys out in Camden harbor, the bells clanging as they swayed with the tide.

———

President William Adams (whom, shockingly, everyone called "Bro," even though he was neither an African American nor a hippie) was new to Colby when I met with him; he'd been inaugurated only that fall. He had said, in his inaugural address, that the primary issue the college needed to address was *diversity* and that we had to commit ourselves to making Colby the kind of community where an increasingly wide range of people would feel welcome.

The wish is granted, I thought as I sat down in his office. *Long live Jambi.*

Bro didn't raise an eyebrow when I explained my situation. I sketched out the issues as I saw them, assured him I would comport myself with dignity, professionalism, and a sense of humor, and handed him a copy of Brown and Rounsley's *True Selves*. (I had purchased a dozen of these "transgender primers" from Amazon and handed them out like pretzels as I spoke with colleagues and administrators over the next several weeks.) I gave Bro a list of resources available in the library and on the Web should he or any other member of the community wish to learn more; I gave him a memo outlining the things that various college officers—particularly the deans of faculty and students, as well as the vice president of personnel—would need to know. And I showed him a photograph of me as Jenny, standing next to Grace and my children and looking more or less like a normal mother of forty-two.

Bro, a good-looking man with a square chin and a mop of black hair, said, "Listen, Jenny, it's my belief that this will be a nonissue at the college. You've clearly given this all a lot of thought, and I'm grateful that you've given so much consideration to the implications of all of this for the institution. Ultimately, it's a private matter. To the extent that it affects the college at all, we can only support you as a professional and a colleague."

Then he smiled. "I will admit, though, that this is the first time I've ever had a conversation like this."

With the support of the president in hand, I proceeded to move through the chain of command at the college. I met with the dean of admissions and the vice president of finance and the director of communications and the dean of students and the dean of faculty and the dean of the college and the vice president of development. Everyone was generous. The dean of students said she was looking forward to a newer and more intimate relationship with me as her "sister."

The dean of faculty, a statistician and a neuropsychologist, went one step further. "You understand," he said, meaning to be generous, "that this is going to have the beneficial effect of increasing the number of female faculty by an *n* of one."

I looked at the dean, nervously. "An *n* of one?" I said. "You're saying an *n* of one. That's beneficial?"

He nodded.

"What's *n*?"

"*n*, Jenny," he said, "stands for the number of persons being referred to."

"Ah," I said.

I was glad we'd worked this out.

As the number of people I talked to increased, it became clearer and clearer that the secret would not hold much longer. So as the date of my coming out drew near, I met with dozens of people each day. I met with the director of creative writing and the head of the English Department and almost all of my colleagues in English. The last meeting I had was with a group of five younger professors. I met them in the conference room in the department; I felt as though I were being interviewed for a new job, which in a way I suppose I was.

On June 14, 2001, I composed an "e-mail bomb." I had decided that coming out in the summertime was best, since it would give the news a chance to settle among the faculty first, before the students returned in fall. By then I hoped to be old news.

Dear Friends:

This letter is being sent to the people at Colby that I'm particularly fond of. Some of you may be surprised to find that you are on this list at all, since perhaps we have barely passed each other in the hallways, or been out of touch for a while. Others of you I count among the people I know, and love, best. In either case, I have been grateful for your presence in my professional life.

In the next week, you will be hearing some rather dramatic news about me. I'm going to attempt to be the one to break it to you myself. Thus, in the next day or two, you will receive a letter I've written, which will be delivered to your home address.

What I wish to share with you is *not* bad news, and I don't wish for this melodramatic e-mail to stir up anxiety at your end. Still, my news will take some getting used to, and I will be eager to discuss it with you.

This e-mail, then, is basically a "heads up" note to let you know that something important is incoming. I'm grateful for your care, and for our ongoing friendship.

Best,
Jim Boylan

I hit send.

Then I picked up 113 copies of my coming out letter—which contained equal measures of Joseph Campbell, John Barth, and Ann Landers—and drove over to the post office in my small Maine town. It was a white clapboard building with a flagpole out front. The flag flapped in the strong wind. The manager of the PO, a kind, efficient Yankee named Val, nodded at me as I slid the envelopes through the brass slot for outgoing mail. Then I got back in the car and waited for the world to explode or to begin.

———————

On the way back from the post office, I stopped off at Nick and Shell's. My guess was, my days of playing piano in crummy bars were over.

"So," said Shell. "Are you finally going to tell us what the fuck's wrong with you?"

"Yes," I said.

"Well, I'm anxious to know what's going on. For the last year you've been looking like you're dying. You know everybody's worried about you."

"I know," I said. "Actually, I'm all right. But I think this means the end of my playing with the band."

"What does?"

So I told her about the whole woman business.

At the end of which she said, "All right, you want to know what I think?"

I said yes.

She said, "I think *Fuck you* if you think you're going to leave the band."

I laughed. Then she went on. "Listen, Jenny—I can start calling you that, right?—I saw some show about this on MSNBC. I think it's cool. You seem like a pretty brave person to me. Nick and me, we've always been crazy about you. We're just glad to know you're okay. As far as I'm concerned, you're you, no matter what."

I told her I was surprised she was taking it so well.

Shell said, "Why? Because we're not college professors, because we're just like normal working people? Listen, you don't have to be a genius to know how to be loyal to the people you love. Your problem isn't going to be us. Your problem is going to be those prissy little office workers at Colby."

Nick came in carrying a brown paper bag. "What's up?" he said.

I just shrugged and said, "I'm having a sex change."

Nick reached into the paper bag and put a fifth of Jameson's Irish whiskey on the table. "Good for you," he said.

"He's not kidding," Shell said.

He reached into the bag again and got out a six-pack of Guinness. He opened two and handed me one. "I know," he said.

"Listen," Shell said. "Can you show me what you look like? As a woman? Or does it take, like, cranes and backhoes and shit?"

"I think I can give you a pretty good idea," I said. "I'll be right back."

I went into the bathroom and I took off my coat and my baggy overshirt and I let my hair loose and I put some earrings in my ears. I walked out of the bathroom and sat at the table again.

"Whoa," Shell said.

Nick took a slug of the whiskey while Shell took a good hard look at me. Then she turned to her husband and said, "All right, Nick, let's have it. What do you think?"

"Of what?" Nick said.

Shell nodded at me. "Of the chick."

He shrugged. "I don't know, what do you think?"

Shell smiled kindly. "Tell you the truth?" she said. "*I'd* fuck her."

Part 3

September 1999 and September 2001:
"Whatever it is," Groucho sang, "I'm against it."

"They Aren't Like Jellyfish at All"

June 2001

To my friends at Colby:

I would like to share some personal information with you. I am known, I suppose, for having a sense of humor, and admit that I once attempted to trick the entire Colby College faculty into calling the "1–800 Oscar Mayer Wiener-dog Hotline" (although Professor Brixton I believe was the only one who actually fell for this). As a result, some of you may think that the information I share with you herewith is a joke. It's not. And comprehending this, in fact, may take a large portion of patience, understanding, and compassion. You are likely, in fact, to need a long time to fully process it.

I am transgender. Specifically, I am a male-to-female transsexual. I have had this condition for my entire life, since before kindergarten, since before language. It is certainly a condition I have had during all the years you have known me, and which has caused me an almost inexpressible degree of private grief.

I have been in therapy, off and on, for my condition, for many years. Since my return from Ireland in 1999, however, it's become clear to me that I cannot proceed with my life without finding union between my body and my spirit.

Fortunately, transsexuality can be treated, and most of those who embark upon the journey of "transition" do go on to live fulfilling and joyful lives. There is a well-established protocol for treating transsexuals that has been adopted by the American Psychiatric Association and other mental health care professionals. This protocol is known as the "Benjamin Standards of Care," and it constitutes a rigorous set of procedures, ensuring that the patient is a proper and appropriate candidate for gender shift.

Carefully following the Benjamin Standards of Care, and under the care of a gender specialist, a clinical social worker, my family doctor, and an endocrinologist, I began taking the steps necessary to shift genders last year. This includes, among other things, a regimen of estrogen and antiandrogen therapy that has, over the last year, rendered my appearance and my body more feminine.

In June of 2001 I began a sabbatical. I will not be in the classroom for the next year, as my transition becomes complete. I am not scheduled to teach in the fall of 2002, but I do anticipate returning to Colby as Professor Jennifer Finney Boylan in the spring of 2003.

Some of you might not have a clear idea what "transgender" means, and that's fine; this is not a subject most people are familiar with. *Transgender* is the preferred term for the whole range of people with gender issues. *Transsexuals*—persons who feel that their body and spirit do not match—are a particular kind of trans person. At any rate, a transsexual is not a cross-dresser, for whom the issue is clothes. ("Transvestite" is now considered a pejorative term for "cross-dressers"; in any case, I am neither of these and would be grateful if you could appreciate this distinction.)

If you've read this far in this note, it's quite possible that you feel that the top of your head is about to blow off. Most of us have no personal experience with transsexuality, and lack even a basic language for talking about it. If you find this strange, or embarrassing, or even wonderful, you should know that your reaction is not atypical.

My wife, Grace, and my children, Luke and Patrick, have supported me throughout this process. Grace, in particular, has found in her heart a depth of love that is nothing short of heroic.

For what it's worth, most people's reaction to my news so far has been remarkable in its compassion and understanding. My sister-in-law, for instance, said, "I'm so glad it's only that you're a woman; I was afraid it was something serious." My mother said, "Love will prevail," and while considering the drama of the changes, also noted, "We will adjust."

Colby's president, Bro Adams—as well as the dean of faculty and the dean of students—have all expressed their respect for the journey I am taking and have pledged that the college will support me in every way it can. I have also been moved by the support of our Affirmative Action/Equal Opportunity officer, Jean Fischman; the director of personnel services, Bob White; the director of creative writing, Debra Spark; and the chair of the English Department, Richard Redd. Given Colby's tradition of honoring diversity, I am confident that my transition at school will be relatively smooth, once the initial surprise dies out. I am eagerly looking forward to getting back to the classroom and to continue the business of being a good teacher, a good writer, and a good friend.

You might be wondering what you can or should do next.

First, if you wish to learn more, you should know our library
has an extensive collection of texts dealing with gender, culture,
and transsexuality in particular. The best first book to read is
True Selves by Chloe Rounsley and Mildred Brown; Eleanor
Brubaker, at the reference desk, will be glad to suggest others to
those interested in this subject.

Second, you should talk this over with those you love. I
would like to assist you in any way I can, both in terms of
helping you to understand gender shift as a whole, and also in
order to reassure you that I am still me, and that the person you
have known for all these years remains, and will remain,
relatively unchanged.

Finally, speaking as an individual whose livelihood has come
in part from her imagination, I want to say it's all right to have a
sense of humor about this. While I would prefer not to be the
object of cruel jokes, I do hope that we can all recognize that
wit and humor are likely to be therapeutic tools for all of us in
this time of transition.

In my classes on story structure and myth, I have often
analyzed the journey of the classic heroine, as she moves
through the stages in her adventure of "departure," "initiation,"
"return," and "reign," following the patterns described by Joseph
Campbell and John Barth. The climax of these stories usually
represents a kind of "moment of truth" for the heroine, when
she must slay the dragon, conquer fear, and attain illumination.

To my students I have always noted that the journey of the
mythic hero appeals to us because this paradigm tells our own
stories as well. In the story of the mythic hero, we see the story
of ourselves.

Which is to say that we all have dragons to slay in life. This
one is mine. I hope that doing so will provide a model to others
on how to find the bravery to be true to oneself, even if it
means doing something that seems impossible.

My adventure in the coming months will require honesty

and courage. I am hopeful that with your help and understanding, I will be able to complete it.

It has been a pleasure to work with, and for, you all over these last thirteen years. I look forward to continuing to serve as your colleague and your friend.

With best wishes,
Jenny Boylan

———

To: Russo <russo@mint.net>
From: Jenny Boylan <jfboylan@mint.net>

Dear Russo,

I have been wondering if I was something of an idiot when I saw you last. Of course, I always wonder this the morning after drinking with you, and so I think perhaps that this is a sign that everything is normal.

Boylan

———

Dear Jenny,

Sarah M——, your former student, here saying hello from Portland, Maine.

I knew you as Jim, back in 1993, and boy did you rock my Colby world. I loved your style, your quirkiness, your gentleness, and your encouraging words to a young writer. I believe I had you for only one class but it imprinted on me. Thank you.

And now I just want to welcome Jenny. A friend of mine gave me the heads-up on your webpage and I found myself deeply touched. I cannot really explain why the emotions came out. Maybe something about witnessing that sort of courage and unabashed integrity. The trueness to yourself. Maybe, too, remembering Jim the professor and knowing that you must have walked around carrying this heavy secret for so long . . . I feel that.

I am so glad that you have chosen to shed that secret, burst out of that chrysalis. Thank you, too, for being a role model, as Jim and now as Jenny. I am sure you will inspire many folks to dig deep and be true to themselves.

Many blessings to you.

Much love, peace, and grace,

Sarah

From: Russo <russo@mint.net>
To: Jenny Boylan <jfboylan@mint.net>

Dear Boylan,

No, you weren't an idiot when you were here last. In many respects it was a more difficult visit than most, in part due to Grace's absence. I'm slowly coming to terms with the way our relationship is changing, and I'm very aware of being less natural with you now, as Jenny, than I was before, as Jim. I miss our former ease and hope that one day we may find some variation on that former theme.

I dislike choosing my words carefully around my best friends, and one of the things I liked best about our old male friendship was that I could be more wide open with you than just about anyone. I hate to think of that ease being lost forever, but the loss seems inevitable for the short term. You're in a very raw and vulnerable place, and you seem to require more sympathy and support than honesty at present, which was why I offered a small portion of the latter very tentatively and then felt horrible about doing so afterward.

But I'm settling in for the long haul, because this period of transition involves not just what you're going through, but also

Grace's transition into something different, and none of it's going
to happen overnight or as the result of any one thing (including
surgery, right?). And, as I think I mentioned to you early on, while
the most important people in my life are all women, I have no
"easy" friendships with women, which suggests that the biggest
challenge to redefining our friendship is probably me.

But then my biggest problem has always been me.

Russo

———————

From: Jenny Boylan <jfboylan@mint.net>
To: Russo <russo@mint.net>

Dear Russo:

That's funny, *my* biggest problem has always been you, too.

Boylan

———————

Dear Boylan:

I think you'll be pleased to know that the general consensus
is that you are still "the best damn teacher on campus." Keep up
the good work.

Noah Charney '02

———————

Prof!

Don't take this the wrong way, but it takes a lot of balls to do
what you're doing. Wow. Without knowing much about your life or
life in general (at the tender age of 24), it sounds like it's going to
be a bumpy road ahead for a while. But I have a feeling you'll get
through it. If you wrote a book about this, it could be one way to

educate people about what you and what must be many others are going through.

Anyway, stay out of trouble. And keep in touch.

John Bishop '99

———————

From: Russo <russo@mint.net>
To: Jenny Boylan <jfboylan@mint.net>

Boylan—

Jesus, I hate to be the bearer of bad tidings all the while, but I'm *not* your worst problem.

Russo

———————

Jenny, You may or may not remember me, but you were my English professor during my first semester at Colby, in the fall of 1989. I just wanted to let you know that a classmate of mine recently forwarded me the link to your official website, that I read about your gender transition, and that I fully support you and the choices you have made.

You are one of the best teachers with whom I have had the good fortune to study, and I mark the beginning of my transition from an adolescent to an adult, intellectually speaking, with your class, in which I learned to read, write, and think at a new, higher level.

When I think about Colby College, I think about the positive experiences I had in your class, and I think warmly about you.

Best Regards,
Matt K———, Program Manager
Upper Chattahoochee Riverkeeper

Professor Boylan,

You are, by far, the most courageous person I have ever met. And I support your decision 100%, not that you were asking for anyone's approval anyhow. I visited your new webpage, and damn, girl, you look good! I hope you are enjoying a somewhat relaxing summer. Mine has been boring (only left San Francisco once to deliver the eulogy at my grandfather's memorial service), but I've been making lots of cash working as a nanny for a wonderful family that lives in my apartment building. I'm ready to return to Colby, though. I have to say I kind of miss Waterville in a very bizarre way.

My very best wishes,
Marley Orr, '04

P.S. What is your feeling on double majoring in English and psychology? My advisor hasn't been much of a help to me, and I welcome any input you might have.

From: Jenny Boylan <jfboylan@mint.net>
To: Russo <russo@mint.net>

Dear Russo:

Okay. Well, listen, Rick, I don't know if I'm any less natural with you now—but I know what you mean. Of course I would like to encourage you to continue to relate to me just as you always have, but maybe this is like encouraging you *not* to see me as a woman.

I think it is hard for me to be with people that I love for whom my transition is something other than a cause for unbridled celebration. I feel great these days, like somebody who just got out of prison after 40 years for something she didn't do, like I got pardoned by the governor. When dear friends deal with me with mixed emotions, it is a little like being told, "Well, Jenny, we're glad you got sprung, really, but quite honestly we did kind of like you better when you were in jail."

And yet, nobody knows better than I do that the consequences of my dealing with being transgender are not a cause for celebration, at least not for those who love me the most. This is just something I have to figure out how to live with. For me it means being patient, accepting a fair amount of ambivalence where there used to be none. And that's hard.

But I think it's part of the deal if I want to move forward. I'm sorry it's so hard. In a way my friends are the ones who are in transition now.

The conversation we had about how and whether people "choose" to be themselves has stayed with me, though—and it is interesting how you spoke of deciding consciously to become yourself. It was interesting that Barb said she couldn't imagine this, and that the idea of choosing fate like that was strange to her. It gave me the helpful insight that I really did "choose" to be Jim every single day, but that once I put my sword down I haven't chosen Jenny at all; I simply wake up and here I am.

J

P.S. The letters are pouring in now that I'm out. I'm up to 150 so far. Do I have to write them all back?

———

[*From Professor Jools Gillson-Ellis. She had been my colleague at University College, Cork.*]

Dear Jenny,

Blimey. It's better than a new hair cut.

I'm so glad you wrote. Yes—it's true, despite teaching lots of stuff to do with transgender identities, your news profoundly unsettled me. I thought about you and your family for days. I think my whole psyche had to rework the Jim I knew when you were here in Ireland. I had a sense that something was held back, when you were here. I guess I just wrote it off as busy young parents.

Vittorio (my lovely honey) and I have bought an old cottage by the sea in East Cork. It needs lots of work, and it's still chaos, but we love it. We've only been here since August 1st, and himself is off in Rome visiting his family. So I am alone with the mad neighbours.

For the first few days here, I was writing a letter to you in my head. It was about navigation, and how we sail through life. It was about the absolute primariness of gender, and the utter invisibility of that. It was about the taste of the journey you've taken, and how I wonder at it. It was about my curiosity, and your writing. It was one of the best letters I've ever not written, in fact.

On the beach this morning we found strange sea creatures. They are small translucent ovals. Around their edges, there is a petrol blue skirt, and tiny tentacles. They aren't like jellyfish at all. No one here knows what they are. We think they are a gift from the Gulf Stream. I brought some back to the cottage and sketched them. Strange things wash up on my shores, and you are not the first. I wish you love and a great imagination(!) If you've got this far, I am sure you have the strength to drag the rest of culture with you. It is fucking brilliant being a girl. Welcome.

You'd better bloody visit soon.

Joolser

––––––––––

To: Jenny Boylan <jfboylan@mint.net>
From: Russo <russo@mint.net>

Boylan—

I too was fascinated by our discussion of choosing to be who we are the last time you were here. I think Barbara was stunned to consider our more fluid and "artful" sense of the self. She possesses very little artifice and even less guile, and she finds these hard to grasp in others. I loved and believed your story about the night you asked Grace to marry you and chose to be James, and I understand, at least theoretically, your metaphor of finally getting out of jail.

What's less convincing, for me at least (and I suspect many of your friends, though I don't want to speak for them), is your claim that Jenny is not a choice—that she just naturally *is,* the way Barbara *is,* or Grace *is.* There are just too many of what seem (again, to me) wrong notes. You say you *are* Jenny, but to me it seems more like Jenny is somebody you need to be and want desperately to be and are determined to be. Like Gatsby, in way. He had to be Gatsby, not Jimmy Gatz, for anything in life to make sense. We've come to use this word *(is)* ironically, to suggest an excellent performance ("Paul Newman *is* Hud!"), even though we know he's an actor. You insist that Jenny is the real you, but you played the other role so long and so convincingly that we can't banish it.

From the beginning of your transition I've been reminded of that fiction writing student we've both had so many times during the course of our teaching careers. He hands in what everyone in the class agrees is an implausible story. Things don't happen this way, we tell him. People don't behave this way. The central plot incident is unbelievable. The kid sits there getting more and more pissed, waiting for his chance to speak. Finally, at the end of the class he says (either to the teacher or the whole workshop), "Yeah, well, you know the thing you say couldn't happen? Well, it really did. And the guy you said wouldn't behave that way? He really did."

And then the kid leaves the room (usually slamming the door), convinced he's made his point about reality and has proven his detractors wrong. Later, in conference, we try to explain that reality isn't much of a defense when it comes to stories, that his main character wasn't consistent, and that his story isn't going to win many admirers until he begins to come to terms with what's gone wrong in the telling.

Your circumstance as a transgender person is not a story, and I don't mean to suggest that it is, but we did agree on the deck that night that there are times when we've made decisions about "who to be." I agreed (then and now) that I've invented (to some significant degree) the self that I use to face the world with. I am, to that extent, a fictional character; the reason I'm reasonably content with the self I created, perhaps, is that, while I'm not an open book, neither am I diametrically different from my fictional self. The reason you became uncomfortable in your created self is that it contained something so far from an essential truth that you couldn't live with it. A change was needed. Granted. Here, you insist, is *the real me,* the me I've kept a secret all these years.

And yet the real you—like the character in the student story—seems mannered, studied, implausible. Your claim that Jenny is real may be true, but it seems almost beside the point. That Jenny is the real you is something that I have to take on faith, because the evidence of my senses suggests the opposite. You may have chosen to be James every day for all those years, but the fact is that you got so good at it that the rest of us can't quite make the shift. You say you were miserable, but that's not what we witnessed. You say Jenny is the real you, but we see an actor learning a role, getting better at it all the time, but it still feels like a role.

It's not that we want you to remain in jail. We just prefer the other story. The one where you seemed happy, where Grace *was* happy. (That you *were* miserable we have to take on faith; that Grace *is* miserable now seems beyond question.) Reality aside (as if this were possible), the workshop (or this one member of it, at least) sees Jenny as not your best work, though it must be conceded (and it's probably the most important point of all) that we're looking at a rough draft, that the real work is ahead in the revision, and that our job is to help the writer arrive at her own conclusion, her own meaning, since finally the story is hers and not ours.

Okay. You said you wanted to know what was going through my mind. Does that still seem like a good idea? Since the afternoon I promised always to be your friend, I've spent a fair amount of time trying to figure out what the hell that might mean. Come to that, to whom did I make that promise? I've often considered honesty to be overrated, and the above may be a poor gift.

Russo

Some Pig

(Fall 2001)

The band was playing in a place in Waterville called the Dog, which was down in the basement of what used to be the post office a hundred years ago. The door to the women's room had the faded words *Civil Service* stenciled on it in black letters. There was a pool table and a jukebox and flashing "Bud" signs on the wall, Shipyard and Geary's on tap.

The scene was the same as always—girls in their twenties, with navel rings and glitter spray and hair stacked high with Ultra Net; older guys at the bar, staring into their Millers; a few college students with dreadlocks and baggy pants; someone's mom at a booth passing around pictures of her grandchildren, women from the Hathaway shirt factory just getting off the late shift and coming in as a single raucous pack.

We opened the first set with "Rock Me Right," followed by Nick singing "Good Golly, Miss Molly." Shell went out into the audience with the remote mike and writhed on people's tables. The veins on her neck bulged as she sang.

Russo and Grace and Barb walked in about halfway through the first set. Shell was dancing on the bar at that point, singing "Respect." As Rick and the women sat at a booth in the back, Shell swung her arm out suddenly and accidentally smashed a glass light fixture. Everyone applauded.

I was at the front of the stage, sitting behind my keys. I was wearing a black T-shirt top and a black-and-blue skirt, black hose.

Grace and Rick had a pitcher of beer at their table. From where I was sitting, I could see them trying to talk over the blasting music, laughing and drinking.

Rick and I hadn't talked much since we'd exchanged our series of perplexing e-mails. I understood, to some degree, what he'd been getting at, but his words—especially those describing me as "studied," "mannered," and "implausible"—stung deeply. I wasn't sure that there was anything I could do or say that would help salvage our friendship. My sense was that if I wanted to have Rick for a friend, I'd just have to get used to accepting his ambivalence. But that wasn't going to be easy—I didn't want my best friend to be ambivalent on the question of my existence. I just wanted to say, like David Tomlinson in *Mary Poppins*, "In the final analysis, it turns out what doesn't exist is *you*." Which was the British way, I suppose, of saying, *Go to hell*.

I'd even decided, in fact, not to introduce him at his Colby reading. Screw him, somebody else could do it. I wasn't in any mood to stand at a podium and sing the praises of a friend who considered me *implausible*.

A guy in a black shirt sat at the bar, watching me. His face was surrounded by cigarette smoke. A big chain attached to his belt loop hung down one hip and curled back up into his back pocket. He had a black beard flecked with gray.

We finished "Respect," and Shell came back up to the stage. "You know what?" she said. "Now that I'm forty, every time I jump up and down? I *pee* a little bit."

There was a chorus of grossed-out laughter.

"Ladies and gentlemen," Nick said, "your host this evening, Miss Shelly LaRoux."

We kicked into "Don't Tell Me No Lies and Keep Your Hands to Yourself."

Immediately the dance floor filled. There, gyrating, were all the young chicks with their navel rings, boys dancing with their beers sloshing out of their glasses. One dude, without a date, hunkered by the front of the stage. "It's my birthday!" he explained. "I'm the birthday boy!"

"Spankin' tunnel," said Shell.

There was applause as the words *spankin' tunnel* were spoken, and the band launched into "Light My Fire," which was a song I loved playing, because I got to do a big solo using the Farfisa.

The time to hesitate is through. / No time to wallow in the mire. . . .

Somewhere in the middle of this, I saw Rick and Barb and Grace get up and quietly leave the bar. As they headed out the door, Rick looked at me and nodded. I nodded back and felt a stab of sorrow. I wished I were with them, heading out into the night, instead of sitting here stuck behind my keys.

Shell got about a dozen members of the audience to form a line. Then she ran the birthday boy through the spankin' tunnel.

The man in the black shirt kept watching me as the night went on. He reminded me of a hyena waiting to pick off a wildebeest.

I went into the ladies' room in between the second and third sets. A girl with a pierced lip stood by the sink. "Can I ask you something? Do I look too pale to you?"

We looked in the mirror. "We *both* look pale," I said. "You think it's the light?"

"It's gotta be," she said. "I don't really look like this."

"It's okay," I said. "I don't look like this, either."

I left the ladies' room and went back on stage. We started the third set with "Sweet Jane," which morphed into "Hot Child in the City," briefly became the *Scooby-Doo* theme song, and wound up, at last, as "Hunka Hunka Burning Love."

The next time I looked over at the bar, the hyena was gone.

The last tune of the night was "Dirty Deeds" by AC/DC, which is a song that I had never written a part for, so I just sat there with the synthesizer and generated senseless machine noise. Everyone seemed to like that.

We were done by one A.M., bar time, and then we had the usual forty-five minutes of tearing down the equipment, wrapping up the cords, getting the instruments back in their cases. Without any word from me, Jack and Nick had begun, around the time of my transition, carrying my amplifier for me, which was good because the Peavey weighed over a hundred pounds and I could no longer lift it.

The bartender poured me a drink and I sat at the bar watching everyone clearing out. The Red Sox were on television, although their pennant hopes had faded yet again.

"This guy's the designated hitter," the bartender said, nodding at the screen. "See, in the American League, they allow you to stick one guy in the rotation who just hits."

"I know what the DH rule is," I said, annoyed.

"He substitutes for the pitcher," the bartender continued.

"I know what the DH rule is."

The bartender dried off a pint glass with a rag. "Purists are against it, you know, but whatever. Keeps the game interesting." He looked over at me. "You like baseball, sweetie?"

Waitresses swept up broken glass with a broom. An old man wiped off the tables. I looked at the booth where Grace and Russo had been sitting, now empty.

Shell split the money and handed it out to each of us. I had everything in my car except my piano stool. "Good night, everybody," I said.

"Good night, Jenny," said Nick, and he came over and gave me a big hug. The feeling of his stubbly face against my neck gave me chills.

"Good night, girlfriend," said Shell. "Chicks rule."

I laughed, picked up my stool, and went out to the parking lot.

It was cold outside, and the wind blew my hair around. I walked to my van and unlocked the back while balancing the piano stool with one hand. It was very quiet. If there are places more dead than Waterville, Maine, at two in the morning, I don't know what they are.

"You need some help with that?" said a voice.

He was leaning against a banged-up Ford, parked next to my van. One of the doors was a different color from the rest of the car. He blew some smoke at me.

"I'm all right," I said, and slammed the hatch. I moved toward my door, but the man with the black T-shirt took a step forward and blocked my way.

"You're sure I can't help you?" he said. "You look like you could use some help."

"I'm all right," I said.

"My name's *Max*."

"Listen," I said. "It's been a long night. I need to go home."

"You want to get to *bed*, is that it, Jenny?"

"Listen—"

"I would love to help you get into bed." He reached out and touched the side of my face.

I shrank back. "Get off of me," I said.

"Aw, loosen up. Don't you want to *party*, Jenny?" he said. I could smell the beer on his breath. He had a space between his front teeth. Max swayed a little bit.

"I'm going home," I said. "Okay?"

"Aw, Jesus, why are you such a fucking *bitch*?" he said, and grabbed me by the wrist. I thought he was going to snap my arm in half.

"Let go of me!"

"Relax already. You can't say you haven't been watching me. All night long, you've been checking me out."

"I haven't," I said. "Please. I just want to go home."

"I tell you what, Jenny, we can do this the easy way, or we can do this the hard way."

"If you don't let go of me, I'm going to fucking scream."

He laughed. "Go on, honey. Scream."

"Help!" I shouted. Somewhere in the back of my mind, even as I shouted, I thought, *Jesus, it's come to this.* My voice echoed off the silent, empty buildings on Main Street. "Help, somebody!"

No one came. "Okay," said Max. "You done?"

"No," I said. "Let me *go.*"

"Come on, you fucking *cunt,*" he said, his face turning red.

This, too, I supposed, was *immersion learning.*

Not expecting much, I shoved Max forward. To my amazement, he fell onto the sidewalk, just like that. Neither of us thought I'd had it in me.

I ran into my car, locked the doors, and started the engine. As I pulled out, Max stood up again. He started pounding on the windows of my minivan. I thought he was going to break them.

I drove home, shaking all over. I kept thinking, *What did I do to him, why did he hate me so much?* Was this what the world was going to be like for me from now on? And another part of me replied, *Yeah, well, when exactly did surprise set in, Jennifer?*

I drove home down Kennedy Memorial Drive and past the three white churches that stand together in a row in Oakland.

As I left Oakland, a pair of headlights appeared in my rearview mirror.

He had his high beams on, and he left them on as he got closer and closer as we drove out into the country. On my left I could see the faint shadows of Snow Pond at the bottom of the hill.

I moved my rearview mirror so that I wouldn't be blinded by the headlights. Still, as I drove at fifty miles an hour toward home, he got closer and closer to me. I wasn't even sure it was Max; I couldn't see the driver's face.

But it was a pretty good bet.

I looked at my gas gauge, well below empty.

The car behind me revved its engine.

I was going to have to stop for gas before I got home, and the only gas station was the Irving station in Belgrade, across from the Town Hall. There wasn't going to be anybody there, either, not at this hour.

I remembered seeing something on television about making a weapon out of your car key, using it as a knife. I imagined trying to do battle with a minivan key. It wasn't going to do much good against a gun. There wasn't much doubt that Max would have a gun in his car, was there?

At the Irving station, a guy with a Harley stood at the pump. I pulled up next to him.

As I got out of my van, Max drove past, leaning on his horn. He held his middle finger up in the air. I heard his horn blaring for a long time as he drove into the distance.

The biker filled his tank and looked at me.

"Nice guy," he said to me. "Friend of yours?"

"No, he's some *asshole*, he's been following me all the way from Waterville."

I was still shaking.

The biker looked over at me. "Hey, honey," he said. "You okay?"

Oh, my God, I thought. Here we go again.

"I'm fine," I said. "I'm just, totally, fine."

He got back on his chopper. "Coulda fooled me," he said.

———

A few days later, I went down to the Town Hall to change my name on my voter registration. By this point I'd done my driver's license, all my credit cards, my Social Security card, a million things, it seemed. One day a notice appeared in the *Kennebec Journal*: "Notice is hereby given by the respective petitioners that they have filed the following petitions. These matters will be heard at 10 AM or as soon thereafter as they may be on the tenth day of September 2001. The requested actions may be taken on or after the hearing date if no sufficient objection be heard. This notice complies with the requirements of 18-A MRSA Section 3–403 and Probate Rule 4. 01–346 James Finney Boylan to Jennifer Finney Boylan."

On the same day I became Jennifer, I noticed, Joseph Alden Wilkins, of Oakland, became Joseph Richard Bannerjee. I wondered what *he* was going through.

The ritual at the Department of Motor Vehicles had been relatively subdued. I arrived at the DMV in Augusta with my paperwork, and I went up to the counter and explained the situation, briefly, to the clerk. She was a young woman with freckles, and she looked over my documents and said, "Okay, great." And proceeded to change my information on the computer screen.

"Oh, and by the way," I said nonchalantly. "Would you mind changing that M to F while you're at it?"

"Hm? Oh, okay," she said. *Click.*

Changing my voter registration was nearly the last of the many legal details I needed to address in changing names and genders. When I explained the situation to our town clerk, I did so in her office. I gathered from the posters on her wall that she was one of our local Democratic representatives. After I explained what I needed, she got a form and handed it to me. I looked at it for a moment, then said, "Wait. This is the wrong form. This is for changing your political party."

"Oh," she said. "I'm sorry. Wrong form."

Then she took that away and gave me another one. When I finished I said to her, "You know, you're being awfully nice about this."

She said, "Whatever, Jennifer. It's no big deal. Just as long as you aren't going *Republican* on us."

Grace and I were driving down to Freeport, to shop at L. L. Bean. I looked over at her. "You're pretty tough, aren't you," I said.

"That's what everybody says," said Grace.

"I can't believe you're so strong."

"I'm not strong," Grace said. "I'm just surviving."

"Well, I think you're amazing. Most people would have left me a long time ago."

"Well, I'm not most people."

"Can I ask about the surgery? Is that okay?"

Grace sighed. "Sure," she said. "We can talk about the surgery."

"Well, you'd said once that you weren't sure how far with me you could go. You'd said that maybe you could stay with me just that far, but that that was the breaking point. Is that still how you feel?"

"Do you want the surgery, Jenny?"

I nodded. "Uh-huh," I said.

"Well, you should have it," she said. "I mean, there's no reason not to."

"Yeah, but— If this one thing would keep us together, I'd be willing not to do it."

Grace laughed sadly. "Jenny, that's not what's keeping us together. It doesn't make any difference at this point, does it?"

I didn't say anything.

"Does it?"

I shook my head.

―――――

We headed up to Freeport Studio, the high-end women's line at Bean's. I was standing before a three-way mirror, examining the fit of a dress, when I heard a voice behind me. "Boy," a woman said, "wouldn't you love to look like *that*?"

I turned around, and there was a customer talking to the sales clerk. The two of them were looking at me. "You're kidding," I said.

"Of course I'm not kidding," the woman said. "I'd *kill* for your body."

"Believe me," I said, turning around. "You don't want this body."

"Isn't this typical of women?" said the customer to the clerk. "We're never satisfied with ourselves."

I took a plane to Wisconsin to meet Dr. Schrang. We had an interesting conversation. "Oh, my patients are all very pleased with their vaginas," he observed. The doctor gave me a unique examination. At length he nodded. "You'll make a nice woman," he said cheerfully. "You're excellent material."

I was excited about the surgery. I was also scared of it—scared of the pain, scared of the unknown. Still, looking at photographs of the results of Dr. Schrang's work, I had to agree that he was very, very good at what he did. Of his patients it was frequently said, "Even your gynecologist can't tell the difference." Or, in the words of trans author Kate Bornstein, "The plumbing works, and so does the electricity."

"I have three goals for you, postsurgery," Schrang said. "I want you to be *sensate*, *mucosal*, and *orgasmic*."

Sensate, mucosal, and orgasmic, I thought. It sounded like the blurb on a book, one I probably wouldn't want to read. At least not in hardcover.

On a Saturday morning a few weeks later, I was drinking Bloody Marys with a dozen of my mother's closest friends, most of whom I had known since I was a child. Mom had decided that the best way to deal with the issue of her problem child was to have a coming out party for me. There were cucumber sandwiches and crackers with cheese.

My mother's friends arrived, one and two at a time, and got a good look at me. One of them exclaimed, "For heaven's sakes, Jennifer. You make a damn fine broad!"

I talked to them all, briefly, about what it meant to be transgender. I then went on to say, "Look, it doesn't really matter if you get this or not. You don't even have to like me. The important thing is Mom needs you right now, and more than ever she deserves the support of her friends." Without exception, they all pledged their love to her and, in some cases, to me.

It took only about fifteen minutes for everyone to loosen up. Following the by-now-standard pattern, her friends there who had no memory of me as a man had nothing to get used to. And the others did their best to follow me to the place I had gone. In the end it was easier than they had expected.

They had come to my mother's house as a favor. Before they left, they were doing my colors and trying to sell me Mary Kay products.

That night, Mom and I went out for dinner. Before we left I gave her a photo album of moments from her entire life, and she was deeply moved by it. I'd even found her high school yearbook photo, and we agreed, with some shock, that I looked now very much the way she had looked in her twenties. Then we made gin and tonics and sat at the piano, the same piano where I'd played "Mrs. Robinson" for the Vietnam Santa over twenty-five years ago.

We sang "My Favorite Things" together. Then we went on to "You Are My Sunshine." The tears rolled down our faces.

At dinner, we sat by a large fire in the crowded restaurant and drank red wine. I finally said something to her like "By the way, Mom, I'm sorry about the whole woman business."

And she said, without missing a beat, "I'm not." She raised her glass. "I am so proud of my beautiful daughter. Cheers."

We clinked glasses.

Later that night I lay in bed, thinking of what she had said. *I am so proud of my beautiful daughter.* It made me feel good. Then I thought, *Jesus, I hope she wasn't talking about my sister.*

Of my sister, all that should be said here is that her reaction to the situation was very different from my mother's. I wrote her a lengthy letter in January of 2001, explaining things as best I could and asking for her understanding and her love. She wrote back a month later, saying she didn't want to know me anymore. She hasn't spoken to me since.

Mom thinks she'll come around, though.

———

One day in the fall, a professor of medieval literature stopped me in the hall and asked if I minded a question. I didn't mind, and since she was a professor of medieval literature, I presumed the question would be interesting, since professors of this period are almost required by the Modern Language Association to be completely insane. The previous professor of medieval literature was a guy with a long ponytail who had written his thesis on the confluence between the works of Chaucer and gangsta rap. He'd been the lead guitarist in Diminished Faculties, in fact, at least until our geologist harmonica player was denied tenure.

Anyway, the professor pulled me aside and said, "Can I just ask you—how do you learn to put on makeup? I mean, can you go to a school?"

I mumbled something about going to the Clinique counter and giving them your credit card.

But she interrupted me and said, "No, no, I mean I own makeup. I just don't know how to wear it, you know? I mean, you look great. Are you wearing makeup right now?"

I allowed as how I might be.

She said, "That's the thing, you don't look like you're wearing makeup. Me, I always look like a little girl playing with her mother's cosmetics. See, you look like a normal woman in makeup. Me, I look strange and artificial. How do you explain that?"

I told her it just took practice, but she wasn't convinced. Fortunately, she had to go teach a class, or we could have been there for a few more hours. I did think, as I walked toward my car, that it was interesting that genetic women didn't necessarily know anything more about this than I did. As it turns out, we're all still learning to be men, or women, all still learning to be ourselves.

———————

One afternoon, Russo and I were back in the Seadog in Camden, drinking Old Gollywobbler. Barbara was out of town. The Yankees were on television. We finished our pints, talking shop for a while.

A waitress came by. "Can I get you anything?" she asked.

"I'll have another pint," Rick said. "And get him whatever he wants."

The waitress looked confused. "Who?"

Rick blushed.

"He's talking about his invisible friend," I said.

"Do you want anything, miss?"

"I'll have another one, too." The waitress walked off.

Rick looked at me, strangely emotional. "Sorry," he said. "You're not invisible, Boylan."

"Well," I said. "Thanks."

"Are we okay?" Russo said. "You and me?"

"I don't know," I said. "Some of those e-mails we swapped were kind of awful, I think."

Russo shook his head. "I was afraid you'd think that. I told you, Boylan, I've never had a very high opinion of the truth."

"I'll tell you what, Rick. I don't mind being called 'studied' and 'mannered.' But 'implausible'? That hurts."

He looked saddened. "Maybe that's the wrong word."

"I mean, *you*—some kid from Gloversville, New York, the glove-making capital of the world, who winds up a famous novelist?—you think *I'm* implausible?"

"Okay, it's *definitely* the wrong word."

"Hell, Rick. Isn't this the reason we become writers, our understanding that all sorts of implausible things turn out to be true? Just because we can't believe them, or understand them, doesn't mean they aren't real."

"You sound like that kid in the workshop again," Rick said.

"I'm not a kid in a workshop, goddammit," I said. "I'm a real person, someone with a condition so strange, it seems to make me into a work of fiction." I was yelling at him now, and I paused to catch my breath. "But I'm not a work of fiction. I'm your friend, and I need you."

Russo was quiet for a long time. "You know what it is," he said at last. "It's not just learning about . . . the woman stuff, that's hard. I've almost caught up with that. But unlearning that you're not a man anymore—that takes longer. I have a long history with you that I don't especially want to give up. Jesus, I *liked* you as a man."

"Rick," I said, "you don't have to give up your history."

"I don't know about that, Boylan. In some ways, I do, at least my history as I understood it at the time. But giving up history isn't the same as giving up memory. It's just hard."

He drank from his pint. "You know what it is? If learning is hard, unlearning is harder. You just have to be patient, all right? I'm a slow unlearner."

I nodded. "Don't worry, Russo," I said. "We'll always have Paris."

A few weeks later, I stood before a roomful of people, introducing my friend, comparing our time at Colby together to life inside the barn in *Charlotte's Web*—the nearness of rats, the friendship of spiders, and the glory of everything. "It's not often you have a good friend who is also a good writer," I said, quoting Wilbur the Pig. "Charlotte was both."

Russo took to the podium as I sat down, and he looked at me sitting there in the audience, smiled, and said, *"Some pig."*

On Halloween I entered Lorimer Chapel with my old friend Charles Bassett; I was wearing a long black dress and a witch's pointed hat, a battery-operated raven on one arm. Bassett, who liked to call

the people he loved "toad," was perhaps Colby's most beloved professor, an adorable old grouch who had pretty much invented American
studies single-handedly. Together we'd been reading ghost stories for
students in the chapel on Halloween for over a dozen years now, and
it was a tradition I wasn't going to give up.

It was the first time most of my students had seen me since transition, though, and as Bassett and I walked down the aisle of the chapel,
the building lit only by candles and jack-o'-lanterns, I felt the weight
of their gaze upon me.

For a moment I thought, *I can't do this. I'm not going to make it.*

Then we arrived on stage. The place was filled. There were students in the organ loft, in the pews, in the upper balconies. Some of
them were even sitting cross-legged on the floor before the pulpit.

According to our tradition, I opened the reading, and Bassett was
the closer. So as he sat in his chair, I went up to the microphone and
said, "Good evening."

Just at that moment I felt a sudden inspiration. I knew I wanted
to say something, but on the other hand, I hadn't wanted to say too
much, either. So I looked over at Charlie and said, "Hey, is it just me,
or does Charlie Bassett look really different from last semester?"

There was some nervous laughter. Bassett rubbed his face with
his palm and muttered, "Don't do this, Jenny."

I was touched he'd remembered to use the right name.

"No, I'm serious," I said into the mike. "Doesn't he look different?
Man, Bassett! You've really changed!"

This time everyone laughed. They got the joke. Bassett sat there
grimacing.

"Oh well," I said. "I guess he's still the same person inside."

And with that, the entire place went nuts. They burst into applause.
They cheered and hollered and stamped their feet. Bassett looked over
at me and smiled.

"Boylan," he said, "you're still a toad."

I went to the credit union to have my name changed on the account I kept there. I told the manager I needed to change my name.

"Did you get married?"

"No."

"Oh—divorced?"

"No. See, the thing is, my name used to be James. Only now it's Jennifer."

The manager looked at me over the top of her glasses. "You were named James?"

I nodded.

She put the glasses on her desk. "I don't understand—did your parents want a boy?"

"My parents— No, wait. See, my parents got a boy. I used to be a boy. Now I'm female. I had my name changed."

"You're saying you used to be a boy?" she said, looking at me very carefully.

"Uh-huh."

"Huh," she said, and started typing into her computer. "Okay, well, this is simple enough. We'll just change your name in the data field here—"

"While you're doing that, can I ask you a question? You know how I have this money deducted from my paycheck and deposited each month? I started doing it when I had a lien on my car, until I paid it off. . . ."

"Right. The Audi."

"Yeah. Well, I'm having surgery this spring—you know, *the* surgery—"

"Mm-hm."

"Well, I wanted to know if I could write one big check for the surgery, and slowly pay it back out of this account. You know, like I did with the car?"

She thought about it. "No, ah—I don't think so."

"But why not?"

"Well, Ms. Boylan—don't you see—with the car we had the car

itself as collateral. If you'd defaulted on the loan, we could have asked for the car back. If you defaulted on this . . . well, what could we take? I mean, what could we get back from you as collateral?"

We looked at each other for a long moment, and then she started to turn deep red. Then we both laughed.

"Well, you can have that, if you want it so badly," I said.

"No, no," she said. "It's just that we'd have to charge you— interest—on it."

"You don't think it would give you any interest?"

She wiped her forehead with a tissue, then went back to her computer screen. "Fortunately," she said, "that's not my department."

Persons Such as Themselves

(Fall 2001)

The first thing we do in support group is go around the circle for "check-in." It's an unusually low turnout this month. We're down to only five of the twenty, plus the therapist who acts as moderator. Ted, the leader, was having a good week. Ted, who used to be Eleanor, has a big black beard and muscles like a lumberjack. He's dating a girl named Candy, who used to consider herself a lesbian but isn't quite sure anymore. Ted has a deep, growly voice and a rich laugh. He was just promoted to foreman at Central Maine Power, where he's worked for years fixing downed power lines.

You'd never know in a million years that Ted used to be a woman. It's hard enough to believe he was ever even clean-shaven.

Millicent was also having a good week. She had her operation nine years ago. Her husband, George, comes to the meetings once in a while, but not to this one. Millicent is a secretary at a law firm, has two children from a previous marriage, and is in an all-women's bowling league called Pins N Needles.

Victoria's doing all right as well, which is good because we worry about Victoria. I don't know Victoria's real name, although no one other than the members of the support group calls her Victoria. She isn't "out" at all and comes to the meeting looking just like another guy you'd see on the street. She has thick stubble, sideburns, hairy arms, a low voice, and one pierced ear. Victoria dreams of the day she too will be female, but she is afraid of losing everything, and this is not so unlikely, given the fact that Victoria's wife has said that she will phone the police if Victoria ever so much as even *mentions* this topic again.

Then there's me. I tell everyone I'm okay but that sometimes I feel incredibly alone. Everyone nods.

Finally we get to Trudy. Trudy is young, about twenty-three. She is shockingly beautiful—about five six, with long blond hair, beautiful legs. Trudy isn't out, either, although how anyone could look at her and see a man is beyond me. On the other hand, I've only seen Trudy as Trudy, so I don't really know what she looks like.

"Well, I've been having a hard time," says Trudy, and she says this in a deep male voice. The voice is Trudy's weak spot. We keep urging her to call my friend Tania, the Bates professor, but Trudy isn't sure. She says she doesn't want to sound all *fakey*.

"Tell us about . . . 'hard time,' " says Andrea, the social worker who sits in at our support group. Andrea is a middle-aged woman with an iron gray braid. She has Benjamin Franklin–type glasses that usually rest on top of her hair like a headband.

"Well, okay," says Trudy. "First of all, like, I got fired at work." This isn't news, since Trudy's been on the verge of termination at the paper factory for some time. She's in charge of quality control for a manufacturer of paper plates, and apparently some of the products she's approved for shipping have had visible pieces of bark and unprocessed pulp in them. "They gave me a warning, then said they wanted to talk to me about the situation, then they just called me in and fired my ass! I went ballistic, punched out Larry, then threw his computer out the window. It was like a bloodbath, with the glass from the window

all over, and Larry running around holding his bloody nose, plus—
you won't believe this—when the computer went out the window
it almost hit this old guy, and now *he's* out shouting on the sidewalk
like I was *aiming* it at him."

Andrea nods her head sympathetically and says, "That sounds
hard, Trudy."

"Fuck yes, it was hard, so they fuckin' fire my ass out of there, tell
me to take my vending machine with me, and not only that but now
I can't get unemployment because you can't get it if you got fired for
whatever you call it, malfeasance? So now I got all these bills comin'
in, and the next thing you know my stupid mother dies, so I had to
go all the way up to Montreal to listen to them go blah blah blah
over *her* dead ass, then I come back here and I'm thinking about this
chick I used to go out with, Melanie, so I start—"

"You're saying your mother died?" says Andrea.

"What? Yeah, yeah, she's dead. The asshole."

"That must be hard, Trudy," says Andrea.

Victoria reaches out and pats Trudy on the thigh. "It's okay,"
Victoria says.

"I'm glad she's dead," says Trudy. "Total fuckwad."

"Let it out," Victoria says.

"Shit for brains," says Trudy.

"It's hard to let go," says Andrea.

"Anyway, so I start wondering about Melanie, whom I haven't,
like, seen for six months, ever since I decided, *Fuck her!*—you know.
Have I talked about Melanie before, and her girlfriend Donna?"

We all look at one another. Quite frankly, we can't really remember
what Trudy has told us and what she hasn't told us. Each month we
get a lot of new information. Me, I'm still back trying to process the
news about her former boss, Larry, getting his computer thrown out
the window of the paper plate factory.

"Maybe you could refresh us," says Andrea.

"Okay," says Trudy. "So Melanie was this chick I met when I
worked at Arby's. She worked the fryer, I was doing the drive-up

window, we used to get off work and go out to Scooters, just close it down?"

Scooters is the name of a marginal bar in Skowhegan, Maine, a town that was also the hometown of Margaret Chase Smith, although my guess is that she never went into Scooters, and if she did, it was just the one time.

"So I got involved in this three-way with Melanie. Her and Donna, they used to have me come back to their place, and Donna would watch us while we fuck, or *I'd* watch them while *they* fuck, or sometimes I'd fuck Donna while Melanie videotaped it, then we'd *all* watch. But Donna was totally, like, fucked in the head, and she kept telling Melanie she'd couldn't see me, or then sometimes she could, but only if Donna was there, and meanwhile, she's coming in for lunches at Arby's and basically sitting there watching us to see if we're doing it while she's making curly fries. So finally I say, Fuck this! and I'm out of there, then Melanie calls me from the hospital a week later, she'd tried to kill herself by leaving the car on in the garage, instead she kills Donna's dog, Freckles. Donna's all pissed off, so she's like, Melanie, you can't live here anymore, and Melanie is like, Fine, whatever! So now Melanie doesn't have a place to live, except I'm like, Do I want to get involved with her at all? But she crashes at my place for a week, and then Donna shows up and just says, Mel, get in the car, and I'm like, Wait, Melanie, don't listen to her, but Melanie just gets her shit and they drive off and I'm left there going, Fuck the both of them, I'm just not talking to them anymore."

"Wait a minute," says Ted. "Did this Melanie know you were trans?"

"Oh sure," says Trudy. "She was cool with it."

Ted nods. "Just askin'."

"So that was this summer. And I'd been doing fine except that I miss Melanie now and again, it's like I never connected to anyone like that before. I mean, it's pretty spooky, like I mean, I never felt like that, ever. I mean, I don't believe in love at first sight and all that crap, but I mean the two of us were just like, *whoa*. It felt like missing part of my fuckin' arm, not seeing her. So after I got back from Mom's funeral I decided I'd do this Internet search for her, and the next thing you know I'm looking at her fuckin' *obituary* from the *Bangor Daily News.* She'd killed herself two weeks after I saw her last, hung herself in her attic."

At this moment I think about pointing out the difference between "hanged" and "hung" but then decided to let it go. There are times when grammar is unimportant, and this is probably one of them.

"Oh, Trudy," says Andrea. "That's hard."

"And I just cried and cried. I mean, what did she go and do that for? I just thought it was all my fault, like I could have saved her if I'd been there."

"You can't think that way," says Ted. "People do all sorts of stupid-ass things. You can't stop them."

"But the thing is, we used to talk about suicide all the time, and she just goes and does it, leaves me behind. I mean, fuck her!"

"I'm sorry," says Victoria.

"So now I'm thinking, basically, of killing myself. I've been giving it a lot of thought. I can tell you exactly the right way to do it. And let me tell you one thing, rope is not the way to do it. That's a totally stupid way to go."

"What is the way to do it?" says Milly.

"Helium," says Trudy. "As it turns out. One big canister of that shit costs you about thirty, forty bucks, and it's very effective. You need about two hundred balloons' worth, and you're done. It's very peaceful."

"Wait," I say. "You've got to fill up two hundred balloons' worth?" I'm picturing Trudy inhaling two hundred balloons of helium, one after the other, and while she is dying, talking in a voice like Minnie Mouse's. *Good-bye, cruel world. Good-bye, Donald. Good-bye, Goofy. I'm like, Fuck you, Mickey!*

"Well, it's better if you hook yourself up to an oxygen mask, you know. That way you just get the continuous effect of it."

"It sounds like you've really researched this," says Andrea, sounding alarmed.

"Oh yeah. I'm basically thinking I'm going to do it any day now. Once I get my life in order."

"I can't believe we're talking about this," I say.

"What can't you believe?" says Trudy.

"That you're talking about killing yourself, and we're all just sitting around listening to this. You can't kill yourself."

"Sure she can," says Ted.

"Thank you, Ted," says Trudy.

"I mean, if she does it, she's an asshole, but she can do it. I mean, she doesn't need your fuckin' permission, Jenny."

Andrea says, "I think what Jenny is saying—"

"Let Jenny speak for herself," says Victoria.

"I'm just saying," I continue. "Listen. When I was about twenty-seven years old, I took this long drive up to Nova Scotia, all by myself. My father had just died. I felt totally alone in the world, like I would never know what it was like to be happy. I thought that being a woman was something that was just impossible, that I'd rather die than have to face that. And I drove all the way up there and I stood by this cliff and I kind of played this game, leaning into the wind, just seeing how far I could lean out into the void before being blown back into the world."

I've got all their attention now. Usually I'm the well-adjusted member of the group. It's a trait that makes me stick out.

"So what happened, Jenny?" says Trudy.

"So I leaned forward, preparing to fall, and then at the last second this big gust of wind knocked me backward, and I thought I felt this presence of . . . I don't know . . ."

"Aw, don't tell me you heard Jesus or some lame-o shit like that," says Ted.

"I don't know what I heard," I say, remembering lying there on the soft moss, looking up into the blue sky. *Son? Are you all right, son?*

"But I knew I wanted to live," I say. "And I left there and I drove all the way home. And on the way back I met Grace, whose love changed my life. And everything that has happened to me since then has made me grateful to be alive, in spite of being trans, in spite of carrying this insane secret, in spite of all the sadness that my coming out is now bringing to the people I love, I am still grateful for this life, and for the time that I've lived since I didn't jump off that cliff."

"Jumping off of a cliff isn't a good way to do it," Trudy says thoughtfully. "A *lot* of people get blown back up." She seems unmoved.

"Listen," I say. "What would you say to your friend if she were here now?"

Trudy thinks about it. "I don't know," she says. "I guess I'd tell her I wished she didn't kill herself."

"Uh-huh," I say.

Trudy shrugs, looks uncomfortable. "Listen, you all shouldn't get all bent out of shape about this. Hell, I never thought I'd live *this* long."

"Trudy, I'm trying to tell you that twenty-three is not old. I know it seems incredibly old to you, but it's not. Your life is really just beginning."

She looks at me, unconvinced.

"Listen," I say. "When I was twenty-six, I went to a therapist who told me I was a transsexual, that I needed to start finding the courage to be a woman. And all I could think of was, The hell with you, I don't want to find the courage to be a woman, I want the courage to *not* be one. I think sometimes that hearing about other people's stories, their own triumphs over sadness or whatever, does us exactly no good. For me, anyway, stories of how other people learned to want to live, or how they came out as women, or whatever, always just depressed me. I wanted to say, Well, fuck you, I'm so glad you worked things out for you, but your story doesn't help me at all, because I'm me and not you."

And now, to my shame, I am starting to cry, and cry hard. It is amazing to me that Trudy, who wants to commit suicide, is sitting there with a shit-eating grin, while I, who love life and am so grateful for all my blessings, am sitting cross-legged on the floor, weeping. I mean, I barely even know Trudy. Why I'm all broken up in tears about her, I can't say. But of course, I think to myself, We're not crying about Trudy, are we?

"It's okay, Jenny," says Victoria, who comes over and sits next to me and pats my thigh. "It's okay."

"It's hard, isn't it?" says Andrea.

And I want to say, *Fuckin'-A it's hard*. Now I am shaking as I cry, and little black rivulets of mascara are coursing down the sides of my cheeks, making me look like Tammy Faye Bakker.

After a pause I say, "Trudy, I don't know if my saying this will make any difference to you at all. But you can't just assume things will always be like they are now. There are all sorts of miracles in the world, and you have to have faith in them."

"Why?" says Trudy.

There's a long silence as everyone waits to see what I'm going to come up with. No one is more anxious to find out what I'm about to say than I am.

"Because," I say, wiping my eyes. "Because life is better than death."

There is another long pause as everyone mulls this over.

"For you, maybe," Trudy says quietly.

Andrea slips into social work mode. "Trudy, are you on medication right now, for depression?"

"Yeah," says Trudy. "They got me on Wellbutrin. Except I can never remember to take it. I keep forgetting. I got ADD, you know, or whatever they call it."

"Mm-hm," says Andrea. "Well, see, if you don't take it, it can't help you."

"I don't know if I want it to help me," says Trudy.

"I tell you what," says Andrea. "Why don't you agree with all of us here that you'll take your medication for one month? Take it every day, like you're supposed to. At the next meeting, we'll see how you feel. But will you agree to not kill yourself for just the one month? And take your meds in the meantime?"

It is a brilliant move, and I suspect heartily that this intervention is taught in social work school. Instead of suggesting, as I was trying to do, that Trudy change her entire view of the world, Andrea is merely trying to buy a month.

"Okay," she says.

Now we are all up on our feet and we are hugging and kissing and we check the clock and the time for the meeting is over. So we all put on our coats and go out to a local Japanese restaurant and drink sake.

We are an interesting party, the five of us—Ted, me, Trudy, Milly, and Victoria. (Andrea never goes out with us, having, as Woody Allen once said, "previous commitments on the planet Earth.") What's interesting is that the five of us look pretty much like three normal women and two normal men—since Ted, Trudy, Milly, and I all look like the sexes we are presenting as, and Victoria looks like a relatively normal man, except for the fact that he is named Victoria, which you wouldn't know just by looking.

We sit at the sushi bar and the chefs say, *"Hei!"* to us and carve off raw fish and create spectacles on our plates that are so beautiful, it seems a shame to eat them. Raw fish, I think, is an unusual medium for expression, and I am grateful, among the many other things that I am grateful for, that I express myself through ink and not tuna.

"Listen, Jenny," says Trudy, salmon roe rolling down her chin. "I wanted to thank you for what you said in there. I mean, you didn't have to say anything."

"Yes, she did," says Ted, who is sitting on my right. "You know she can't help herself."

"What do you mean, Ted?" says Milly.

"Aw, you know the professor, it's always blah blah blah."

"Thank you, Ted," I say. I know he means this nicely.

"Well, I'm grateful, okay?" says Trudy. "You don't have to worry about me."

"Hey, Trudy, can I ask you about something?" I say. "When you were talking about getting fired from the paper plate factory, you mentioned something about how you had to go and take your vending machine with you. Did I hear that right? What does that mean, you had to take your vending machine?"

"I got a line of vending machines," Trudy says. "I got about fifty units. Gumball, soft drink, encapsulated prizes, snacks. I had a soft drink unit at the mill, and they told me I had to take it with me."

"Wait," I say. "You've got your own line of—vending machines?"

"Yeah," says Trudy, and suddenly this look of complete happiness comes over her face. The sushi chefs look at each other and exchange comments in Japanese.

"I *love* vending machines," says Trudy. "I've *always* loved vending machines. I fell in love with them when I was fifteen, and it's only gotten more intense since then. I love everything about vending machines! The sound the quarter makes when you put it in the slot, the clicking it makes as it falls into the mechanism, the efficiency of the delivery of the product when the machine is working right. I mean, there's nothing in the world like a vending machine that's tuned properly."

I sip some sake. "You tune them?" I say. "Like a piano?"

"No, no, it's more like a car. You know, it takes a lot to keep them running right."

"Wait," says Milly. "How much money do you make from a vending machine each week?"

"Well, depends on the unit, and it depends where it's placed. Sodas are very high maintenance, and there's not a lot of profit margin. People know how much a soda is supposed to cost, so they won't put in much more than a buck, a buck twenty-five, for a can of soda. Gumballs, though, you can ask anything for a gumball, and people just shovel it in. Plus, a case of gumballs only costs like ten or twelve dollars. And you don't have to refrigerate them. Profitwise, all vending machines aspire to gumball."

Trudy's face is full of light. Her eyes are focused somewhere far off.

"There's this one machine," she says, "called Gonzo's Wild Ride. Have you ever seen those, like, pinball machines in airports where a single ball rolls through a whole series of, like, channels, bounces off of drumheads and xylophones, gets carried up a ramp, and so on?"

"There's one of those in Logan," says Victoria.

"I saw one at the Museum of Science," says Ted.

"Right. Well, in Gonzo's Wild Ride, for a dollar you send a jaw-breaker on a journey like that, it rolls all the way through this whole obstacle course before it gets vended out to the consumer. It is the Mercedes of vending machines. A dollar, for a jawbreaker! It's totally beautiful, it's just one of the most beautiful things I know about."

As I look at Trudy, I can't help but think that for the first time all night, she seems completely animated, full of life.

"Do you have that one?" I say.

"No," she says. "Not yet."

"Trudy," I say, "did you hear yourself? You just said 'yet.' "

"So?"

"So that's the first time you've talked like there's a certain future, and that you're going to be in it."

"Well, duh, Jenny," says Trudy. "Do you really think I'd kill myself before I get Gonzo's Wild Ride? I mean, get real!"

Get real, I think. It sounds so easy.

"I don't know how long I have to live," says Trudy. "But I know I'm getting fuckin' *Gonzo* before I go."

Drunken Noodles

(January 2002)

On New Year's Eve 2001–2002, I played with the band at Scooters in Skowhegan, the same place Trudy used to go with her dead friend, Melanie, after they got finished working the deep-fat fryer at Arby's. Halfway through the first set, Shell announced, "All waitresses on top of the bar, *now!*" and a moment later, they were.

I wasn't crazy about playing out on New Year's Eve, but Grace had encouraged me to go. She and the boys had been invited to the house of our friends Frank and Sandra, the same couple who had had the millennium party two years ago. I remembered standing by the frozen lake with Luke in my arms, watching the distant fireworks, his breath coming out in clouds.

Shelley worked the bar's large, raucous crowd and declared her intention of crowning someone "Baby New Year." She soon found a willing volunteer, whom she diapered with a giant Depends, an oversize baby bonnet, and a small sign that read "Happy 2002." For his humility the band gave the young man—a University of Maine at Farmington student—a George Foreman minigrill as a token of our gratitude. Ten minutes later, though, he and his grill had stolen out of Scooters and into the night, perhaps forever scarred from his moments before the cheering crowd in a giant diaper. It left the rest of us asking plaintively for the ensuing hours, "Hey, man. Whatever *happened* to Baby New Year?"

The band launched into "Psycho Killer." In the midst of this a guy came up to me and started *lurking* in front of the keys. "I'm in looove with your haaair," he explained, and reached out for me.

The bouncer, a very large man in a white T-shirt and a shaved head, pulled him away from me.

The band sang, "Fa fa fa *fa* fa-fa, *fa*-fa *fa* fa fa."

A moment later he was back, closer this time. He explained things again. "I want to *play* in your *haaair*."

He reached out for me. Less than two seconds after that, the bouncer had him. Mr. Clean hauled the young man halfway across the bar, at which location the young man was dropped onto the floor. The bouncer stepped on the boy's neck with his large black boots. Shortly after that, my suitor was outside in the snow.

During the break, I said to the bouncer, "Did you *have* to hurt him like that?"

He shrugged apologetically. "Sorry, ma'am," he said. "It's our policy."

———

At nine A.M. the next morning, Grace said, "Jenny, wake up. It's next year."

I opened my eyes to see her standing bedside with a very large pile of pancakes and syrup. "Hi," I said. My voice was hoarse. My hair smelled like smoke.

"Here, eat these," she said. "We're climbing a mountain in forty-five minutes."

I ate the cakes.

Forty-five minutes later we were ascending French's Mountain in

Rome, Maine. We'd done this with our friends Loretta and Dave every New Year's Day for a couple of years running. By midmorning we were at the summit, and we looked around at the lakes shimmering with ice and the snow-covered hills that surrounded us. The kids threw snowballs and fought with icicles as if they were swords.

Loretta talked about the first time she'd climbed French's Mountain on New Year's. "This old woman I know, Mrs. Voron, used to climb up here with all her women friends every year. The time she took me, she handed us all little squares of paper. When we got to the top, everybody made a wish, and then the wind came and blew the paper away."

Loretta paused to look out at the frozen lakes.

"Then, at that moment," Loretta said, "a red-tailed hawk swooped down, *whoosh*, just like that, and right after *that*, a sudden snow squall passed through. It was totally freaky."

Our children climbed trees as the grown-ups looked out at the horizon and handed around a thermos of hot cocoa. Lucy the dog stood at the edge of the precipice, gazing at the abyss.

When it was time to go, I picked up a handful of powdery snow and held it in my mitten. I thought about the coming year, the year of finally having surgery, of all the trials that lay ahead. I closed my eyes and wished that my family would be protected from the world by our love for one another.

The snow blew out of my hand.

———————

That night, Grace and I got a baby-sitter and went out for Thai food and a showing of *Lord of the Rings*.

I asked Grace how she felt about the year to come. She was eating drunken noodles and spicy chili fish, along with a side dish of plad mun.

Grace looked at me and said, "I know you always ask me how I feel, but there are times when I think it doesn't matter."

"Of course it matters," I said.

"Jenny, shhh," she said. "This time you listen."

She poured herself some tea.

"You're good at asking me how I feel, Jenny, about trying to have a conversation about your transition, but you know what I think sometimes? I think, What's the difference. Since day one you've pretty much had an idea in your head of exactly what you wanted to do, and when you'd do it. All I've ever said all along was, Wait, please, stop, slow down, and to that you've responded with all sorts of words about your suffering, about what you've been through, about how you don't have any choice, about how this is mostly a medical issue and all that. It seems like no matter what I say it doesn't matter, because it's all been decided a long time ago. You've just been on a freight train for two years now. You're going where you feel like you need to go. For me, it's just like I'm standing here watching."

Tears filled Grace's eyes, dripped down her face, and fell into her drunken noodles.

"Do you believe," I asked her slowly, "that all of this is necessary for me?"

She wiped her eyes.

"Yes, I suppose so," she said. "But you can't expect me to feel the way you do about this. I can't imagine what it's like for you, even now. I'm not the one who's trapped in the wrong body, in the wrong life, in the wrong place. At least I didn't used to be. No matter what happens from here on out, I lose."

Her lower lip trembled.

"I'm sorry," I said.

"I know you're sorry," Grace said. "But what can I say to you? You don't want to be the person I married." She shrugged. "I do love you. But this isn't what I signed up for. This isn't what I had in mind, when I spent the last twelve years, building something."

"It was something I built, too," I said.

We both sat there for a long time then, not saying anything.

"For all that," Grace said, "I still believe that being together is better than being apart. I still want to be with you."

I said quietly, "No, Grace. What you want is to be with Jim."

"No," she said. "What I want is to be with *you*."

We were silent again for a little while.

"But being with you can't mean what it used to mean. I'm always going to miss my boyfriend, the person I married, the person I love. The fact that all of this is necessary for you doesn't make that any less hard for me. But I know I want us to be together. I know I will always be close to you, Jenny. I'm just not sure . . . how near."

"Do you want me to move into the guest room?" I asked. "Do you want me to move out of the house?"

"No," she said. "I don't."

We were silent again for a long while.

"But," I said, "that doesn't mean you ever want to have a relationship with me again? That just means we're like *sisters*, for the rest of our lives?"

"I don't know what it means, Jenny. I'm not sure what we are. It's like you get to be happy, and me—well, we all just wait for me to get over it. But I can't get over it. I'm always going to feel betrayed by you, abandoned, like our little family was not enough. You know how I feel? Gypped.

"You asked me if I thought this was necessary, and yes, I do. I think it's taken incredible bravery and courage for you to be the person you need to be, and I'm not going to stand in the way of that. I would never keep the person I love from being who she needs to be. But I can't be glad for you, Jenny. Every success you've had as a woman is also a loss for me. I mean, I'm proud of you—you're a beautiful woman, you've come so far. But all of that success for you just feels like failure to me. I can't feel the way about your transition that you do; I'll never feel that way. All of the good things that have happened to you—your acceptance at Colby, with the band, with the school—to me, they all just mean one more thing I've lost.

"And I didn't get to participate in this at all. I didn't get to choose when you started hormones, or when you went full-time, or when you'll have surgery. I mean, you consulted me, you included me, and we talked about it all again and again and again—but it didn't *really* matter what I said about any of it, did it? I mean, really?"

The waitress came by and asked if there was anything she could get for us.

We said that we were fine.

Later we sat in a darkened movie theater watching *The Lord of the Rings*. About an hour into the film I found my eyes suddenly filling with tears, and the next thing I knew I was sobbing uncontrollably.

It was the scene at the end of the Council of Elrond, when Frodo accepts his burden.

"I will take the Ring," he says. *"I will go to Mordor. Although I do not know the way."*

I wept so hard that people in the next row glanced over at me. I reached out and held Grace's hand. I held it for a long time.

Then my tears stopped for a while.

They started again when Frodo reunites with old Bilbo Baggins in Rivendell and Bilbo tries to get Frodo to show him the Ring. For a moment Bilbo seems transformed into Gollum. Then he diminishes, and a look of exhaustion and horror comes over him.

"I understand now," Bilbo says. *"Put it away! I am sorry. Sorry you have come in for this burden, sorry about everything."*

Part 4

June 2001. Okay, I thought. Enough.

The Yankee-Doodle Girl

In 1987, while I was living in Washington, my mother came down for a visit. We went over to the Lincoln Memorial. As we drove, she reminisced about coming to America as a child, her memories of Ellis Island and Depression-era New Jersey. It wasn't a topic she visited often.

"No matter what else you say," she said, "you have to love America."

"I have to?" I said. "I don't have a choice about this?"

"No, Jim," she said. "As a matter of fact, you don't."

I parked the car near the Mall. Together we walked through the rain up the steps. There was Abe, sitting on his marble throne. It was quiet.

Visiting the Lincoln Memorial is sort of like being sent to the principal. You feel ashamed of yourself for being such a shithead. You want to tell him, *I'm sorry about being a woman, Mr. President. Honest I am.* Lincoln looked at me, his melancholy face ravaged and discouraged: *I'm not angry. I'm just terribly, terribly disappointed.*

"Boy," my mother said. "He's ugly."

Fifteen years later, Grace and Russo and I walked by the train tracks in a Wisconsin town we'll call Egypt. Behind me, my suitcase on wheels went clackety-clack across the sidewalk. To our right was the small river that flowed through Egypt, paper factories built upon its banks.

A gritty diesel groaned past us, hauling boxcars: *Georgia Pacific, Chessie System, Southern Serves the South.*

We'd arrived the night before, checked into a hotel that was decorated with the work of an artist named Remington, the "Cowboy Sculptor." I'd never heard of him before, but Grace and Rick had. There were broncos bucking dudes with big hats, bison staring down guys in chaps.

Grace and Russo and I walked into a brightly lit office. On the door were the words *Dr. Eugene Schrang, Cosmetic Surgery.* For all that, it was a place like many others. The waiting room included stacks of old magazines, a television tuned to CNN.

The three of us went into Dr. Schrang's chambers.

"Jennifer," he said, standing up to shake my hand. He wore a three-piece suit and a white lab coat over that. Schrang exuded a kind of imperious dignity, as well as a not displeasing measure of eccentricity.

"This is my partner, Grace," I said, "and my friend Rick Russo."

We all shook hands, sat down. For a moment it was silent.

"I've read your novel," Schrang said. He meant Russo's. "It's good."

"Thank you," said Rick.

It was quiet in the office for a moment. I was waiting for Dr. Schrang to examine me further, to brief my partner and my friend on the surgery that would be performed the next day.

Schrang got up, went over to the bookcase. He pulled out a copy of *Empire Falls* and gave it to Rick. On the cover were the words *Winner of the Pulitzer Prize.*

Empire Falls had done all right.

"You wouldn't mind . . . signing this for me, would you?"

"Sure," Rick said with a forced smile. He opened the novel to the title page. For a moment I thought I heard the gears turning around in his head as he tried to find words appropriate to the occasion.

"How'd you become a novelist, anyway?" Schrang asked Rick. "Is it something that just came naturally to you?"

"Oh no," Rick said. "It took a long time to figure out how to do it right."

"Well," said Schrang, "figuring out how to do sexual reassignment surgery was like that, too."

Rick rubbed his chin, having never realized how much his work and Dr. Schrang's had in common.

Schrang got up, removed three more books from a shelf, and handed one to each of us. The title was *The Great Communicators.* It appeared to be the work of a vanity press, a collection of essays about personal communications. A much younger Eugene Schrang was on the cover. He beckoned toward the reader with one hand, like a magician about to produce a rabbit.

I opened the book, and on the first page was a huge photograph of Ronald Reagan. "This book is dedicated to President Ronald Reagan, the Great Communicator," read the inscription.

"Yikes," I said.

"You don't think you're the only one who wrote a book, do you?" said Schrang with a dignified smile. He was talking to Russo.

"Listen, I don't know if I should tell you this before the surgery, but I'm a Democrat," I said. The doctor looked at me, not sure if I was kidding.

"Oh, that's all right," he said. I was glad he was being so nice about it. Of course, Dr. Schrang dealt with transsexuals every day. Democrats probably weren't that much worse.

"Hey, where are *my* books?" I said.

Dr. Schrang looked at me as if I had spoken a foreign language. It was clear, at that moment, that he had no idea I'd ever written anything.

"I'll send you one," I said.

"I'd like that."

It was silent again.

"Well, do you have, like, any . . . questions for us?" I said. "Or any more examinations you have to do before tomorrow?"

"Nah," said the doctor. "Since you were out here in November, I know all that I need to know. You're going to do fine."

"What are some of the things that could . . . go wrong?" said Grace.

"Well, the biggest danger is a fistula, you know, a fissure between the vagina and the rectum. That's the worst-case scenario. If that happens, I'll have to put in a colostomy. I see that all the time, in patients who've had their surgeries done somewhere else, a fistula. Oh, there's a lot of junk out there, you wouldn't believe some of the junk I've had to correct." He looked at the three of us. "Do you want to see some slides, some pictures of some of the junk I've had to fix?"

"No," all three of us shouted.

"Is that going to happen to me?" I said. "A fistula?"

"I sure hope not," said the doctor.

"Do you want to talk with the doctor privately?" Grace said.

"I think I ought to," I said. "You know, just so we do it."

"Okay," said Grace and Russo. They stood, took their books, shook the doctor's hand. "See you tomorrow."

The door to the office closed. I sat back down.

"What do you get for a Pulitzer Prize, anyway?" he asked after a moment. "Is it money? Or a medal, or what?"

"I think it's money," I said. "I don't know how much, though."

"You think it's a lot?"

"I bet it is," I said. Dr. Schrang looked troubled. "But I don't know for sure. I know you get a certificate, like a diploma. I think Rick got a paperweight, too."

"That's nice, a paperweight," said Dr. Schrang. He smiled, all those years in medical school seeming worthwhile again.

"So, like," I said. "Surgery's tomorrow and everything."

"How are you feeling?" Dr. Schrang asked.

"I guess I'm excited. Kind of nervous. Afraid of the pain, of the unknown. I don't know, it's like you open a door, thinking you know what's on the other side. But you don't really know. I mean, I've done my research, I think I have a good idea of what to expect. But I won't really know for sure until it's all done, you know?"

Dr. Schrang nodded. "It's okay to be afraid. Most people are."

"Okay," I said. "So you're saying I'm normal?"

He nodded. "That's right, Jenny, you're normal."

I had a strange affection for Eugene Schrang. He was an eccentric, perhaps, but he was also a genius. It must be hard, I thought, to be the pioneer of a field so arcane.

Gingerly, almost shyly, he showed me some slides of the operation, which initially struck me as being about as appealing as watching a car accident. Yet as I sat there in the dark, it was impossible not to find something beautiful about these slides as well. I recalled the words I had so often heard used to describe Schrang's work: *Even your gynecologist can't tell the difference.* It was remarkable.

"And you say I'll be orgasmic?" I said quietly. "I mean, *really*?"

"Well, that's the goal," Schrang said. "We want you to see stars and comets. The whole nine yards."

I nodded. That would be nice, stars and comets. Dr. Schrang reviewed some more slides. I could sense his pride as he described the intricacies of his handiwork. "You see that?" he said, pointing to a slide with his pen. "Nobody else makes a urethra like that, *nobody*!"

Eventually the last slide clicked in its carousel, and the screen went blank. We were silent for a moment, Eugene Schrang and I.

"Jenny," said Dr. Schrang, "you're going to be all right. You're going to sail through."

"I hope so," I said.

"You will." He put his hand out to shake. I put my arms around him and hugged him. He wasn't a large man, and as I embraced my doctor I had to bend my knees. That way I could reach him.

———————

On the Fourth of July 1968, our neighbors the Staineses had a bicycle contest. They were from Tennessee. The father, Verge, chain-smoked L&Ms and had a deep voice and cracks in his face that looked as if they'd been cut by running water.

We all decorated our bikes, threading red, white, and blue crepe paper through the spokes. It was good that the Staineses were doing this for the Fourth because it was becoming more and more self-evident, even to the children, that the country was down the drain. The loss of Martin Luther King that spring had torn something open that seemed unlikely to heal. My parents and I had sat around the radio in the kitchen, listening to Bobby Kennedy address the crowd in Indianapolis: *"What we need in the United States is not division; what we need in the United States is not hatred; what we need in the United States is not violence or lawlessness; but love and wisdom, and compassion toward one another, and a feeling of justice toward those who still suffer. . . ."*

They were still voting for Nelson Rockefeller, though.

The Staineses lived at the bottom of a steep hill, and their driveway was long and treacherous. For some reason, they erected the judging stand at the bottom of the hill, so that all the children participating in the bicycle parade had to jam their brakes on the whole way down Mount Staines.

I was last in line. Alone, I stood at the top of the driveway, looking at the grown-ups far below, sitting behind a row of card tables covered with bunting. Verge Staines was playing John Philip Sousa marches on a small phonograph. His wife was pouring out glasses of lemonade.

Then I began my approach. I saw the reviewing stand rush toward me. I saw my fingers, loosely holding, but not applying, the hand brakes. I couldn't understand why I wasn't slowing myself down; it didn't make any sense.

With the force of an impending asteroid, I slammed into the reviewing stand. Card tables and bunting and glasses of lemonade went
flying through the air, as did Verge Staines and our next-door neighbor, Mr. Wheeler (who came from Texas and once fired a shotgun
over the heads of my sister and me when we decided, out of sheer
cussedness, to defecate in his garden). Also airborne was our other
neighbor, Dr. Wheeler, to whom, strangely, Mr. Wheeler was not related. Dr. Wheeler liked to walk alone in the vast woods of the Earle
Estate, and now and again I would run into him when I was over
there playing girl planet. *What are you doing?* he'd ask me.

Oh, nothing.

Years later, I wondered whether Dr. Wheeler was playing his own
version of girl planet.

Tables, bunting, glasses of lemonade, phonographs, Staineses,
Wheelers, Wheelers, and I all fell to earth with a loud thump. No
one was killed, apparently. I lay on my back, the wheels of my bike
spinning around and around nearby, as adults gathered around me.

"Is he all right?" I just lay there listening to the voices of the
grown-ups, a weird smile on my face. My father held me in his arms.
"Are you all right, son?"

———

We arrived at the hospital. There was some trouble finding the en-
trance. No one seemed to know where the front door was.

At length, Grace and Russo and I got as far as the admissions desk
on the second floor. They were expecting me. I filled out some papers,
gave permission for an AIDS test, gave them a copy of my living will.

Then they took me down the hallway to my room. Grace and
Russo walked behind me. There were two beds in the room, and in
the bed by the window was another patient of Dr. Schrang's, a pale
woman with black hair. A nurse sat on a chair by the window, reading
a copy of *GQ*. The magazine contained an article I'd written about
the woman business. There were some big Diane Arbus–type photos
of me in the magazine, taken by *The New Yorker*'s Martin Schoeller.

"Whoa," said the patient. "It *is* you. It's me, Melanie Seymour, from Virginia. Remember we swapped a couple of e-mails?"

Actually, I didn't remember her particularly well. I got a *lot* of e-mail.

"Hi, Melanie," I said.

"I can't believe it's you," said the nurse, looking up from the magazine, comparing me with my photo. "A celebrity, right here on my ward."

"I know, I'm sorry."

"Where do you want this stuff?" said Rick. He was still carrying my suitcase. It was nice that this time *I* was the celebrity for a change, even if my constituency seemed to be limited to a pale, bedridden transsexual and her scrub nurse.

"Anywhere is fine," I said.

"You can use that locker," said the nurse. "That's for all your personal effects." She got out a hospital johnny. "You'll want to put this on."

I *didn't* want to put on the johnny, actually. We puttered around the room, moving in. I got a stuffed moose doll out of my suitcase and put him on the pillow.

"Now *that's* going to come in handy," Russo noted.

"Listen, Jenny, we should let you get settled," said Grace.

"Okay," I said. "I know." I was in no mood for them to leave me there, though. Grace and Rick each gave me a hug.

"We'll be back after dinner, all right?"

"Okay," I said.

Grace hugged me again.

"Okay."

They walked off down the hall, and for a moment I lay on the bed, holding my moose in one hand. The nurse said, "You ring if there's anything you need."

Then I took off my skirt and hose, peeled off my blouse, and slipped into the hospital gown. I hung up my things in the locker, then lay back on the bed. I realized I wouldn't be wearing my own clothes again for a long time, over a week. All sorts of things would have happened once I got my own clothes back.

"So, Melanie," I said. "You had the operation when? A couple days ago?"

"Last Friday," she said.

"How are you feeling?"

She nodded. "Okay," she said tremulously.

"It's hard, isn't it?"

Melanie nodded gravely. "But if I can get through it, you can get through it."

I wasn't sure this was true, but for now I left it at that. It was better, maybe, not to know just how hard the coming week would be.

By nightfall, Melanie's spirits had fallen considerably. "Why did I do this?" she said softly. "I wish I were dead."

———————

I went with Zero to an Alice Cooper concert in 1974, just a few months before Nixon resigned. Frank Zappa was supposed to make a surprise appearance, but he didn't. That left us stuck with Alice. There was this big toothbrush that chased him around. Later he cut off his own head with a guillotine—Alice, I mean. Turned out later he was okay.

Zero looked over at me about halfway through the concert. We'd been smoking pot. "Are you okay?" he said. I was holding one cupped hand next to my thigh, then slapping it on the top. "Seriously. Are you all right?"

"I'm dissolving," I explained sadly.

———————

I was painted with iodine, filled with magnesium. A nurse shaved me with an electric razor. I drank a gallon of an electrolyte solution that emptied me of my contents. Blood was drawn, and drawn again. The night came on, and I was sedated and I slept.

The day before we'd come to Egypt, I'd taken a long walk up a mountain in our hometown. I walked the ridge above Great Pond, watching the boats dotting the lake below me. I saw eagles circling the sky above Long Pond. A gentle summer breeze shook the sugar maples and white pines.

I reached the top of the mountain and sat there for a long time. I had wanted, I suppose, to engage in some sort of final farewell to manhood, to create an appropriate ritual that would mark my final passing into the world of women. Yet every rite I could think of seemed arbitrary or foolish. Anyway, there was very little about being a man that I had not already surrendered.

All I could think about was Grace, and how I loved her still, and the terrible grief and guilt I felt for all the losses in her life. I realized I would never regret being female. But I would probably always regret not being Grace's husband.

Then I stood up and, for the last time, peed against a tree.

Okay, I thought. *Enough*.

————

In the morning, Melanie was watching the World Cup on television, England versus Argentina. We talked about ham for a while, the way certain Virginians will if you get them going. I didn't mind. The way I figured, if she wanted to talk about ham, I might as well listen. It was better than having to hear about Second Manassas all over again. She allowed as how a Smithfield ham was best, but it had to be soaked before cooking. When Grace and Rick arrived, we were still discussing ham.

"You like ham?" Melanie asked Grace.

Grace nodded. "I'm partial to it," she said.

A man in green arrived at my door with a gurney. "Jennifer," he said, "I'm here for you."

I said okay and got out of my bed, which had no wheels, and got into this other one, which did.

Russo squeezed my hand. Grace hugged me. "Are you ready?" she asked me. I nodded.

We went out into the hallway, and the man in green pushed the down button. The elevator kept opening, but it was always filled with people. "I'm going to wait until we can get one of our own," he said.

I began to sing "Everything's Coming Up Roses."

"You'll be swell!" I said. "You'll be great! / Gonna have the whole world on a plate! . . ."

"Is that Ethel Merman she's doing?" said Russo.

"I think so," Grace said, shaking her head.

Russo looked at the orderly. "This isn't the . . . usual reaction, is it?"

"We get all kinds of reactions," said the man in green.

It was silent for a moment, then I started in on "I'm Gonna Wash That Man Right Out of My Hair."

"Man," said Russo. "You know who I pity, is her anesthesiologist."

The doors opened on an empty elevator.

"Okay," I said to my wife and my best friend. "I'll see you later."

"We'll be here," said Grace. Rick nodded. I was rolled in. The elevator doors closed.

It was quiet in there. I didn't sing.

"Your friends are nice," said the man in the green scrubs. We descended.

"They are," I said. "They're about the two most amazing people in the world."

He didn't know what to say to that, so he didn't say anything.

The doors opened, and I was rolled to a kind of holding area just outside the OR. "Okay," said the orderly. "They'll be taking you in to surgery in just a few minutes."

And then he left me there.

It was silent in this place. There were half a dozen other gurneys all around me, but they didn't have people on them. Across the hall from me was a supply cabinet. Nurses and doctors walked down the hall now and again, glancing over at me as if I were a work forged by the Cowboy Sculptor.

The anesthesiologist came over to me, introduced himself. He told me to call him by his first name, which was Jeff. He connected a tube to the IV line on the back of my hand. We talked for a while. "I've got you on a mild sedative right now; we'll increase it later, once we get you into the OR."

"Am I going to sleep?"

"Chances are, you're not going to remember anything, Jenny. You'll be lying here one moment and the next thing you know it will be this afternoon."

"That's so weird," I said. "It's as if the way we medicate pain now is not by removing the pain, but by removing the memory of it."

Jeff smiled. "That's so wrong?" he said. He had a nice face. "I'm going to see if everything's ready in the OR. Is it all right if I just leave you here for a couple minutes?"

"It's fine."

I didn't mind. I just lay there in my little bed. I looked at the clock. It was 8:40 A.M., June 6, 2002.

I felt like an airplane sitting at the end of a runway, waiting for clearance from the tower.

Jeff was gone for more than a couple of minutes. I felt very peaceful. Quietly I sang "In the Still of the Night."

Shoo-doop, dooby doo. Shoo-doop, dooby doo . . .

I lay there singing, thinking about everything.

'Tis a good life, the life at sea.

"Okay," said Jeff, returning at ten after nine. "Sorry you had to wait. You're the second surgery this morning, and the first one went long."

"That's all right," I said. "I've been fine."

"You've been singing?" he said, wheeling me into the operating room.

"Yeah."

The OR had green tiles on the wall. There were a lot of machines in it. It was brightly lit. A woman in the corner with a face mask was washing her hands. I didn't recognize her. I hadn't seen her before.

One night in 1987 the phone rang. It was a friend from college, who'd heard I'd died. I thought about Aunt Nora. Maybe what I needed was to drink some milk.

I explained to my friend that I was not dead. Someone had seen a notice in *The New York Times*, he said, and my entire peer group up in Boston was now in mourning for me. They couldn't believe it. I'd been so young.

"Oh," I said. "That was my father who died."

That cleared things up.

That night I attended a performance of a play I'd written called *Big Baby*. It was about a baby that gets big. After the performance, the playwrights had to get up on stage and talk about their work. Edward Albee was in the audience, and he raised his hand and said, Listen, Mr. Boylan, about this baby in your play. Why is it so large? He seemed annoyed with me, although I do note that fifteen years later he *also* wrote a play about a baby. His was better than mine, though.

I explained that the size of the baby was intended to create a comedic effect.

At that moment, a tile fell out of the ceiling and hit me on the head, and I fell down *klunk* on the floor. This, incidentally, was much more effective at producing a comedic effect than my play had been.

People offered to take me to the hospital, but I fended them off. I was all right. I had a big bump, though.

Later, the series of events had me worried. I thought about the possibility that there was some sort of curse on me now, the result of people mourning for me under false pretenses. It's because there's this rumor I'm dead, I thought. It's going to kill me.

Surely the effects of enough people believing something, even if that something is untrue, are not without consequence.

The next day I arrived at the airport to fly to Boston, to visit my friend Moynihan. There, on the tarmac, was my plane—a single-engine puddle jumper. As I looked at this questionable aircraft, I understood clearly what all the premonitions had been about. It was in this plane, surely, that I would make my final journey.

I got on board.

The propellers began to whirl. The tiny plane took off and flew up the East Coast of the United States.

I looked out the window at all the places I had lived before my unfortunate demise. There was Philadelphia to the west, where I had grown up. Then there was New York, where I lived after college. I thought I could even pick out my old apartment building on 108th Street. To the east was Long Island, and now I could see, in the sparkling sun, the coast of Fire Island, where an old girlfriend's family had a summer house. We traveled north and crossed Connecticut, and I could see the bend in the Connecticut River and Wesleyan University on the hills of Middletown.

There was every place I'd ever lived. I said farewell. I felt all right about everything, even about dying. Okay, so you never got to be a woman, I thought. But you did all right.

We landed safely in Boston. Again I had failed to die. It was something I wasn't very good at, as it turned out. I got my bags and jumped into a cab, sailing off to Moynihan's house.

In Somerville, Moynihan's door opened wide and a girl stood there. It was Grace Finney.

I hadn't seen her since the memorial service for Tim Alcock at Wesleyan, the one where I'd been too sad to sing "Beautiful Dreamer."

"Hey, James Boylan," Grace said, surprised. "I didn't know you were coming." She looked embarrassed. "I heard you were dead."

———

We were in the hallway, rolling. "Jenny," said Grace.

It was Grace, and we were rolling. We were in the hallway. I was Jenny.

"You're all right," she said. "It all went perfectly."

"*It's? It's?*" It was Jenny, and she was rolling. Grace was in the hallway.

"It's over," said Russo. "The doctor came out and talked to us. He said he couldn't be happier."

"You'll be swell! You'll be . . ."

"You're going back to the room now. We're here with you. You're all right."

"You'll be swell! You'll be . . . great . . ."

The phone rang, and I talked to someone. It was Zero, it was my mother, it was Grace's sister Bonnie, who had died of ovarian cancer two months earlier. I'd read a Galway Kinnell poem at her funeral. My hospital room was filled with flowers, from Grace, from my mother, from my friends. A card read "It's a girl!"

"Grace," I said, "can you sing me a song?"

Grace looked over at Russo, who shrugged and looked back at her as if to say *You're on your own here.*

"Okay," said Grace. "What do you want to hear?"

"One of those . . . falling asleep songs you sing the children."

Grace looked out the window, thinking about the songs she knew.

"Do you think I could leave you crying?" she then sang, taking my hand.

> *When there's room on my horse for two?*
> *Climb up here, Jack, quit your crying,*
> *We'll mend up your horse with glue.*
> *When we grow up we'll both be soldiers*
> *And our horses will not be toys.*
> *Maybe then we'll remember*
> *When we were two little boys.*

———————

I was awake, then I was asleep again, then I was awake. Grace was on the phone, talking to someone. "Whatever else you say about my husband," she said, "she's a remarkable woman."

Then it was late at night, and Russo was sitting by my bed and

Grace was gone. "Where did she go?" I asked. My voice was slightly hoarse. I'd had a tube down my throat, but it wasn't there now.

"Grace went back to the hotel," Russo said. "We went out to dinner. I told her to go get some rest."

"Were you drinking? I hope you were . . . drinking. . . ."

Russo smiled. "We might have had a couple."

"Is she all right?" I said. "Is she really okay?"

"She's doing great," said Russo. "She's very proud of you. Apparently you sailed through. Schrang says you were amazing."

"Do you think . . . he's nuts?" I said.

Russo smiled. "Well, all we know is that he's very, very good at one thing. And fortunately for you, it's the thing you needed him to be good at."

"Russo . . . it's done. It's over. I did it."

"You sure as hell did. You *did* it, Boylan." He smiled. "I'm proud of you, too, Jenny."

"I can't believe," I said. "It's over."

He smiled. "Are you okay? Do you feel okay?"

I beamed. "I think so. I keep dozing off, though. I think I'm on . . ." I felt a wave of pain. I picked up my Demerol drip and hit the magic button that released the drug. It dinged, as if I were at a gas station and I'd driven over the hose. "I keep, you know . . . waking up and . . ."

"You look like you're doing incredibly well."

"Really?" I said.

"Yeah. Quite frankly, it's a little eerie. You seem so happy. To tell you the truth, it's a pretty powerful thing to see, how happy you are."

"It's just that I'm so relieved, Rick," I said. "I was afraid . . . I was going to wake up . . . and have a sense of regret. Instead, I just feel glad. I feel so . . . grateful."

"Is there anything I can do for you right now?"

"Would you read me something?" I had *Empire Falls* lying on the nightstand. "Read me some of this, would you?"

He looked about as glad to read his own work at my bedside as he'd been to sign a copy of it for Dr. Schrang. But he did it.

My friend read me the beginning of chapter 14 of his great novel, a scene in which Miles Roby and his father are driving in their car.

On general principle his father was dead set against swerving to avoid obstacles. . . . Once, the year before . . . , they'd encountered a cardboard box sitting square in the middle of their lane on a narrow country road. Since no one was coming toward them and no one was following, and since there was plenty of time to slow down and maneuver around the box, Miles was surprised when his father actually accelerated into it. He braced for something like an explosion, but the box, thankfully empty, was sucked under the car, where it got caught in the driveshaft and made a hell of a racket for a hundred yards or so before it flapped away, mangled and reduced to two dimensions, into a ditch.

"What if that box had been full of rocks?" Miles asked.

"What would a box full of rocks be doing sitting in the middle of the road?" Max wondered back, pushing in the cigarette lighter on the dash and patting his shirt pocket for his pack of Luckies.

Miles was tempted to reply, "Waiting for an idiot to hit it doing sixty miles an hour," but he said instead, "If it had been full of rocks, we might both be dead."

Max considered this. "What would you have done?"

Miles sensed a trap in this innocent question, but at sixteen he continued to play the hand he'd been dealt, confident he had enough to trump with. "I might've stopped to see what was in the box before I hit it."

Max nodded. "What if it was full of rattlesnakes? Then when you opened it, you'd be dead."

Miles had not grown up in his father's intermittent company

for nothing. "What would a box full of rattlesnakes be doing sitting in the middle of the road?"

"Waiting for some dumbbell like you to stop and look inside," Max said.

———

Grace and Rick returned to Maine on Sunday, June 9, leaving me to recover a few days longer in an Egyptian hotel. One day, I decided to kill a few hours by taking a taxi several miles north to the Houdini Museum, in Appleton.

The Houdini Museum consisted, for the most part, of a collection of shackles, handcuffs, and straitjackets that the great magician had eluded over eighty years previously. There weren't a lot of other people there that day, and as I rolled in my wheelchair around the museum's environs, it was hard not to be struck with a sense of infinite loneliness. This feeling was amplified by the juxtaposition of the Houdini material with a very large exhibit in the main hall, a retrospective on Wisconsin's own junior senator entitled "Joe McCarthy: An American Tragedy." There were entries in a guest book such as this one: "Joe McCarthy was right—his only fault lay in not going *far enough*!"

On the wall by the handcuffs was a tattered poster: "HOUDINI: ORIGINAL INTRODUCER OF THE METAMORPHOSIS! *Changing places with his wife in 3 seconds!* The Greatest Mystery the World Has Ever Seen!"

From the next room came the recorded voice of Senator McCarthy harassing a witness, attacking his patriotism: "Will you tell us the names of these sympathizers, or will you not? By five o'clock today?" Before me, in a wooden box, were half a dozen loose handcuffs and a straitjacket on a hanger. "Slip on these shackles! Try the straitjacket on for size!" read the sign. "And see if *you* can escape."

———

I flew home on Father's Day. My children met me at the door with a big sign that read "WELCOME HOME, MADDY" as well as a box containing the Milton Bradley game Battleship, tied up with a bow. Grace had a bottle of champagne on ice, a lobster dinner on the stove.

A few weeks later, we got a package in the mail from Melanie, my roommate in Egypt. What did she send us? A ham.

On the Fourth of July, Grace and I were in Boothbay Harbor, attending the wedding of our friend Frank's daughter. The ceremony was performed down by the water, as yachts and lobster boats sailed by.

There we were, two women in our early forties, wearing our summer dresses, watching our friends and their children walk down the aisle as a man in a white tuxedo played Pachelbel's Canon in D. Wind blew across a microphone. The sound of the ocean was picked up by the PA system. Gulls flew in circles over our heads.

The groom, a sweet-faced young man, came down the aisle in his white jacket and bow tie. The bride followed, on her father's arm. In one hand she held a bouquet of white tulips.

The ceremony combined the two families' Jewish and Christian traditions; a minister officiated, but the vows were exchanged beneath a *chupa*, and a glass was broken. "We do this," explained a rabbi by the minister's side, "to remind us of the destruction of the Temple, to remind us that even in the midst of joy there is sorrow." As if this were something we could ever, possibly, forget.

Those two young people looked in each other's eyes and shyly, softly, promised to love each other "as you are, and as you shall be." They promised to make each other's needs their own.

After the ceremony, we sat inside a rustic lodge that overlooked the harbor, eating salmon and drinking champagne. Our friend Frank, a tall, burly, elegant man, stood before the gathered crowd at the side of the woman he had divorced twenty years earlier and toasted his daughter and his new son-in-law. His eyes filled with tears as he raised his glass, and as the big man cried, so did everyone else.

Between the two of us, Grace and I had only one napkin, and we kept snatching it back from each other in order to dab at our eyes. After a few minutes we got up, still crying, and went outside. Salt air was blowing in across the harbor, and the moon was rising above the sea.

Throughout that evening, I had felt the eyes of strangers upon us, silently asking the question for which we ourselves still had no answer: *What are you two?* Clearly we were not husband and wife; on just that much we could all agree. But neither, by any stretch of the imagination, were we a lesbian couple. We were parents, yes, of two remarkable and resilient children, both of whom had apparently inherited the unsinkable optimism and faith of their grandmother, the woman whose motto was "Love will prevail." Were Grace and I "sisters," then, two siblings somehow born to different parents? Was that what we had become?

We were still legally married and could remain so even though I was now female. Although we could not legally have *gotten* married now, if we were to meet and fall in love for the first time, we were allowed under the law to *remain* married, for as long as that suited us both. If we chose to divorce and remarry, however, I could legally marry only a man. If I then divorced that man and Grace married him, then Grace's ex-husband and her husband's ex-wife would both be the same person. I smiled as I tried to make sense of all this and thought of the song I used to sing to my children, "I'm My Own Grampa."

What were we? For her part, Grace was still a beautiful woman, still able to whistle with two fingers in her mouth as her eyes crinkled with devilish laughter. Even now, men still looked at her as she passed through a crowd and thought, just as I had twenty-five years earlier, *Whoa. Who was that?*

As for myself, I had begun, to my own shock, to see men through different eyes. Dr. Schrang's hope that I would be orgasmic postsurgery had been fulfilled. The sensation—which I'd cautiously, curiously, produced all on my own—was like nothing I'd experienced, and yet, sure, it was familiar. The Greek prophet Tiresias, who was said to have lived as both a man and a woman, claimed that "the pleasure for a woman is ten times that of the man." To this, all I can add is that what it reminds me of, more than anything else, is the difference between Spanish and Italian.

I had always imagined that post-transition my sexuality would remain constant, that I would remain fascinated by women no matter what form my own body took. Yet somehow, without any conscious thought, the object of my desire was gently shifting. Now, looking around at the world, I would occasionally think, Jeez. Look at all these *men*. Surely they haven't been here all this time? Where did they all *come from*?

Occasionally a man would give me a hug, and the sensation of his stubbly face against my soft neck and cheek made the hairs on my arm stand on end. Women no longer struck me as creatures of such wonder. Their world seemed like the one I knew, like the one into which I woke each morning. Men, on the other hand—to me they now seemed like a mystery.

It was inevitable, I suppose, that one or the other of us, at some point, would take a first tentative step in a new direction. Yet that time was not upon us, and it was impossible to know whether it would come months from now, or years, or never. In some sense, I think we both dreaded that moment as much as we hoped for it. Where on earth would either of us find men that we adored as much as we had adored each other? How could we want, even after all these losses, to ever wake up beneath a roof that did not cover the other as well?

We knew what we were *not*—we were not husband and wife; we were not lesbians; we were not merely friends. We knew that we were not all these things. But what were we?

"Are you all right?" I said to Grace.

"I'll be fine," she said. "What about you?"

I nodded. "I'm okay."

Grace turned to me.

"Jenny," she said softly.

"Grace."

I had no idea what it was she was going to say next. It could have been anything—I want you to move out.... I want a divorce.... I want you to climb a mountain in Nova Scotia and allow yourself to be blown off a cliff by the wind. Nothing would have surprised me, I thought, with the exception, perhaps, of the one thing Grace did say to me then, the thing she said after all these years together.

"So, Jenny," she said. "Do you want to dance?"

For a moment I didn't know how to respond; she had caught me completely off guard. Then I said something I had said to her a long time ago, in the National Cathedral, in Washington. I said, "I do."

We went back inside and walked up to the dance floor, where scores of other couples were rocking out. The band was playing a Paul Simon song, "Late in the Evening."

And we danced.

A conga line formed, and we snaked through the inn. Everyone was laughing and dancing, clapping their hands. We all formed a big circle, and at its center Frank danced with his daughter, and the groom danced with Sandra.

A moment later, a man I did not know put his hand around my waist and spun me into the middle of the dance floor. He wanted to dance close, and all I could think of was, *He's got the wrong hand out and the wrong hand on my waist*—until I realized that as a woman I had to do everything I had done before, only in reverse.

I thought hurriedly, Am I leading?

Well, I guess I'd been in love before, and once or twice I been on the floor.
But I never loved no one the way that I loved you.

The man spun me with one hand, and I saw faces I recognized whirling around me in a blur. There was Grace and Russo, Dr. Schrang and Hilda Watson and my sister, Donna Fierenza, Dr.

Wheeler, even Seamus O'Twotimes. *He just walked right out into space. Into space.*

A moment later I was by Grace's side, back in the outer circle again. "Well, I'm back," I said.

———————

Exactly twenty-six years earlier, on the evening of the American bicentennial, I was once more in Surf City, New Jersey, sitting on the beach with my friend Tad Pennypacker and his girlfriend, Lois. Before me was the very jetty on whose tip I had stood as a child, watching the hurricane blow up, the waves crashing against the rocks. Where would you get, I asked myself, if you went directly east from Surf City, New Jersey?

SPAIN, said my grandmother to the medical student who was examining her. SPAIN.

Whoop?

Fireworks were exploding above the sea. Tad and Lois and I sat there on the beach, drinking a bottle of Mateus rosé. Through a series of incidents we could hardly have explained, Gerald Ford was president. People kept trying to assassinate him, but he was having none of it. I admired that.

I was sitting in the middle, halfway between Tad and Lois. Drunkenly we sang "In the Still of the Night."

A few miles north of us was New York Harbor, filled with the masts of tall ships. As I lay there watching the fireworks light up the sky, I thought, What a beautiful night it is, what a beautiful country.

Tad and Lois and I all had our arms around one another. I hadn't been cured by love yet, but at that moment I felt as if I might be, if only I sat there long enough.

Conundra, or The Sick Arab

The best piece of writing ever published on the subject of transsexuality bears the title "*Conundrum*," a clever Latinate word meaning "a puzzle whose solution involves a joke or riddle." I am referring here *not* to Jan Morris's classic 1973 narrative of her own transition, but to the even more classic trashing of same by Nora Ephron, collected in a sprightly Ephronasaurus published by Avon in 1984.

Of the many autobiographies published by my gamy and tawdry colleagues, none reached quite so large an audience as Morris's. This is, perhaps, because as James Morris, she was a widely respected travel writer; her work on Venice remains one of the best books ever written on the subject. She also emerged at a time when the culture, American culture anyhow, was first turning its attention toward the issue of civil rights for gays and lesbians. The time had come to add transsexuality to the rock pile, and add it she did.

Conundrum was an instant smash; it was reviewed on the front cover of the Sunday *New York Times Book Review*; it became one of the standard texts in hundreds of college courses examining gender; it remains the one book on transsexuality that has been most frequently read by persons who otherwise would prefer live burial to "gender studies."

Morris showed that a transsexual can be mature, wise, dignified, and literary. Single-handedly her book demonstrated that transsexuals as a *people* were not lurid, crazy, or marginal, at least not necessarily. *Conundrum* generated (and continues to generate) tremendous respect. Jan Morris did more to advance public understanding of transsexuals than any other figure, including the pioneer of this odd domain, Christine Jorgensen, the former GI whose groundbreaking surgery in the 1950s shocked the Eisenhower administration into bombing Korea.

For all that, it's hard not to be amused by Ephron's trashing of *Conundrum*. "I always wanted to be a girl, too," writes Ephron. "I, too, felt I was born into the wrong body, a body that refused, in spite of every imprecation and exercise I could imagine, to become anything but the boyish, lean thing it was. . . . I wanted more than anything to be something I will never be—feminine, and feminine in the worst way. Submissive. Dependent. Soft-spoken. Coquettish. I was no good at any of it, no good at being a girl; on the other hand I am not half bad at being a woman. In contrast, Jan Morris is perfectly awful at being a woman; what she has become instead is exactly what James Morris wanted to become those many years ago. A girl. And worse, a forty-seven-year-old girl. And worst of all, a forty-seven-year-old *Cosmopolitan* girl."

I personally do not know how Morris feels about *Conundrum* now, nearly thirty years after its publication. Like most former transsexuals, she seems to be interested in being judged now more for what is between her ears than between her legs. (A well-regarded writer friend of mine who attempted to interview Morris for a book she was writing received the terse, one-sentence rebuff "When I hear the word *gender* I reach for my pistol.") My guess is that she is proud of the work for the huge step forward it marked in the public's understanding of transsexuality. At the same time, I wouldn't be surprised at all if Morris felt that *Conundrum* reflected a sensibility that was—and I do mean this generously—somewhat adolescent.

Transsexuals going through transition resemble nothing so much as gawky, wonder-struck teenagers, amazed and perplexed by their bodies, startled by an awareness of themselves as men or women, as if they have invented the whole business single-handedly then and there. This book of mine, in fact, almost surely commits this sin again and again, for which I can only say I am truly sorry. It does no good to tell a transsexual that this is all old ground and to get over yourself, any more than it does to tell this to a fifteen-year-old.

There is nothing as annoying as someone for whom the world is new. At least to those for whom the world is old.

For most forty-three-year-old women, many of the trappings of womanhood have long lost their wonder. One friend of mine said, "You know what it's like, Jenny? It's like gum that's lost its flavor. By the time you're forty, c'mon, let's face it—*the party's over.*"

For me, of course, the party was just beginning—and I refer, of course, to the experience of being in this body, not to the accompanying losses and grief, which were anything but a *party.* I wore makeup on Sundays. I wore skirts when most other mothers were wearing yesterday's blue jeans. I put polish on my toes. I read fashion magazines. Other women, especially Grace, looked on all this activity with annoyance, and who could blame them, or her? Indeed, I did, at times, not seem intent so much on being a woman as on being a *girl.*

A transsexual's womanhood is examined, considered, and criticized much more relentlessly than that of other women. In my early days, people would often look at me and conclude, if my clothes were too feminine, for instance, that this was because *I just didn't know what I was doing,* and of course in many ways they were correct.

Yet plenty of other women—including forty-three-year-olds—behave in ways much more embarrassing than I did. Women *born* women are given the right to define womanhood on their own terms. Dolly Parton and Janet Reno, to name two, represent different interpretations of the fact of womanhood, and while one might question either of their sartorial styles, no sane person would ever conclude that Dolly and Janet are not *women*.

Male-to-female transsexuals, on the other hand, have begun their lives as boys, and many of the things that partly define a woman's life—menstrual cycles, pregnancy, and an oppositional relationship to men—are things that we know nothing about. For many people, transgender or not, womanhood is thought, wrongly, to be synonymous with femininity—with makeup and stretchy T-shirts and an obsession with Brad Pitt. None of this has a damn thing to do with it, of course, and in the long run, a transsexual who hopes to build a life around high heels and sponge cake is in for something of a disappointment.

I moved forward into transition not in order to be Dolly Parton (or, for that matter, Janet Reno), but in order to be Jenny Boylan. There are aspects of me that are feminine now, but I was feminine when I was a man, for that matter. I still retain a number of masculine affects that I am not ashamed of, and which many other women possess as well. I like to drink beer on a hot summer afternoon; I like to watch baseball, at least late in the season; and I still like to hike in the Maine woods and go camping. I prefer music to be loud; I like to tell jokes; and I have been known to swear like a Barbary pirate. Had I been born female, no one would remark upon these things—but since I was not, any masculine affect is considered a vestigial link to a previous life; conversely, any feminine affect that seems excessive can be hauled out as evidence that I, like Morris, have arrived at middle age just in time to be fourteen years old.

As time has gone by, I have become more mellow about the whole damn business, content to let the primary concerns of my life—children, teaching, music, my relationship with Grace, friendships with Russo and Zero and others—take up my attention. Whether these things are masculine or feminine is not particularly important to me anymore. They are simply what I do.

Most of all, perhaps, I have let go of constantly trying to explain what this is all about. Early in transition, it was essential to me that everyone understand the condition of transsexuality—that they grasp the horror of the dilemma, that they understand its medical components, that they know I had done all I could to remain the person they had known and loved, and so on. I had an answer ready for every objection.

What I have come to realize is that no matter how much light one attempts to throw on this condition, it remains a mystery.

Worse, it is a mystery that everyone has an *opinion* about. "Hey, man, cutting off your arm doesn't make you Lord Nelson," said one helpful academic. My sister said, "Why can't you just wait until Mom is dead?" Another friend said, "I don't see why you get to be a woman just because you think you are. I mean, what if you thought you were a cat? Would you walk around with little paste-on whiskers and a tail?"

All I could say to such comments, in the end, was, "Well, I'm not a cat."

Quite frankly, there are times when I think about transsexuality and I just have to shrug. I'm sorry I can't make it make more sense to you, I told Zero. But it is what it is. Whether I "really" am a woman, or whether I "had a choice" or not, or whether *anything*, no longer matters. Having an opinion about transsexuality is about as useful as having an opinion on blindness. You can think whatever you like about it, but in the end, your friend is still blind and surely deserves to see. Whether one thinks transsexuals are heroes or lunatics will not help to bring these people solace. All we can do in the face of this enormous, infinite anguish is to have compassion.

As Dr. Schrang said, "I'll tell you one thing. These people who object to transsexuality. They wouldn't like it, either, if they were the ones who had it. They wouldn't like it one bit."

As a teacher and a writer, I found the inscrutability of the topic absolutely frustrating. I am used to being able to convince people of something I believe to be true, if only I have a few minutes and the proper rhetorical argument at hand. That there was nothing I could say to make this dilemma—which for me was so huge and all-encompassing—clear to people was an absolute frustration.

Furthermore, I am above all else a skeptic. There are very few things, I think, that should be exempt from satire. The domain of the transgender struck me as a land where one had to be so serious and respectful and empathetic that one more often than not found oneself having to sit there straight-faced while someone says things like "Actually I believe my 'true' self to be a two-year-old baby." (Yes, someone really did say this to me.)

"That's hard," I'd have to say. "That's so hard."

"Just tell me this," said my friend Tim Kreider. "When you started in on hormones, was irony the first thing to go?"

I no longer hope that everyone will be able to understand what this condition is about. It seems to elude an accurate description. It is a medical condition, but it is not solely medical; it is a behavioral condition, but it is not solely psychological. Whatever it is, it is widespread. Professor Lynn Conway at the University of Michigan estimates that there are forty thousand trans male-to-females in this country, and that counts only the ones who have *already had the surgery*. According to Professor Conway, that makes the condition more common than cleft palate and multiple sclerosis. This figure revises a statistic generated at Johns Hopkins decades ago—and still constantly quoted in the media—that the number of transsexuals is astronomically small. But by almost any measure, it's not.

So why don't we see more transsexuals in our daily travails? Why are those who suffer from the condition thought to be such rarities? Simply because most transsexuals look unremarkable; having resolved their situation as best they can, they then proceed to essentially vanish off the radar. Unfortunately, the public's primary perception of transsexuals as a population is defined by the extremely small fringe of the community that feels driven to behave badly on *The Jerry Springer Show*. In the meantime, tens of thousands of other extremely well adjusted individuals have gone about the business of their lives, doing their jobs, raising their children. Remarkably, they seem to have done so even without the benefit of anyone else's theory about their existence.

As Zero wrote me once, "It must be hard, Jenny, to have to keep proving to people that you exist."

I wrote back, "I don't care about *people*. I would settle for you."

Toward the end of transition, I found myself reading Katherine Anne Porter's "Noon Wine," a short novel about a farmer whose failing farm is resuscitated by the sudden appearance of a hardworking Swedish migrant worker. After several years, a bounty hunter named Hatch appears, claiming the Swede is a wanted man. The farmer tries to get between his man and Mr. Hatch and winds up murdering the bounty hunter; the Swede disappears. In an ensuing trial, the farmer is found innocent by reason of self-defense, but in the years following, he spends his life suffering from the fact that his neighbors no longer think of him as "one of us." He drives around in his pickup, from farm to farm, trying to "explain how it was," to assure them that not only was he *found* innocent, he *was* innocent.

His neighbors don't want to know about it.

In the end, the farmer shoots himself in the head with his rifle, just like my friend John Flyte.

It's a cheerful little story.

What I've taken away from this, however, is the way in which we can become obsessed with clearing our good name, even after our innocence has been established. It is a very human impulse, but it's ultimately fraught with peril. The more we feel compelled to keep explaining ourselves, the less like others we become. As Zero said to me, rather late in transition, "Listen, Jenny, I don't mind you being a woman. But don't you think you could shut up about it once in a while?"

In the end, the best thing seemed to be to keep my head high, to maintain a sense of humor, and to be forgiving. I was treated as a woman by most people and basked once in a while in the glow of their love. Everyone was nice about it, even if occasionally they betrayed the fact that my extraordinary history made them uneasy. I felt like Jim in *The Adventures of Huck Finn*, who is disguised by the duke in order to prevent him from being carried off into slavery. "Blamed if he warn't the horriblest looking outrage I ever see," writes Huck. "Then the duke took and wrote out a sign on a shingle so:

"Sick Arab—but harmless when not out of his head."

Explosive Bolts

I.

May 3, 2002

Mr. Patrick O'Keefe, Head Administrator
National Aeronautics and Space Administration
Washington, D.C. 20546

Dear Mr. O'Keefe:

I am writing you from Waterville, Maine, where I am co-chair of the English Department at Colby College. I am not sure if you know much about Colby, but it is one of the finest liberal arts colleges in the nation. Doris Kearns Goodwin went here, and we are very proud of her, except for that recent

business about her stealing some of her books from other
historians. She didn't learn *THAT* at Colby, I can promise you.

I am writing to ask if I might become the first transsexual
in space.

Although you may think this request is facetious, allow me
to quickly state that my desire to educate the country about
gender issues from the environment of zero gravity is sincere. I
hope you will allow me to explain exactly how a transsexual in
space would be something the whole nation might be proud of.
A "giant leap for personkind," as it were. I bet you have heard
that phrase somewhere before!

First, I want to say I have been a lifelong fan of NASA and
all of its brave enterprises. I was born in 1958, which means that
I grew up during the Gemini project, and Apollo, of course. I
do not understand why no one talks about the Gemini launches
any more, unless of course it is because of all the trouble you
had getting the Atlas booster off the ground. In particular I
recall Gemini 6 which, at the moment of countdown, just sat
there smoldering, and kids all across America were so annoyed
with you. NASA tried launching Gemini 6 a few days later, and
guess what: same result. In fact, if I recall correctly, Gemini 7
actually took off *before* Gemini 6—now *that* was embarrassing.
There were reports of Lyndon Johnson storming around the
Rose Garden describing the administrator of NASA in very
colorful terms. Aren't you glad it wasn't you?

Still, eventually you "had liftoff" of Gemini 6, and the
astronauts orbited for a week or so and even got to wave out
the window at the crew of Gemini 7, with whom they
"rendezvoused in space." I thought that was so cool, four guys
in two Gemini capsules orbiting a few feet away from each
other way out in space. I always figured it made them less lonely,
having friends a few feet away, even though of course they still
had to eat creamed spinach out of tubes and dock with the

AGENA docking module, which (again, if I recall correctly) started spinning haplessly out of control only minutes after docking, forcing Frank Borman to land his capsule then and there, and catching everyone in the South Pacific off guard.

Anyway, I have here the printout from the NASA Web page concerning "Astronaut Candidate Training." If I can read this material properly (and I have to admit that my eyesight is pretty bad)—the position I am applying for is "mission specialist." I would be in charge, I believe, of "Orbiter onboard systems, performing space walks, and operation of the remote manipulator system."

Listen, Mr. O'Keefe—I'm an English professor—"remote manipulation" is what I do best! Although I do not have, as you require (I think), a degree in astrophysics, I can certainly recite from memory a wide range of English Romantic poetry, particularly that of John Keats, who observed, among other useful things, that "truth is beauty, beauty truth. That is all ye know on earth and all ye need to know." I think this would be true in space, too, but of course we won't know until we actually send an English professor up there, will we?

As for the usefulness of a transsexual in space, I think this is self-evident. We all know that the astronaut corps over the years has included many valiant *men*, including our first American, Alan B. Shepard. (Aha! You thought I was going to say John Glenn, didn't you—well, I know all about Colonel Shepard—he was my favorite of the Mercury Seven, in part because he was such a grouch, and in part because NASA told him to pee in his pants just before the launch of Friendship 7. Boy, I bet you guys were sweating that out! Weren't you afraid he'd cause a short?

I also know about Gus Grissom and how his capsule sank. Man, you guys have had a rough time of it, haven't you. First Shepard peeing in his pants, then Grissom sinking the capsule. A transsexual wouldn't have blown the explosive bolts off *her* capsule prematurely, I can promise you that! Most of us, alas, spend most of our lives trying to keep our explosive bolts from blowing—and as a result, are extraordinarily well suited at withstanding nearly unbearable pressure.

Anyway, so yes, you have had all these heroic men, and then twenty-five years later you allowed as how maybe it would be okay to send up a *woman*, and you managed to find an astronaut named "Sally Ride" to fly the shuttle. (Although very few Americans, I hate to be the one to tell you, actually believed that was her real name; surely this is just the chorus from "Mustang Sally," a song that, by the way, I have played in all sorts of seedy bars with my rock-and-roll band.)

As I recall, Sally Ride had to wear a special electronic bra in zero gravity. Gosh, I bet your boys in R&D had fun designing *that*. They even, no doubt, had to try it on *themselves* first, just to make sure it wouldn't short out if Alan B. Shepard peed on it by accident (or, knowing Shepard, on purpose).

Listen, I want your engineers to know, there is *nothing wrong with wanting to wear an electronic bra*—not if that's the way you feel! I did not choose to be a transsexual any more than your research boys choose to be pencil-protector-wearing, Band-Aid-holding-their-glasses-together, Neil Diamond–enjoying, Chevy Nova–driving toads. It's just the way we are!

I believe that God makes us all a certain way, and that the adventure of life is largely the challenge to find the courage to become ourselves. For many of us, the challenge that is given us is to find that courage, to be brave, and to stand up for the truth.

This is a message that the astronauts of NASA have bravely sent since 1962. The citizens of this country have always taken pride in your accomplishments. (Although we *were* a little annoyed that the Russians got off the ground first. Be honest— do you guys still wake up at night worried about Yuri Gagarin? I know *I* do.)

Anyway, I would like, should you honor me with your consideration, to join the chorus of courage to which the astronaut corps has given voice.

Were I honored with the pleasure of being the first transsexual in space (that we know of—personally, I always had my doubts about Buzz Aldrin, but that's just me), I would perform the responsibilities of mission specialist with grace and aplomb. And I would also, if possible, say a few things to the young people of the world.

What would I say? Well, *Dare to be brave*, for one. For another, *Find the courage to become yourself. And above all, *The three most important things an astronaut, a transsexual, or anyone can have are dignity, self-respect, and a sense of humor.*

I hope that you will give me the opportunity to share these insights from the rarefied atmosphere of the *Orbiter*'s interior. It would be an honor to serve my country.

In the meantime, I remain, very sincerely

Your humble servant,

Jennifer Finney Boylan
Co-chair, English Department
Colby College

P.S. It also says here that in order to go into space I have to pass a swimming test, which if you ask me is a rather odd requirement, unless you're expecting the whole sinking-capsule problem to repeat itself. Quite frankly, I had hoped you had solved this back in 1962. At any rate, I can swim across Long Pond, here in Central Maine, in about ten minutes. Maine really is a lovely state, Mr. O'Keefe. I hope if you ever come up here with your family that you will feel welcome to stop in and visit.

II.

Ms. Jennifer Finney Boylan
Chair, English Department
Colby College
5264 Mayflower Hill
Waterville, ME 04901–8852

Dear Ms. Boylan:

Thank you for your letter of May 3, 2002, to NASA
Administrator Sean O'Keefe expressing your interest in flying
aboard the Space Shuttle as the first mission specialist
"transsexual" and educating the country about gender issues
from the environment of zero gravity.

NASA continually receives numerous letters from citizens
offering their services to the space program. We hope the day
will come when everyone will have the opportunity to go to
space. For now, however, as with any rare commodity that is in
great demand, NASA has the responsibility and obligation to
maximize taxpayer return, in the form of scientific and
operational knowledge, from both the Space Shuttle and the
International Space Station. Therefore, flight opportunities are
not available for persons other than NASA astronauts (pilots and
mission specialists) and payload specialists.

You mentioned an interest in becoming a mission specialist.
They are selected for a particular mission based on mission
requirements and objectives and their educational backgrounds
and skills. Before becoming members of the Shuttle crew, all of
these individuals must meet certain medical standards, which are
dictated by the existing flight systems training and operational
constraints. The next opportunity to apply for the class of

mission specialists will be released in the media as well as posted
to our Web site: (http://www.spaceflight.nasa.gov or www.edu
.nasa.gov).

Thank you for your interest in the space program.

Cordially,
Winfield Hooker
Associate Administrator for Space Flight

The Death of Houdini

(Late Summer 2002)

We headed over to the Magic Shop, the four of us, Grace, me, Luke, and Patrick. Luke was reading a book about Houdini. "Boy, I'd like to do some of *these* tricks," he said from the backseat. "Do we have a trunk, Maddy?"

"A trunk?" I said. I was looking out the window at the Boston suburbs. We were down for the weekend, visiting friends in Arlington.

"He tied himself up, then got locked in a trunk, and they threw it into the ocean. He was free in less than *one minute*."

"Luke," Grace said from behind the wheel, "you're not tying yourself up, okay?"

"It's just a trick," Luke said.

"*I* would throw you in the ocean," Patrick said to his brother.

"Houdini could hold his breath for *five minutes*."

"How long can you hold your breath for, Luke?" said the six-year-old.

Luke huffed and puffed, then held his breath.

"Ah, peace at last," muttered Patrick.

We drove through Somerville, looking for the Magic Shop. I was wearing a blue skirt and a white T-shirt. Grace had on blue jeans and a turtleneck.

I looked over at her. Grace had always been the driver on family trips; she loved driving as much as I loved playing the piano. She had a number of superpowers as a driver, too, including 1) the ability to talk her way out of any ticket, and 2) the ability to parallel park in virtually any space.

Her face was still the face of the woman James had married in 1988, her eyes bright, her forehead crinkled with lines that seemed to come from equal measures wisdom, grief, and humor. Small star-and-moon earrings swung from her earlobes. I reached out for her and touched her elbow.

She quickly pulled her arm away. "Don't," she said, irritated. "Just don't."

I looked out the window, saddened.

Luke, in the backseat, started making suffocating noises.

Grace glanced over at me. "Remember our rule for this trip, Jenny?"

"Which rule?"

"No pouting."

"I'm not pouting."

She looked at me and smiled. "The hell you're not."

"It's just . . . ," I said. "You shouldn't snap at me when I'm trying to comfort you."

Grace looked back at the road. Her face darkened. She didn't say anything for a while. "There isn't any 'should,' " she said.

"*Paahh!*" shouted Luke, gasping for breath. "How long was that?"

"Okay," I said to Grace. "I know."

"Maddy," said Luke, "how long was that?"

"How long was what?"

"How long did I hold my breath for?"

"I don't know, Luke," I said softly. "Was I supposed to be timing you?"

"Oh, man," said the eight-year-old. "That's the whole point? Timing me?"

"I'll throw you in the ocean, Luke," Patrick said again, softly.

"Where is this place?" Grace said, checking the street numbers. "It's supposed to be right here."

"Maybe it disappeared," said Patrick. "Get it? Disappeared? Magic Shop? Disappeared?"

"That's very funny, Paddy," I said. "Both of you are very funny."

"You take after Maddy, Luke," Grace said. She didn't sound happy about it.

I had often thought this about my boys, particularly Luke, who in so many ways struck me as Jim without tears. On some level it took some of the sting out of my sense that I had stolen James out of the world, knowing that Luke was still in it. Yet Luke will be himself, not some nether-version of myself, and any adult who looks to her children to redress the losses of her own life should probably get out of the parenting business for good.

"Yeah," said Luke. "I'm just not going to be a girl, that's all."

I spun around. "You know that, right?" I said. "What happened to me is not going to happen to you."

Luke rolled his eyes. "I *know*," he said, and opened his Houdini book again.

"It's a very rare thing," I said. "Boys turning into girls. It can't happen unless you want it to. You both know that?"

Patrick looked out the window and didn't say anything.

"Both of you know you can always talk about this, right?" said Grace. "It's okay to talk about. It's a hard thing for some people to get used to."

"I got used to it," said Luke.

"Tell me something, Luke. Don't you ever feel bad, not having a daddy like the other kids?"

"Yes," he said.

"I'm sorry about that," I said. "I know it's not easy, having me for a parent."

"I don't mind," he said. "I like you this way."

He unbuckled his seat belt and climbed into my lap and hugged me. "I love you, Maddy," he said.

"Luke," said Grace, "can you get back in your seat, please?"

Then he snuggled over into Grace's lap and hugged her. "Lukey," she said, "I'm glad you're such a loving boy. It's a wonderful thing. But when we're driving I need for you to be in your seat with the seat belt buckled."

"Okay," said Luke, and climbed back into his seat. We heard the snap of the buckle clicking into place.

"Why don't you hold your breath again, Luke?" Patrick said.

"You know how Houdini died, Maddy?" said Luke. "He got punched."

"You can't die from punching," said Patrick.

"Can so," said Luke. "Look." He pointed to a picture in his book, in which Houdini was falling to the floor, clutching his stomach. "These guys came up to him and asked him if it was true that people could really punch him as hard as they could without it hurting him, and he said it was true, and just like that they punched him and he fell onto the floor and died a couple days after that."

"Boys?" said Grace. "I don't think we're going to be able to go to this Magic Store. It's not where it's supposed to be." She looked at me. "The street numbers around here make no sense."

"Then you know what, Maddy?"

"I see a digger," said Patrick.

"What number are we looking for?"

"Maddy, you know what?"

"Eighty-seven. But it goes straight from seventy-two to ninety."

"That's weird."

"Maddy."

"What is it, Luke, what?"

"You know what Houdini said to his wife, to Mrs. Houdini?"

"What, honey?"

"He said that if there was such a thing as life after death, that he'd come back from the dead as a ghost and talk to her."

Patrick began to speak like Dracula. *"I am the haunted voice!"* he said.

"What should we do?" I said to Grace. "Should we just go home?"

She looked at me, her jaw set. "You know I don't give up easy," she said, and I knew she wasn't talking about the Magic Shop anymore.

I nodded. "I know that, Grace."

She drove around the block again.

"So, Maddy, guess what. They all had this thing, a seense—"

"A *say*-ance," I said. "It's pronounced séance."

"A say-onns. And they like, waited for Houdini to come back? And they waited, and waited, but he never showed up?"

"I am the haunted voice!"

"But then, a little bit later, his wife claimed that she got this one word from him. It came to her in a secret code."

"There it is, across the street," Grace said triumphantly. "I get it. The numbers switch from odd to even here."

"What was the word, Luke?"

Grace parallel parked the minivan effortlessly, wedging us between two rental trucks.

"The word was *believe,*" said Luke.

"Believe what?" said Grace, shutting off the engine.

"I don't know," said Luke. "Just *believe.*"

"I am the haunted voice!" said Patrick.

"Come on, haunted voices," said Grace, opening the door. "Let's check this place out."

We walked into the Magic Shop, which felt like a movie set. There were posters from the 1930s on the walls, framed autographed photos of famous magicians. Expensive kits for various tricks lay in glass display cases. Every square inch of the store was covered with tricks, top hats, hand-painted vaudeville signs. A young man in a muscle T-shirt stood behind the counter.

"Good morning," he said. He was a strong young thing; he looked like Sylvester Stallone in the first *Rocky* movie. Not exactly the magician type. "And what do we have here?"

"Two young magicians," I said.

"Luke's reading about Houdini," said Grace.

The magician looked reverential. "The greatest escape artist of all time."

"He came back from the dead," Luke commented.

The magician looked concerned. "Well, no one knows about that, do they?"

I cleared my throat. "We're looking for some simple tricks the boys can learn."

"Excellent," said the magician. He pulled out a deck of cards, fanned them before our eyes. "Pick a card," he said. "Any card."

Luke picked out the six of diamonds.

"Don't show me the card," said the magician. "Put it back in the deck." Luke slid it into the middle of the pile. Then the magician shuffled the cards. He had Patrick cut the deck. Then he pulled the six of diamonds off the top. "Was *this* your card?"

Luke smiled. "Wow. How'd you do that?"

"It's a special deck," the magician said. He turned the cards over. They were all sixes of diamonds.

"That's nine ninety-five," he said. "Then we have the levitating rope." He put a length of rope in a small vase. He had Luke pull on it to show it could move freely. Then he waved his hands over the vase.

"Presto change-o," he said.

Grace looked over at me.

He turned the vase upside down. The rope hung there, suspended in space.

Luke smiled. Patrick had already lost interest and was now exploring the rest of the store. He was gazing down a corridor at the back of the shop. Voices echoed from down the hall.

"There's a small ball in the bottom of the vase," explained Rocky. "When you turn the vase upside down, it traps the rope." He put this on the counter next to the trick card deck. "That's six ninety-five."

"Luke," Patrick whispered. He looked frightened by the thing he saw. He ushered Luke toward him with his hand. *"C'mere."*

Luke walked toward his brother. The two of them looked down the long hallway toward the distant voices in the next room. I caught snatches of conversation. It sounded like two old magicians talking, a man and a woman.

"Boys," Grace said. "Come here." They didn't.

"Now this one is very popular," said the magician. He stuffed a violet silk handkerchief into one hand. He waved his hand over his fist, then opened it. The handkerchief was gone. Then he closed his fist again, waved his hand. The handkerchief reappeared.

"Wow," I said. "I like that one."

Grace went over to where the boys were standing. The magician looked after her. "You two sisters?" he said to me. It took a moment for me to realize what he was talking about.

"Yes," I said. "We're sisters." I looked at Grace and the boys. The three of them stared down the hallway. A look of surprise crossed Grace's face, as if she were seeing something she had neither expected, nor desired, to see. She took a step forward, holding the children's hands, and vanished down the corridor.

"I thought you was sisters," said Rocky. He looked at the wedding ring on my finger, the ring given to me by my mother.

"You want to know the secret?" Rocky said.

"Yes," I said. "I want to know the secret." I wasn't sure what we were talking about now. Rocky leaned in very close to me. It felt like a strangely intimate moment.

"Plastic thumb," the magician said, placing a skin-colored fake thumb on the counter. "You stuff the handkerchief in here, then when you pull your thumb out of your fist, no one sees the thumb, they just see that the handkerchief is gone."

"Wow," I said. "I like that one. I think that's great! A fake thumb!"

"Four ninety-five," said the magician. "A classic. The hanky's not included." He got out a box from behind the counter. "Then there's the disappearing egg." The magician put the egg cup on the countertop, put a small ovoid sphere into it.

"Whoa," I said. "I remember this one! The disappearing egg! I used to have this when I was a kid! I could never get it to work, though." I thought about Gammie and Hilda Watson and Aunt Nora, about the day I had stood below the boardwalk and looked at the rising sea and prayed that my life would be changed by the redeeming powers of love. I thought about Houdini, sending his wife a coded message from the place he had gone to. *Believe.*

"Hey, Grace," I said. "Look at this! The disappearing egg! I had this when I was a kid!" I looked over in the direction where Grace had been.

But my wife wasn't there anymore.

The New Equator

Trudy killed herself on Thanksgiving. She'd spent the day eating turkey and stuffing and sweet potato puff with her family, told her parents that she loved them, then went back to her apartment and threw a noose over one of the rafters. Apparently this was more efficient, when the time came, than helium.

She never got Gonzo's Wild Ride, either.

I don't know. Maybe they have vending machines where she is now.

————

I knew a guy at Wesleyan named Huang who manufactured his own LSD in the chemistry laboratory. It was sad. Chemistry wasn't his major.

Things went from bad to worse. One day he showed up at my dorm room pulling a little red wagon. My guess was he'd stolen it from a child.

The wagon was packed full of books. A change of clothes. "The new ice age is coming, man," he told me in a thin, wavering voice. "The poles have come off center. All the magnetism is out of control."

Huang leaned forward. "I wanted to tell you in advance, man. I'm only letting a couple people in on it. The people who deserve to survive. Before the new ice caps start forming."

"Well, thanks, Huang," I said. "You're nice to include me."

"Of course I'm including you, Boylan," he said. "I mean, the eyes I've got now—I can see *into* people."

Then, as if to demonstrate, he looked into me with his X-ray vision. It was a little bit frightening for both of us. "Whoa," he said as he riffled through my interior.

"What?" I said nervously. "What do you see?"

"Boylan," he said pityingly, "I never knew."

"What?" I said. "What?"

He reached out for my hand. "It's okay," he said. "Don't worry. It's not the worst thing in the world. Having secrets."

I didn't know what to say. I asked him if he was all right.

Huang looked at me as if I were insane. "Of course I'm all *right*, man. Aren't you listening? I'm giving you a *chance*."

"Okay," I said. "What am I supposed to do?"

"Get everything you want to last. Go up in the graveyard. It'll be all right there."

"The graveyard?" I said. There was this big eighteenth-century graveyard near the college. "What's going on there?"

"Well, you'll be *fine* there, man," he said as if I were an idiot. "That's going to be the new *equator*."

————

From: Jenny Boylan <jfboylan@mint.net>
To: Russo <russo@mint.net>

Dear Russo:

I was thinking earlier today about how you have had to prove your love for me, or some such damn thing, in this last year or two. I am, of course, inexpressibly grateful.

The thing is, though, that you know that if our positions were reversed, somehow—that I would be there, just as you were, when you needed me.

I guess what I'm observing is that of the two of us, only you have had to actually answer the summons. That you did, under such tough circumstances, is something I will be considering the rest of my life. But that I have not had the opportunity to do the same for you leaves me, in equal measures, both thankful and restless— deprived, on some weird level, of the opportunity to show you I wasn't goddamn kidding, either, when I said I was your friend.

I am also aware that since you were on *MacNeil/Lehrer* tonight, this e-mail will be buried along with about eight million other good wishes, and people asking for a piece of you. Which is as it should be, I guess.

I love ya, big dummy.

J

From: Russo <russo@mint.net>
To: Jenny Boylan <jfboylan@mint.net>

Boylan—

I have always known, and never doubted, that if I called you'd be right there. I had no idea you'd show up in heels, but that's hardly the point, is it? Remember that early scene in *The Godfather*? "The day may come when I will require a service, but until that day . . ."

Yours is the first message about *Lehrer,* actually. I'd heard it was going to be on, but I'm far too squeamish.

Anxious to see you and Grace on Friday.

R

One morning toward the end of transition, I was in a pickup truck, driving toward Ithaca, New York, with Grace's brother, Tex. We drove past a graveyard, an old one. That cemetery got me thinking. I remembered the night I'd walked through the pitch dark with Russo, the sound of the ocean coming all muffled through the trees. Then I told Tex the story of seeing my father's ghost, when he'd stood by my bedside and spoken my name for the first time.

"Wait a minute," said Tex. "What was that your daddy said to you, in this dream you had?"

"My father said he wasn't going to look out for me anymore. If I became a woman, that is. I was so annoyed with him."

"How do you figure that?"

"Well, I thought it was a kind of manipulative thing to say, for a ghost. Like he isn't going to watch out for me anymore."

We drove on in silence for a while.

"I tell you what," he said. "I think you've got that all wrong, Jennifer."

"What do I have wrong?"

"About how he meant that, about him not looking out for you anymore." Tex looked at me with his kind, well-lined face. "The way I see it, he was saying, Jenny, once you're a woman, he won't *have* to."

Sabbatical over, I returned to Colby in the fall of 2002. I resumed my academic career as the co-chair of the English Department, a job I assumed along with a brilliant, charming colleague named Peter Harris, whom I had once almost killed during a hike along the Knife Edge trail up Mount Katahdin, although not on purpose. Peter had never quite forgiven me for nearly allowing him to fall to his death on that occasion, which I felt ensured that we would probably have a good relationship as the department's co-directors. It's hard to trust anyone you haven't nearly murdered, at least in academia it is.

The week before school started, a young woman appeared at my door. She had short hair and big clunky black boots.

"Professor Boylan?" she said.

"Yes?"

She came into my office. "I'm Diane Bloomfield?"

"I'm Jenny Boylan?"

"I wanted to know if I could ask you to sponsor me for this independent study I want to do?"

I invited her to sit down.

"I'm a double major in women's studies and English? And I had this idea to do a project on women in contemporary American novels, and how they, you know, transcend our understanding of the archetypes of femininity and womanhood?"

I nodded. "That sounds interesting," I said. "But you know, I'm a professor of creative writing, a novelist. You really ought to ask one of the Americanists, like Cedric or Katherine."

She looked alarmed. "But I want *you*!" she said. "I mean, I've put together this whole reading list! And I have a sample of a paper I wrote, last year, for you to look at if you want. I'm a good writer. I mean, you're the perfect person to do this project!" She paused. "Please?"

I thought about it for a moment. "Diane," I said, "is the reason you want to work with me because I'm . . . well, you know, because of my history, because of my issues?"

She looked uncertain. "What do you mean?" she said.

"You know," I said. "Because I'm transgender—or because I used to be. Is that why you think I've got some particular insight into these works?"

Her forehead crinkled. "You're trans . . . what?"

Diane looked at me like a pitcher shaking off bad signals from a catcher. Then she looked embarrassed. "I don't know anything about that. I just thought—"

"Wait," I said. "You didn't know? You hadn't heard?"

She shrugged. "No." Then she added quickly, "Not that it makes any difference or anything—it's just—"

"Well, why me, then? Why not one of the American literature professors?"

She shrugged. "Everyone says you're a good teacher, that's all. I just wanted to work with you. I didn't know anything about the other stuff."

"Oh," I said.

"Everybody says you're funny." She smiled hopefully.

I nodded. "I'm funny all right," I said.

When Diane finally left my office—I convinced her it'd be in her best interest to approach my other colleagues first—I sat there for a moment, in wonder. I looked up at the poster on the wall. Groucho, Harpo, and Chico.

Whatever it is, Groucho sang, *I'm against it!*

I picked up the telephone and dialed information.

"In Freedom, Maine? The last name is Brown, Stacey?" I wrote the number down. A moment or two later, I listened to a phone ringing.

"Hello?" said a woman's voice.

"Stacey?" I said.

"Yeah, who's this?"

"You probably don't remember me," I said. "But my name's Jenny Boylan. I picked you up last year, when you were hitchhiking, you and your roommate. I drove you over to that guy Speed Racer's house, when you went to buy the pit bull?"

"Oh, hi!" said Stacey, as if we were old friends. "How have you been? I saw the Roy Hudsons playing in a bar a couple months back, thought about you. Are you still playing with them?"

"Actually, I haven't played out with them since that time I picked you guys up. I should call them sometime."

"Well, it's great to hear your voice," she said, and started coughing.

"I was calling about your roommate, Lee—I was wondering if she was there."

"Oh, no, she doesn't live here anymore. She moved in with Mike last winter."

"Mike?" I said.

"Yeah, you know, her old boyfriend. They let him out of prison early, for good behavior, if you can believe that."

"Oh," I said. "Well, okay. It's none of my business anyway. I just wanted to encourage her . . . you know, if she wanted someone to encourage her . . . to go back to school, finish her degree."

"You know, she was talking about that when Mike got out. I don't know if she'll still do it, though. Mike's got all kinds of plans. He wants to get married, have kids, you know, all that."

"Well," I said. "Whatever. It's none of my business anyway. It's just that the last thing she said to me before she got out of the car was that she wanted to talk sometime. I didn't know if she really meant it, or whatever, but I wanted to encourage her, as best I could, you know?"

"Oh," said Stacey. "Man, well, that's awfully nice of you. I mean, it is true that it's hard to find people to talk to sometimes—"

In the background, there was a deep growling. This was followed by the sound of something hitting the floor and breaking into lots of small pieces.

"Hey, Jenny, I have to get off the phone, okay?" She sounded annoyed. I wondered if she'd made the mistake of leaving a remote control out where the dog could see it.

"Hey, wait," I said. "Is that the pit bull? You've still got her?"

"Yeah," said Stacey. "I got her. Like I said, I gotta go—"

"Let me ask you something—I know you have to go, but can I just ask you one more thing?"

Stacey sighed. "Sure."

"What did you name the dog? Remember when you picked her up, we forgot to ask what her name was?"

The dog barked again.

"Spike," she said. "We named her *Spike*."

In the fall, the band played at a bar in Mexico, Maine, called Mrs. Whatsit's. The bar was not far from one of the largest paper plants in the state. Even inside the tavern, you could smell the mill. We took a break at ten, and I went to the bar to get a drink. As I waited, a man with a mustache came up to me and put his arm around my waist and announced, "You're a beautiful blonde."

I took a step backward and gave him his arm back.

"Thanks," I said with contempt.

Jake the drummer, who was leaning against a pole and watching this interchange, laughed quietly to himself.

"What?" I said.

"Nothing," he said. He gave me a strange look I hadn't noticed before. Now that I thought about it, Jake the drummer was cute. He had sparkling eyes and a peg leg.

"C'mon," said Jake the drummer, and finished his beer. "Let's play."

Back on stage, sitting down behind the keys of the synthesizer, I felt safe.

Jake, who was sitting closest to me on stage, leaned over and said, "Hey, Jenny."

"Hey what?"

"She's not there," he said.

"Who?"

"No," said Jake. "The song. 'She's Not There.' " It wasn't a song we usually did, but Jake counted it off and sang.

———

We were tearing down the equipment. Mrs. Whatsit was walking through her tavern, giving the malingerers a particular *look* she'd perfected. This expression made it unnecessary to shout, "Closing time." When Mrs. Whatsit gave you that look, you put your coat on. No one knew what would happen if you didn't. In all the years that she had been running the bar, no one had ever risked finding out.

On stage the band was disassembling the lights, putting all the guitars back in the cases. Shell collapsed the tripods that held up the PA speakers. I detached the music stand from the Kurzweil and looked out at the dissipating crowd. My ears were still ringing. It had been a good night.

A man named Pete, who wore a T-shirt that read "Desert Storm Vets," came over to Nick, holding a pint of Shipyard. "Here you go, Nick," he said. "Last beer in the state of Maine."

Pete had known me as a guy, years ago, and had heard the rumors I'd been sick. He didn't recognize me now.

"And who is *this*?" he said, looking over in my direction.

"That's Jenny," said Nick. "Jenny, this is Pete."

"Hi, Pete," I said.

"Well, hel-*lo*, Jenny," he said.

"By the way," Nick said, "I don't think I told you, I finally found out what was wrong with Jim Boylan."

"Yeah?" said Pete. "And what was that?"

My friend took a deep draft of Shipyard before answering. He looked at me and smiled.

"Not a damn thing," he said.

———————

One winter night, Luke swallowed a marble. I called Poison Control. "How is he, ma'am?" the woman asked. "Can he breathe? Is the object lodged in his lungs?"

"Luke," I said, "can you breathe?"

"Of course I can breathe," he said, annoyed. He looked up from his Game Boy.

"He says he can breathe," I said.

"Can he talk?"

"Luke, can you talk?"

"Maddy . . . ," he said, annoyed.

"He can talk."

"Well," said Poison Control, "he sounds all right. You could take him to the doctor, but if you want my opinion, you can probably just wait for it to come out by itself."

"Uh-huh," I said. I had a pretty good idea what she was getting at.

When Gammie died, she'd left me her good silver. This was just before she gave herself to science. I kept the silver in its wooden box on the lowest shelf in the hutch. There were dozens of salad forks and demitasse spoons and pie slicers in there, all engraved with an ornate *B*.

In the days that followed, I found a new use for the silver serving fork, one unimagined by my grandmother. Each evening I examined that which Luke produced, using the fork as my instrument. I felt like a California forty-niner during the leanest days of the gold rush. Patiently I searched for Luke's marble, but each night my panning efforts proved nugatory. I decided, after a while, that I probably wouldn't be seeing that marble again. The thought made me restless, though. What had become of it? Is it possible for things to just vanish inside us? That hadn't been my experience.

Then we awoke one morning to find the ground covered with snow, all the color taken out of the world. Pieces of lawn furniture and sandboxes nudged above the surface, like the dorsal fins of sharks. The snow crystals sparkled in the sun. Grace came into the bedroom with two cups of coffee, and we sat on the edge of the bed, looking out the window at the changed world.

That evening, my efforts bore fruit. The marble rolled around the metal bowl I was using as a sieve. I washed off the marble and held it in the palm of my hand. It was small, the marble. It was surprising how small it was.

It was late at night, and I was the last one up. I'd set the coffee robot for five-thirty A.M. I'd made the children's lunches for school, put them into the Jimmy Neutron lunchboxes, and placed these in the refrigerator, next to the Go-Gurt bars and the juice boxes and the cheese sticks.

I walked into Luke's room, a forty-four-year-old woman with bifocals, and I sat on the edge of my son's bed. He was already asleep, and his long eyelashes fluttered in dream.

I ran my fingers through the blond mop of his hair. Luke looked a lot like I had when I was eight. I remembered the moment he was born, Grace hearing the cry and whispering, "That's amazing."

The house was full of sleeping creatures. Patrick lay in his Buzz Lightyear sheets, clutching Big Pig and Big Pig's friend Mystic, a unicorn. Lucy, the dog, lay on the floor of Patrick's room, barking in her dreams. Grace was upstairs, the *New York Times* crossword on her stomach, a pen in one hand, her eyes shut. The fish swam in their tank.

The chimes of Aunt Nora's clock rang from the living room. There were faint embers glowing in the fireplace.

Luke opened his eyes and looked at me. "Hi, Maddy," he whispered.

"Hello, Luke," I said.

We stared at each other for a moment.

"You're a pretty great kid, you know that?" I said, my voice catching slightly.

He smiled. "So . . . are you in here for any particular reason?" he said.

I opened my palm. "Does this look familiar?"

He sat up. "Whoa," he said. "Is that the marble?"

"That's it all right."

"But wait. Maddy?" He looked confused. "This isn't the one I swallowed."

"What do you mean?" I said. "Believe me, it's the one you swallowed. Unless you swallowed two."

"But this marble isn't blue," he said. "It's red. The marble I swallowed was blue."

We sat there for a moment, thinking things over.

"Well, somehow it changed, inside you," I said. "I can't explain it."

Luke looked at me with his wide, young eyes. The winter wind blew against his window.

"Maybe it's a miracle," he said.

I kissed my boy. "Maybe," I said.

Afterword:
Imagining Jenny

by Richard Russo

September 2002. "Don't worry, Russo," I said.
"We'll always have Paris."

I.

Jenny had been given to understand she'd have a private hospital room in which to convalesce. The next day she'd be operated on by Dr. Eugene Schrang, who'd pioneered "gender reassignment surgery," a term that still cracked me up (if it didn't work out, you'd be reassigned again, this time to the motor pool). I don't know if Schrang was the one who actually came up with the idea of using a penis to create a vagina, of turning one highly sensate organ in upon itself to produce another, but if so, he gets points for imagination in my book. Either that or he just lived through the Depression and, like my maternal grandmother, hated to waste anything. He was also very expensive, though as Jenny herself pointed out to me, if you're in the market for new genitalia, you really don't want to shop in the bargain basement. Still, I had some doubts about the good doctor. His Web site featured a giant vagina on its home page, and I'd begun to think of him as "Big Pussy," like the character on *The Sopranos.* One thing was for sure. He had a thriving practice. Dr. Schrang did some eighty male-to-female gender reassignment surgeries a year, and June had apparently been a particularly busy month. When we arrived in Egypt, he had a wardful of postop transsexuals, which meant that Jenny would have a roommate.

Her name was Melanie, and to Jenny, she couldn't have been more encouraging. "Don't be scared, hon, you're doing the right thing," she counseled in a southern drawl from behind the drawn curtain that divided the room. Pay no attention to that man behind the curtain, I thought, wishing I could whisper this advice to Jenny, who shared my devotion to *The Wizard of Oz*. Over the last two years there'd been plenty of tense, strained moments in our friendship, and lately we clung to laughter like drowning men (*sic*) to an inner tube. It usually wasn't long after an argument that I'd get an e-mail from Jenny that would restore our equilibrium. One such said, "Russo. I've come up with a title for Larry Fine's autobiography. It's *Moe, You Bastard, You Bastard, Moe, You Bastard*." Reading it, I found myself grinning from ear to ear, and not just because at age fifty-three I still took pleasure in the Three Stooges. It was, of course, the way Jim and I had communicated right from the start—that is, elliptically. To be Larry Fine was to be poked in the eye, cuffed in the head, knocked down, ridiculed, and buffeted by a malicious force of nature over the course of a lifetime, and never to know why. By the time you came to writing your autobiography, all you'd know is that you'd had enough. Moe, you bastard.

Melanie's operation had gone well enough, but her recovery had been dicey. Since her catheter had been removed, she explained to us, disappearing into the small bathroom located on Jenny's side of the curtain, she actually had to stand on the commode to pee. How the added elevation could possibly help in this enterprise I neither understood nor wanted to understand. When the door closed behind her, we could hear the seat drop and Melanie climb aboard. "It's worth it, though," she assured Jenny ten minutes later as she limped back to her own bed, bathed in sweat from the fruitless exertion. "It's *so* worth it."

In what sense? was what I wanted to ask, but I bit my tongue. Jenny, herself in a hospital gown now, was beginning to look panicked, all too ready for the sedative she'd been promised. Grace sat on the edge of the bed and took her hand. "How do you feel?"

"Terrified," Jenny admitted, her voice all but inaudible. "Brave. I couldn't do this without you." Her eyes shifted, kindly, to include me. I searched for something to say, failing utterly, and not for the last time in Egypt. It was language—easy, thoughtless words between friends—that I'd most felt the loss of over the long months. We value our friendships in part, I suspect, according to their ease, and Boylan and I had hit it off from the start. Ten years earlier he'd been the very first visitor to our rented camp on Great Pond, where we were staying until we could find a house in Waterville. He'd arrived, bearded then, with a six-pack of beer by way of a calling card, to welcome me to Colby College after I'd been given a job he himself had applied for. He might have been coming to check me out, the way you'd look over the guy your wife left you for, but by the time we'd shaken hands, I'd known this wasn't the case. By the time we'd drunk half of that first beer, our feet up on the railing of the deck, before I'd read his two sad, hilarious companion novels (*The Planets* and *The Constellations*) about souls adrift in the wide universe, I knew I'd made a friend. Here was a man (I thought) who spoke my language, to whom I would seldom have to explain myself, who was predisposed to give me the benefit of every doubt. By the time we'd finished that beer, we'd formed, it seemed to me, an unspoken pact, the exact nature of which we'd figure out later, the details being unimportant. It'd be easy. And until recently it had been. Now, though, I had to watch every word I said, especially the pronouns, not because Jenny got upset when I messed up (she never did), but because my mistakes, especially public, social ones, caused her both pain and embarrassment. Worse, such blunders were evidence that I missed my old pal Jim and wanted him—and our old, thoughtless ease—back again. Which I did.

"You know what?" Grace said later, when we left the hospital in search of whatever the town might have to offer by way of dinner. "She's going to get *all* the good drugs. We're not going to get any."

———————

Barbara, my wife, happened to be away visiting family when Jim told me. She returned a couple of days later, and I drove down to Portland to meet her evening flight. We'd spoken a couple of times, but I'd said nothing about Boylan because it wasn't the sort of news you impart over the phone and also because I myself had only begun to process what I'd been told. The first person I always want to tell important news to is Barbara, partly because I can trust her reactions, which are often more generous than my own, and partly because I often don't know what I truly think about things until I *do* tell her. Which was why it now felt so strange to possess knowledge that I badly wanted to conceal from her.

I waited until we'd loaded her luggage into the trunk of the car, gotten through the worst of the Portland traffic and safely onto I-95 pointed north, and only then, when the other cars fell away and the tall, dark pines began to enclose us, did I lean forward, turn off the radio, and tell my wife to prepare for a shock. ("This is not about us," I hastened to assure her, fearing she would leap to some terrible conclusion.) As I told her that our friend Jim Boylan believed himself to be a woman; that he'd understood this to be the case all his life and was only now discovering the courage to admit it; that Grace knew and was, of course, devastated; that he'd consulted doctors who had diagnosed his condition; that he intended to enter into a "transition" from male to female, from Jim to Jenny, that would involve hormone therapy and, quite possibly, gender surgery—Barbara said nothing until my voice finally fell. Then she said, "Oh, this is just insane. There *has* to be something else going on. We *know* this man." She was looking over at me now, though it was very dark in the car, as if I, too, at any moment, might be revealed to her as a stranger. I understood all too well what the news was doing to her. What she knew—what she *knew* she knew—was being challenged. The ground beneath her feet had shifted, was no longer stable. Of all the couples we knew, the Boylans had the marriage most like our own, and if Grace had not known the truth, never even suspected it, then what in the wide world was truly knowable? If you can be so wrong about something so fundamental, what could you trust? Or, more to the point, who?

We drove on for many minutes, adrift in time and space. I speak here not in metaphor. We were supposed to have gotten off the interstate at Brunswick and taken Route 1 up the coast to Camden, but I'd missed our exit. I know now that this is what must have happened. At the time, though, we were simply flying down the pitch black interstate, peering out the windshield at a newly unfamiliar world. It occurred to me that what I'd told my wife—that none of this was about us—wasn't true. It *was* about us.

II.

Over the long months that followed, as Jim confided in more and more people, it became clear that, as one friend remarked, he'd become a walking Rorschach test. As he revealed who he was, we revealed who we were as well, and in doing so, I suspect, surprised ourselves almost as much as Jim had surprised us. When Barbara and I talked about it—and it was impossible not to—we often ended up clinging to each other, reassuring each other that everything was okay with *us*, that we *did* know each other, that we weren't harboring some terrible secret capable of atomizing our marriage should it ever come to light. But every now and then I'd catch Barbara regarding me strangely (or, more likely, I'd imagine her doing so) and immediately conclude that she'd been thinking about Jim and Grace and the fact that nothing in the world was quite as certain as she'd once imagined.

When things spin out of control, when the familiar becomes suddenly chimerical, our instinct is to restore order. Jim's sister, conservative by nature and efficient by habit, immediately set her own world aright by telling her brother she wanted nothing further to do with him. Problem solved, order restored. For the rest of us, encumbered by decency and affection, it wasn't so simple, though I suspect most of us, in our own ways, also would have preferred "the problem" to go away. Looking into our crystal balls, we concluded there was no way Grace and Jim's marriage could weather a storm of this magnitude. Sure, they loved each other, were devoted to each other, but they would end up divorced. Thinking of Grace, we decided that sooner would probably be better than later. She was going to have to invent a new life, a new happiness, and the sooner she got started on this necessary task, the better. It was Jim we always imagined moving away, to New York or Washington, some big city where he would find "a support group" of people who had themselves survived their own transsexuality, or were in the process of doing so. Interestingly, we didn't immediately see ourselves as Jim's natural support group, nor did we imagine that Grace would be the one to move to New York or Washington, because that scenario did nothing to restore order to *our* world.

My own Rorschach reaction to Jim's revelation was both surprising and disturbing because it revealed an emotional conservatism in my character I'd have surely denied had anyone accused me of it. After the day Jim first trusted me with the truth and I'd promised always to be his friend, I began to wonder if I'd made a promise I'd be unable to keep. Almost immediately, I began to feel like Nick Carraway after Gatsby's murder; I wanted the world to be "uniform and at a sort of moral attention." Jim had explained, and at some level I even believed, that his was a medical condition, not a moral one, but I discovered I was unable to sever that medical condition from its moral consequences. When I asked myself if he (I had not yet even begun to think of my friend as "she") didn't have the same right to the pursuit of happiness as anyone else, my response was no, not if it meant Grace's *un*happiness, not if it put their children at risk. He'd *made* his choice when he took Grace, to have and to hold, until death. "Conduct,"

Nick Carraway says, "may be founded on the hard rock or the wet marshes, but after a certain point I don't care what it's founded on," and I agreed, almost proud that my tolerance, like Nick's, had found a limit. My friend's moral duty was to be a man, in every sense of that term. I tried to imagine myself telling him this. Saying the words: *Be a man*.

Of course, my emotional conservatism, if that's what it was, had more than one source. I was not just a recovering Catholic and, as such, prone to see the world in moral terms, but also a fiction writer, and no matter how liberal a writer's politics may be, the act of storytelling is not an inherently liberal enterprise for the simple reason that storytellers believe in free will. A plot, I used to remind my students, is not merely a sequence of events: "A" followed by "B" followed by "C" followed by "D." Rather, it's a series of events linked by cause and effect: "A" *causes* "B," which *causes* "C," and so on. True, a person's (or a fictional character's) destiny may be more than the sum of his choices—fate and luck play a role as well—but only scientists (and not all of them) believe that free will is a sham. People in life—and therefore in fiction—must choose, and their choices must have meaningful consequences. Otherwise, there's no story. Jim's medical condition—his insistence that it was a medical condition and nothing more—was pure fate; if what he claimed was true, then his circumstance was preordained, which removed the whole thing from the realm of narrative, and doing so ran contrary to my own belief system, not just to my residual Catholicism, but also to my novelist's sensibility.

Of course, Jim himself was a novelist, a fine one. As Professor Boylan of Colby College, he too had sought solace and understanding in narrative. Not surprisingly, as this memoir details, he'd been drawn to imaginative literature, the heroic quest, which so often involves a revelation of the hero's true identity. Only when the hero thoroughly understands who he is can his final dragons be slain. Such stories, of course, are not the only ones in Western literature that deal with transformation, and just as Jim had been drawn by his circumstance to a certain type of story, I found myself drawn by my own to another sort. Probably no people embrace change more enthusiastically, at least in theory, than Americans. Who we are at birth is less important to us than who we will become. We are expected—indeed, obligated—not just to be, but to become. This, in a nutshell, is the American dream. But we are also by nature a cautious, pragmatic people. After all, Gatsby's need to transform, to reinvent himself, is his downfall. We are, Fitzgerald suggests, what we are, regardless of our need to be otherwise. Ironically, this was what Jenny herself kept reminding us, though she was applying the wisdom differently.

I wish I could honestly say it was exclusively great literature I turned to for understanding, but the truth is that I was equally attracted to more lurid, archetypal fictions, especially in the language of film, which has for decades provided numerous cautionary parables of transformation, of men who turn into wolves, into vampires, even into insects. Often these stories are not just about the man who is transformed, but also about the faithful, loving woman his transformation will inevitably endanger. At the climax of these stories, the "creature" must choose between what he's become (a monster) and what he was (a man, someone's lover). Often he's asked by his beloved to deny his new nature, to remember who and what he used to be, and to be a man again. In these stories it is always clear that the creature is not to blame for his cruel fate. He did not ask to be bitten by the wolf, the vampire, the spider. He cannot make himself human again. Rather, the man he was is still "in there," and it is to this former self that the heroine appeals. *Remember,* she begs him. Remember me. Remember love. Do not harm me. Even now, changed though you may be, you have a choice.

Such is our credo. As social and natural scientists continue to erode our *belief* in free will by revealing the extent of our genetic and cultural programming, novelists continue to hold people accountable for their actions and the consequences of those actions. This is the fiction writer's manifesto, because without it, there's no story.

III.

Jenny's operation seemed almost an anticlimax. For her it was a natural conclusion, a resolution, really. She wasn't "changing genders" or "becoming a woman." She's always been a woman. A skilled surgeon was simply going to help her move about in the world. If the surgery was scary, well, all surgery was scary. Even for Grace, Egypt wasn't as dramatic as I'd imagined it would be. For her, the point of no return had come and gone incrementally, undramatically, over the long months during which she'd come to understand that this operation was going to happen because it had to. Also, as if to suggest that nothing all that momentous was occurring, the operation itself went without a hitch. Jenny'd been wheeled into the operating room singing "I'm Gonna Wash That Man Right Out of My Hair" and come out clutching a button that controlled her intravenous pain medication. (Grace had been right. Jenny did get all the good drugs.) Within two hours of being wheeled back into her room, she'd talked to her mother and several friends who'd called to find out how the operation had gone. Her voice didn't have much strength (we could hear Melanie moaning as she stood atop the commode on the other side of the bathroom door more clearly), but she laughed and joked on the phone and clicked her button, and by the next morning she had no memory of any of it. She seemed, more than anything, very, very happy. "Jim was always The Golden Boy," Grace remarked wistfully when Jenny nodded off into another morphine dream. "And Jenny's going to be The Golden Girl." From inside the bathroom came the sound of Melanie climbing off the commode, then she herself emerged without a flush, suggesting that again no business had been conducted.

You had only to look at Melanie, now haggard and frightened and dispirited, to know that she'd never been a golden boy and wouldn't be a golden girl, either. She'd not had a boob job to go along with her GRS, as many transsexuals did when hormones left them flat chested, and as a result, she did not look, postop, much different from the way she'd looked a year before when some guys on the basketball court had offered to kick the shit out of her because she looked like a girl. She claimed to be content with an androgynous look, but I had my doubts, since she also admitted to having spent very nearly her last dime on her surgery. She'd come to Egypt alone, the way she'd done her entire transition. Her family and friends, after organizing an intervention in the hopes of preventing her from going through with the operation, kept on belittling her right up to the moment she boarded the plane and continued, incredibly, even now, to call her at the hospital to belittle her further.

As a result, she was starved for human kindness, and she attached herself not just to Jenny, a natural ally, but more surprisingly to Grace and me. The sliding curtain that divided the room and had been drawn when we first arrived was now thrown open so that when we visited, Melanie could be part of the conversation, which among other things helped take her mind off the fact that she couldn't pee. "They're not going to let me out of here until I do," she confided sadly, as if she'd spent her entire life disappointing people as a man and was now doing the same thing as a woman. She'd been scheduled to be released from the hospital the day before, and she had no idea how she'd be able to pay for the additional stay, not to mention the several outpatient days she'd be required to spend at a nearby hotel, the same one where Grace and I were staying.

For me, Melanie, like the other transsexuals on the ward, posed a paradox. They might not look much like women, but I had little trouble thinking of them as female, whereas Jenny, who could (and did) pass for a woman anywhere, even before her surgery, still seemed like my old pal Jim in drag. As I regarded the two of them in their adjacent beds, I began to suspect that I might be lacking in imagination, the very quality in which, as a novelist, I most prided myself.

No doubt one of the reasons I was among the first people Jim confided in was that if anyone was equipped, by both training and inclination, to understand his plight, it was a friend who also happened to be a novelist, whose stock in trade is moral imagination. The problem, as this memoir illustrates, is that the transgender person's experience is not really "like" anything, and Jim was to discover, alas, that no one would have more trouble imagining what he wanted us to imagine than his closest friends, and that my being a novelist counted for less, at least in the beginning, than either of us could have guessed. It wasn't that I was unable to imagine anything or that my imagination had taken a holiday when confronted with intractable reality. Quite the opposite. From the start I discovered myself to be in imaginative overdrive. During the first week of my new knowledge, my imaginings were so powerful and relentless that I had trouble sleeping. Though I knew Grace to be a strong woman, I imagined her shattered as she watched her husband disappear, like an old photographic image, into terrible blank whiteness. I imagined their children ridiculed in the schoolyard, told by adults that they were no longer suitable friends for their own children. During this period, I was working on *Empire Falls*, a novel about the terrible weight that kids today have to bear, and it was not difficult to imagine Luke and Patrick, thus tormented, driven darkly inward, like my fictional victims, by what they could not explain, even to themselves. And worse. The Boylans lived out in the country, and it was easy to imagine them awakened in the night as rednecks in pickup trucks with the windows rolled down, full of last-call courage, bellowed their unsolicited opinions into the still night. And even worse. Three-in-the-morning night terrors that were only slightly less lurid than werewolf tales, but full of "respectable," real-world violence. Gradually, they went away.

But as I regarded Jenny and Melanie in their adjacent beds, I realized that banishing phantasms is not the same as imagining a happy ending, something I'd somehow written off as impossible from the start. I'm not talking here about the kind of happy ending that makes everything all right, that negates loss, that squints at reality in order to substitute a fantasy. Rather, I mean the kind of qualified happy endings that my friend and I had always managed to eke out in our own novels, the kind that allows Huck Finn, after witnessing just about the worst that human nature has to offer, to "light out for the territories" armed with little but his own hard-won decency for a moral compass, as fine and true an ending to a comic novel as we're ever likely to see. That's what Boylan and I were, after all—comic novelists—and comic novelists traffic in hope. More important, this was the kind of imagination that Jim had asked of me from the start, and it was what Jenny needed of me now. She needed those who loved her to share her ridiculous, buoyant hope for her future, for the future of her family. The problem was, I not only hadn't imagined a hopeful future for Jenny. I hadn't really begun to imagine Jenny.

IV.

A couple of days after the surgery, Grace and I began to take turns at Jenny's bedside. The tiny hospital room accommodated two visitors only if one of them stood, and having two visitors at the same time was also more tiring for Jenny, who, whacked-out on painkillers, felt the need to entertain us. So Grace and I would both drop by in the morning, then I'd leave the two of them alone, returning an hour or two later to take a shift while Grace grabbed something to eat or returned phone calls.

One afternoon when I returned to the hotel from lunch, there was a voice mail message. "Don't forget to check on Melanie," Grace reminded me. The day before, Melanie had finally peed and by way of reward had been discharged from the hospital.

I had not forgotten. Actually, after lunch I'd taken a stroll through town and picked up a couple of things for her at the drugstore. When Grace had spoken to her earlier that morning, Melanie had complained of a headache and a terribly parched throat. Could we stop

by later with some lemon candies? Well, of course we could. "We"
was, to my way of thinking, the operative word, and since Grace was
just then at the hospital, there was no "we" available to check on her,
just "me." I was already late for my afternoon shift at Jenny's bedside,
having dallied over lunch and spent too long talking to my wife and
daughters on the cell phone. If I went directly to the hospital, I could
spend a few hours with Jenny, give Grace her break, and then "we"
could drop by Melanie's room on our way to dinner that evening.
That had been my plan.

Melanie's room was right across from the elevator. I pressed down,
then, while I awaited the elevator's arrival, went over to her door to
listen for sounds. Music. The television. Something. If she was sleeping,
I told myself, Melanie'd need the rest more than the bag of hard candy
I held in my hand. I paused, considered, then finally knocked. Behind
me the elevator dinged, and when the doors opened a middle-aged
couple got off, smiled at me, rather quizzically I thought, as if trying to
connect a man like me with the sick transsexual they'd seen wheeled
into 302 yesterday. Just dropping off this bag of candies, I wanted to
explain as they slipped their card key into the door to 304. Inside
302, not a sound. I'd done my duty, had I not? I could tell Grace
I'd stopped by the room, knocked, and gotten no reply. Melanie was
either resting or she'd gone out for a walk. Except she hadn't gone
out for a walk. She was still far too weak for that, and I'd knocked
loudly enough to wake her unless she'd been sleeping very soundly. I
knocked again.

Unless *she'd* been sleeping very soundly. Odd, but I hadn't slipped
with Melanie, not once referred to her as "he." I'd goofed twice with
Jenny just that morning. My only consolation was that Grace still
messed up occasionally herself. Still, was it stubbornness on my part?
Refusal to let go, even now, of Jim? To all appearances Jenny had been,
these many months, a woman. People who didn't know she'd been a
man were slack jawed with amazement when told. Now, postsurgery,
she was anatomically a woman as well. Between me and full acceptance stood only geneticists and fundamentalist Christians, two groups

whose wisdom I'd never before paused in rejecting. It was clearly past time for me to jettison what was holding me back, that midwestern, Nick Carraway desire to see the world stand at moral attention that, when allowed to thrive unchecked, turned otherwise decent people into someone like John Ashcroft, who couldn't bear to be in a room with a statue of naked Justice, who had to cloak her lest she corrupt him, poor, pathetic boob that he was.

These were my thoughts when I heard, finally, stumbling movement behind the door of room 302. When it opened, I took a quick, involuntary step back. The woman who stood framed in the doorway was Rochester's mad wife, down from the attic, barefoot, her hair wild, her eyes frantic and unfocused, clad in a thin nightshirt.

"Melanie?" I croaked, but her eyes had rolled back in her head and she slumped, first sideways into the door frame, then forward into my arms.

V.

Story endings, I used to tell my students, are often inherent in their beginnings. In the year that preceded our journey to Egypt, I'd found I was able to imagine the past—that is, imagine the young Jim Boylan before he and I had met. True, my initial reaction to my friend's news may have been, as I said, conservative, but I soon discovered I had little patience with people who were more sternly moralistic than I when they learned of Jim's circumstance. When someone asked how he could have kept such a secret from Grace all those years ago, I found I knew the answer. As I said, to the novelist, life—both fictional and real—is a series of dramatic moments, and this was one I had little trouble imagining. Jim, tormented since childhood and diagnosed with a condition he simply refused to accept, one day meets the very woman he's been dreaming of and praying for since he was that small boy beneath the pier, watching the approaching storm—the woman who frees him from himself. For the first time in his life, he himself simply doesn't matter anymore. *She* matters. She is not merely Grace, she is *his* grace—that gift from God that can never be earned, but must be rather freely and gratefully accepted. Perfectly radiant, she is not just the love of his life, she is his cure. When she smiles, he can feel what he's always regarded as his illness melting away. It's not just women's clothes he gathers together from his closet for disposal before he proposes marriage, it's a shameful self that can now be shed, *like a suit of clothes.* Not just hidden out of sight, but swept clean away.

Who *cannot* imagine such a moment? The weight of the self simply vanishing, banished by the power of longed-for love, the promise of family, of normality. Does he tell her about the clothes in the Dumpster? The *self* in the Dumpster? To do so would be to suggest that maybe those clothes are not really gone, that the discarded self may one day reemerge. To tell is to doubt the power of the love he can feel coursing through his veins, routing the virus, making him well. What patient does not want to believe the treatment has worked, that he's clean, that he can now live a normal life? *Tell* his beloved that he's been ill for a very long time, that the illness may return, even though he's convinced it never will? *Tell* her, now that his faith, which has never flagged since he was a child, has finally been rewarded? No, and it's in his *not* telling, surely, that we recognize our shared humanity. This is what I attempted to explain to people, barely containing my annoyance that such an explanation should be necessary.

But of course it begged a question. If I could imagine the past with compassion, why couldn't I breathe hope into an imagined future?

It was Saturday, but Dr. Schrang was in his office, and he answered his own phone. "Rick," he sounded pleased. "Of course I remember you."

"Melanie's in bad shape," I told him. "She's burning up."

"Put her on. Let me talk to her."

"Well, that's the thing. She keeps passing out. Also, she's sort of hallucinating."

"That doesn't sound good."

Do you think it could have anything to do with the fact that you cut her dick off last week? I didn't actually say this, just thought it.

"Bring her over," Schrang suggested. "Let me have a look at her."

"I don't have a car, doctor," I reminded him. *Also,* I wanted to add, *this is not my transsexual. This is a whole other transsexual from the one I came here with. Jenny Boylan is mine. This one's yours.*

"Use the hotel van," he advised, perhaps as an alternative to slinging Melanie over my shoulder and walking the half dozen blocks through traffic. I hung up and told Melanie, who was now stretched out across the bed, her eyes twitching, that I'd be right back. She groaned.

There was a young man on the desk in the lobby. "I'm going to need your help," I told him, and my expression must have revealed that I was dead serious, that I wasn't giving him an option, that he wasn't going to enjoy the task I had in mind for him, that I knew that it wasn't any more a part of his job description than it was part of mine. "We're going to need a wheelchair, and you're going to want to pull the van right up outside the front door. Room 302," I added.

He seemed to know what that meant.

———————

To my surprise, Grace was in the waiting room half an hour later when I came out of Schrang's office. "I realized after I left the voice mail, it wasn't fair to ask you to do it alone," she said. She'd been to the hotel, heard what had transpired there.

"I almost didn't," I confessed, feeling the chill of that truth.

Later in the afternoon, we abandoned Jenny altogether in order to visit Melanie in the emergency room. A massive infection was the diagnosis. But Grace suspected there was more, and she was right. Late that morning, Melanie had gotten yet another phone call from home, from a loved one who wanted her to understand that she was now a freak. Already feverish and shivering and light-headed, she'd been about to call the hospital. Now instead she drew the curtains against the harsh sunlight, crawled under the covers, and went to sleep. Another couple of hours and her kidneys might have failed. "I could have died," she told us. "If it hadn't been for the two of you ..."

When Grace went over and took her hand, Melanie broke down. "My partner," she said, sobbing, "she's not a bad woman. This is just so hard for her." Incredibly, she seemed to have little comprehension of the fact that the woman she was confiding in knew precisely how hard it was. "But my friends," Melanie went on, looking more like a frightened little girl than a woman, "I don't understand why they have to say such terrible things. Why do they have to make me feel like this, over and over?" She was regarding me now, as if I might know the answer to this one. I thought about the advice I'd nearly given my friend. Be a man.

And suddenly I was as angry as I could remember being in years. Angry at those friends of Melanie's who'd allowed her to come here alone, because of course it was easy to be angry at them, having never met them. And angry at Jenny's sister, also for not being here where she belonged, and because I'd never met her, either. Even angry at Melanie herself for being so oblivious, for thinking she needed to explain to Grace how hard it was for the wife of a transgender person to accept her loss. And, I had to admit, angry at myself for not once having fully imagined how afraid and lonely Jenny had been throughout much of her life. I'd grasped it intellectually, but I'd somehow not felt it until I saw that fear and loneliness reflected in the eyes of a stranger. And finally angry at the whole brutally unfair world, which distributes its blessings and burdens so unequally. Moe, you bastard.

———————

Back in Jenny's room, we gave her the good news (that Melanie was going to be okay) and the bad (that after Jenny's one blissful day in a single room, Melanie was specifically requesting to move back into her old room with her old roomie). "If that's okay with you," the nurse added.

"Of course it is," Jenny said, as if the question were absurd, as if people were never unkind, or intolerant, or selfish, or ignorant, as if she'd heard once as a child that people could be this way, but never witnessed such behavior personally. It was, of course, the same generosity of spirit, neither masculine nor feminine, that Jim had shown in welcoming me to Colby College, to a job that should have been his, the same generosity that had for too long allowed him to suffer alone rather than share his burden, that allowed him to forgive, again and again, those who trespassed against him. Against her.

And so, an hour later, Melanie, looking sheepish, was wheeled in, and we again pulled back the sliding curtain so we could all be one big happy family.

VI.

According to Flannery O'Connor, the fiction writer's material falls into two categories: mystery and manners. The latter are, for the most part, observable human behaviors, often socially constructed (like gender, some would argue), while the former, which reside at our human center, constitute the deeper truths of our being. These truths we often keep secret, because to reveal them makes us vulnerable. To my mind, an even deeper mystery than the secrets we keep is the mystery of the way our hearts incline toward this person and not that one, how one soul selects another for its company, how we recognize companion souls as we make our way through the world in awkward bodies that betray us at every turn. This is not the special dilemma of the transgender person; it's all of us.

Two days after Melanie returned to Jenny's room, Grace and I boarded the plane that would take us home. I had less than twenty-four hours before I was to embark on a long, grueling book tour. Grace was returning to work and the children and a life she was re-inventing, a life she'd *been* reinventing now for nearly two years. As she stared out the window at the flat midwestern landscape below, I regarded her with wonder. Years earlier, her heart had inclined in the direction of another soul, and now, against the advice of many friends and well-wishers, she'd had the wisdom to understand that when our hearts incline—often in defiance of duty, blood, rationality, justice, indeed every value we hold dear—it's pointless to object. We love whom we love. In the past two years, for Grace, everything had changed and nothing had changed. Her heart still inclined, as was its habit.

The same was true for Jenny. I'd witnessed this earlier in the week, the night of her surgery, at the end of the very long day she'd been envisioning, in one way or another, for forty years. She'd been slipping in and out of drugged sleep all afternoon and evening, awakening with a joke to tell and then falling asleep again in the middle of its punch line. Finally, as it got later, she grew serious. Time, she knew, for Grace and me to return to the hotel. When her eyes filled with tears, Grace went around the side of the bed and took her hand, leaned down, and kissed her on the cheek. "Grace," Jenny whispered, "sing me a song." As she began to sing "Two Little Boys," a lullaby she often sang to Luke and Patrick at bedtime, her voice sweet and low, the words themselves inaudible to me, I found myself backing toward the open door. Jenny was gazing directly into Grace's eyes, Grace into Jenny's, and their intimacy in that moment was so wholly unguarded that I felt myself to be an intruder. At the doorway I stopped, though, unwilling, perhaps unable, to leave.

What I was witnessing, I realized, was a great love story. Jenny had told me, many times, about how he—Jim—as a boy had walked beneath the Surf City pier as the storm approached and there prayed for love to save him. As I watched the tableau before me, it was hard to ignore the possibility that this prayer *had* been answered, ironically, of course, the way our prayers are all too often answered, the result perhaps of our not understanding what to ask for, or how to ask for it. And it occurred to me, too, that if this *was* a great love story, I had no idea where we were on its time line. For all I knew, we might be nearer its beginning than its end. How was it that I'd failed to imagine a scene such as the one I was witnessing? Was it so implausible? Hadn't I been witnessing this same love and tenderness throughout all the years I'd known these lovers?—for that's clearly what they still were, in the sense that mattered most. Is it the fact that the world so often disappoints us that makes hope seem so far-fetched? What makes imagining the worst so easy? Is it really so much more plausible? Or, frightened children that we are, do we imagine the worst as a kind of totemic magic, in the hopes of fending it off in reality?

When the lullaby was finished, Jenny, still holding Grace's hand, looked over at me. She was visibly exhausted, no more than a second or two from deep sleep, though a small, impish smile creased her lips. "Russo," she said, "sing me a song?"

It was a joke, of course, which was just as well. Sing? I could barely speak.

Afterthoughts, 2013

Mt. Katahdin, Maine, 2012.
Grace turned to me. "Did you hear that?" she asked.

The Life at Sea

Epilogue: Ten Years Later

My mother was dead, to begin with. There is no doubt whatever about that.

A few days before Christmas 2011, we walked into her old house for the last time. Steam hissed through the radiators.

"Oh, Jenny," said Grace, carrying a picnic basket. "It's so dark." In the basket were some chocolates, a soft pretzel, a bottle of Irish whiskey, and a book.

To our right was Mom's kitchen, empty now. Once I'd rushed into that room and startled my father, who was sipping Virginia Gentleman from a jelly jar. *Dad,* I said. *I got into Wesleyan.*

In November large men had come and carried my parents' things into moving vans. Some of them were loaded onto a container ship and delivered to my sister's house in the UK; others went north, to my office at Colby College or our house in Belgrade Lakes, Maine. Grace and I hadn't taken a lot of stuff. Some needlepointed pillows.

A couple of chairs and a desk. A tiny brass cowboy hat that doubled as an ashtray.

The biggest thing we'd kept was the old piano, the same one I once played for Vietnam Santa, the Cable-Nelson with the cracked ivory keys upon which, back in 1974, I'd performed a crazy jam for Onion in the key of G.

Mom had died on the fifth of July. The night before, my sister and I had sat on the back porch, drinking wine, listening to the crickets, while distant fireworks flickered in the sky. It was only the second time we'd been together in ten years.

"This whole world is about to go *psssh*," my sister had said.

Now, from an upper floor, Grace and I heard footsteps.

"You are fettered," said Scrooge, trembling. "Tell me why?"

"I wear the chain I forged in life," replied the Ghost.

Grace turned to me. "Did you hear that?" she asked.

It was bad enough losing my mother, but putting her house up for sale had nearly snapped me in half. Briefly, I'd considered moving our family back to Pennsylvania, quitting my job at Colby and taking up residence in the old mansion, beginning the last third of my life as a Main Line matron after spending the first third there as a schoolboy.

But that wasn't going to happen.

We'd found buyers for Mom's house in record time, a beautiful couple with three children all under the age of six. The oldest of the three was a beautiful blond boy, not so unlike my own mop-topped self circa 1964. As he'd entered my old bedroom, his face had lit up. "Daddy!" he shouted. "I want this to be *my* room!"

It's all for the best, I told everyone. *It's time to let go.*

Letting go, however, has never been my strong suit. I wound up spending a lot of the fall of 2011 staring out my office window at the college, blinking back tears, holding that little brass cowboy hat in one hand. One afternoon I found myself in the midst of a lecture, suddenly unable to speak. *I'm sorry,* I explained to my students. *It's just I miss my mom.*

It was my religious, conservative mother, of course, who'd responded to the news of my transition by taking me in her arms and saying, "Love will prevail." I can't say I learned everything I know about being a woman from her, but I can say she taught me, more than any other soul, what it means to love, and what it means to forgive. *Won't it be a scandal,* I'd asked her, *when everyone finds out I'm your daughter now?*

Well, yes, she'd replied. *But I will adjust.*

Then she quoted First Corinthians: *Faith, hope, love, abideth these three; but the greatest of these is love.*

A month after she died, aged ninety-four, I went to a concert, and when the pianist performed "Someone to Watch Over Me," I was so suddenly convulsed with grief that I was afraid someone was going to have to take me to the hospital, to inject me with anti-crying medicine, assuming such a thing even existed.

"What is it, ma'am?" said a sympathetic stranger sitting next to me. "What's wrong?"

I was grateful for the man's kindness, but wasn't my problem obvious? *After all these years,* I thought, *there isn't anyone watching over me anymore.*

As it turns out, of course, I was dead wrong about this, but that was nothing new. Over the course of my long and happy life, I've been wrong about lots of things.

———

Our plan was this: on the third floor of Mom's house, Grace and I would eat something sweet, and remember sweet things. On the second floor, we'd eat something bitter, and recall our losses. And on the ground floor, we'd eat something salty, and consider life's flavor, and its continuation. Our hope was that by saying farewell in this grandiose fashion, it'd be easier to move forward.

So we tromped up the creaking stairs to the third floor. To my right was my old bedroom, now empty except for a few spiderwebs hanging from the ceiling. Once there had been hidden panels in the wall, secret hidey-holes in which I'd kept a pair of earrings, a copy of the *Feminine Mystique*, a peasant blouse. I had been able to imagine myself as young and beautiful back then, when I closed my eyes and prayed to God to make me female. But I had never dreamed of myself as the woman I finally became—a middle-aged English teacher with bifocals.

I was reminded of Russo's observation that our dreams so often come true ironically, the result of our not knowing what to ask for, or how to ask for it.

As a teenager, while the rest of my family was out, I had sat in my red chair in that room *en femme*, reading *Tonio Kröger*. One afternoon, while thus engaged, I'd heard a car door slam out in the driveway, and I'd gone to the window and peered through the lace curtains. Down in the driveway my mother and sister were arriving home. My sister looked up at my window, and for a single second she seemed to see my eyes, staring down at her through the lace.

James? her face seemed to ask. *Is that you?*

"Here we go, Jenny," said Grace now, and she pushed play on the iPod.

There is a young cowboy, who lives on the range . . .

"All right, then," said Grace. "So what can we think of that's sweet?"

"Happy Maddy's Day," said Patrick, and he gave me an origami dragon. This was back in June, on what most people would have called Father's Day. The four of us had been sitting in a hammock by the banks of Long Pond near our home in Maine. While my back was turned, our sons had turned into teenagers—Patrick was fifteen, and Luke was now seventeen. They had dimples, and wide smiles, and crazy hair.

"This is from Mommy and me," said Luke, and he gave me a small box that contained a pair of earrings. The stones on them sparkled in the late-afternoon light.

There was a splash from the water. Grace had thrown a tennis ball out into the lake, and our two black Labs dove in after it. They love to swim, those dogs, but even more than this they love to chase after things and bring them safely back to us. The dogs—Indigo and Ranger—could do this for hours. (Lucy, our Kennebec Valley Flycatcher, breathed her last in 2005.)

Luke began to sing, "In the town, where I was born . . ."

Patrick and I joined in. We sang "Yellow Submarine" as the loons called and the dogs dove into Long Pond again and again. After "Yellow Submarine" we sang "Swing Low, Sweet Chariot." Then "You Are My Sunshine." Then "The Circle Game."

As I listened to their sweet voices, I looked with wonder at my sons. They were not perfect children any more than we had been perfect parents. But they had done well enough. Having me as a father—and later as "Maddy"—had done them no harm. It was even possible that coming from a nontraditional family had made them more compassionate, had given them more sympathy for the world's outliers and wastrels.

But I don't know. In the years since transition, I've heard from many trans people whose children have suffered at the hands of ironhearted bullies. Some of the tales have nearly burned off my ears—children unable to go to class, parents forced into hiding, boys and girls afraid to state the fundamental truth about themselves or the people they love.

Why didn't any of this happen to Patrick and Luke? I wish I could tell you for certain, but the truth is that I don't really know for sure. It may be that we made more good decisions than bad ones, the four of us. Or it may have had something to do with Maine itself, a place where people tend to respect one another's privacy. Some of this was surely part of it.

But I also wonder whether our family, above all, has eluded misfortune because of the love we share. Is it possible that the blueprint for our future had really been best imagined by my ninety-four-year-old mother when she took me in her arms and said that *love would prevail*?

Back inside the house were the makings for three pizzas. That had been another late-breaking effect of estrogen: I'd become a mozzarella artist. That night we were having a deep dish with andouille sausage, jalapeño peppers, and provolone; a classic pie with pepperoni and green peppers; and a grilled pesto pizza with caramelized onions, exotic mushrooms, and Gorgonzola.

There was a reason I'd gained ten pounds since transition.

That Maddy's Day—just a few days before my fifty-third birthday—we sat by the lake and sang songs as the sun went down over the ridge. Exhausted at last, the dogs lay down at our feet, tennis balls still clenched between their teeth.

"I've got a song," said Grace.

We all turned to her. She hadn't been doing much singing, leaving most of this to the boys and me, but she had a song now.

"Do you think I could leave you crying?" she sang.

When there's room on my horse for two?
Climb up here, Jack, quit your crying,
We'll mend up your horse with glue.
When we grow up we'll both be soldiers
And our horses will not be toys.
Maybe then we'll remember—
When—

Her throat closed up.

For a moment there was silence. Loons called to one another on the lake.

Then Patrick and Luke completed the verse for her.

"When we were two little boys," they sang.

It was a song from their childhood, of course. But now our sons' voices were those of young men.

In November, Luke had burst into our kitchen, a letter in one hand. "Maddy!" he shouted. "I got in."

"What?" I said, stunned. He'd applied to Vassar, early decision. I was drinking whiskey from a jelly jar.

He spread his arms wide. "I got in, Maddy," he said. "I got in to college!"

"You—" My mouth dropped open.

He nodded, and we hugged. Then he lifted me into the air and spun me around. *How is it possible,* I wondered, *that my own son is now capable of lifting me off the ground?*

But then my sons are capable of lots of things.

Patrick, a sophomore, had settled comfortably into the top of his class at school. He loved chess, and soccer, and playing his French horn, and the trumpet, and our dogs, and folding origami. He was part of several honors bands, including the Mid Maine Youth Orchestra. The family had spent a pleasant afternoon the previous summer listening to Paddy perform with an orchestra at a summer music camp. He'd played "Jupiter" from Holst's *The Planets*, and Grieg's "In the Hall of the Mountain King," and a composition by Peter Schickele titled "Grand Serenade for an Awful Lot of Winds and Percussion." During this last composition, the clarinetists had inserted the ends of their instruments into glasses of water and bubbled.

If we appeared smug about our sons' success, Grace and I hoped to be forgiven. Over and over, during the time of transition, we'd heard things like, *Oh, I feel sorry for the poor children,* as if boys having Grace and me for parents could only be objects of pity. The only phrase we'd heard more frequently, in the wake of *She's Not There*, was *Oh, I feel sorry for the poor wife. She's the real hero!*

Grace did not feel like a hero. Mostly she felt like a working mom married to someone she loved. She was still a social worker, dividing her time between teaching in the social work program at the

University of Maine and working as a counselor in the local schools. It made me feel good that these young people had Grace looking out for them.

At the end of the day, we'd sit by the fire together drinking martinis, talking about our sons, our work, our plans for the future. Sometimes we said nothing at all, and just read our books by the fire—or sat on the deck at the lake, when the days were warm.

Looking back now at the year or two immediately after my transition, I was sometimes frightened by how close we'd come to the edge. Everything seemed fragile and uncertain then, and we really had no idea how we were going to survive. Rereading the closing chapters of *She's Not There* now, ten years later, I see two people stepping out onto very thin ice.

How it was we did not fall through? Mostly we kept walking forward, day by day, until this strange new world began to seem familiar. It hadn't been easy. There were times when it seemed as if we were taking our marriage not just day by day, but hour by hour.

We had been married twenty-three years—twelve as husband and wife, eleven as wife and wife. And yet you couldn't call us lesbians now, at least not in the way that most people use the word. We did not have a particularly intimate relationship, if by "intimate" you mean girl-on-girl action and the smoking of Virginia Slims. Still, there was no shortage of intimacy in the life that Grace and I shared. It wasn't that we didn't miss regular sex. How could we not? But we'd found other forms of intimacy that mostly made up for its loss. And in this compromise, I think it's fair to say we had plenty of company among middle-aged couples who have been married for almost a quarter century. As I occasionally found myself saying to audiences of young people aghast at the particulars of our marriage: *Hey, man. Your parents aren't having sex, either.*

I'm not trying to be deliberately glib about this very serious issue, and I admit that there are times that the absence of sex makes us each feel mournful and hollow. But anyone who views our marriage only in terms of its loss is missing the point.

To be sure, we had plenty of friends who failed to believe we could possibly be happy with the odd connection we had invented—a state I sometimes call *quas-bians*. Readers of *She's Not There* and some of my other work would occasionally write me brittle letters, accusing me of "holding Grace hostage" or calling her a "martyr," as if Grace had not stayed with me out of her own choice, or as if a life with me could only be interpreted as a sad, pitiable existence.

"Fortunately," Grace liked to point out, "you're not married to any of those people. You're married to me."

"But why?" I'd ask her sometimes, when the vapors had laid me low. "Why not find a better life?"

"Because I love you?" Grace would say, as if this explanation could only fail to be obvious to the willfully blind. "Because this is the life I want. This life with us together."

What could a person say, in response to this kind of love?

'Tis, a good life, the life at sea.

———

"Sweet Baby James" came to a conclusion. It was time to leave the third floor. "Are you okay, Jenny?" said Grace.

I wiped the tears away. "Yeah," I said, and got to my feet.

"This is supposed to be the sweet floor," said Grace, packing up the chocolate. "The second floor is the floor for bitterness."

"I know," I said. As I sat there on the floor of the hallway, looking into my old bedroom, it occurred to me that once, in this very room, I had *been* a James, although whether I had ever been a *Sweet Baby* is probably not for me to say. "Just because it's sweet doesn't mean I can't cry."

Grace hugged me. "I know," she said, and we descended the creaking stairs. I looked at the third-floor hallway for the last time. The door to my room stood half-open. I wouldn't be closing it anymore. "On to the bitter."

———

We pulled into a hotel in London after an all-night flight from Boston in 2007. Grace had slept on the plane, but I hadn't. I was too wound up. I was excited about this trip—for one thing, I was going back to give a speech at University College Cork. I hadn't been to Ireland since The Troubles. My old friend Eoin, who was sponsoring my talk at UCC, had promised that afterward we'd take over Reidy's Wine Vaults. He had high hopes that as the night drew on I'd sing "Fooba Wooba John," or possibly even "The Dog Crapped on the Whiskey," if everything turned out just so.

"And what's the one about the chicken that's so instructive?" Eoin asked. "You could do justice to that one as well, I'm sure."

"You mean, 'That's the Way You Spell Chicken'?" I said. "I can't believe you remember me singing that."

"Oh, I've tried to forget," said Eoin. "Believe me."

Before that, we were to spend the evening in an art gallery in London, as Rick and Barb Russo's daughter Kate swapped marriage vows with a wry young man named Tom. I think Russo was hoping for some singing, too. After all these years, Rick was still one of my dearest friends. We saw less of each other after he and Barb moved to Camden, and after they bought a winter place in a warmer location (Boston?!), we saw less of them still. The Russos, as empty nesters, had entered a different phase of their lives than Grace and I, who for the last ten years had ridden the bucking bronco of our sons' adolescence. Still, Boylans and Russos convened every other month or so, to raise a few glasses and spend an evening eating a glorious meal, usually one cooked by Russo himself. He was still quite a chef.

Remembering our days of camaraderie at Colby, back in the early 1990s, it was hard not to be amazed by the divergence in our careers as writers. Rick, for his part, had settled down into literary fame as one of the country's best-loved novelists. He'd published a great complex novel, titled *Bridge of Sighs*, in 2007. That was followed by *That Old Cape Magic* in 2009.

As for me, the publication of *She's Not There* had brought about a different kind of literary fame. True, I hadn't won the Pulitzer, but on the other hand, I'd been imitated by Will Forte on *Saturday Night Live*. "You know what, Boylan?" Rick said to me. "He does you better than you do."

One afternoon, Russo and I had wound up at a party at Don McLean's house. (Don't ask.) On the way back from the bathroom, I'd taken a wrong turn and wound up in a beautiful, lavish chamber that was clearly the composer's man cave. In one corner was a bust of our host, the author of "American Pie." There was a lei around its neck.

In a bar after the party, I told Rick about what I'd seen, and, following our long-established pattern, I began to taunt him a little bit. "Sure, you won the Pulitzer," I said. "But you don't have a bust of yourself in your house, do you, Russo?"

"You've got me there, Boylan," Rick said, staring into his beer and wondering how much longer *this* was going to go on.

"Seriously, Russo. Don't you ever wake up in the morning and go, 'Man, I have to get me a bust!'?"

"Well, Boylan," said Rick, his face breaking into a grin, "I know *you* did."

On the day of Kate Russo's wedding, in the lobby of our London hotel, there had also been a long-planned rendezvous.

My sister and I had not seen each other for seven years. But we were seeing each other now.

Writing about this is awkward, because Lydia's exasperation with me was not only about the woman trouble. It was also about the books I'd written, not least the original edition of this one. She'd found my transition galling enough at the time, and had long held fast to her rule that our children and her own could not speak to one another and that my existence was not to be acknowledged in my mother's presence. But worse than this, I think, was the fact that I'd been so public, that I'd dragged the family name into the ditch and caused such a stink that if a person sniffed hard enough, one could smell all the way across the Atlantic, where she now lived with her husband and four kids.

My heart pounded as we stood there in our hotel lobby waiting. It had been a long time since I'd had to "unveil" myself to anybody.

At last my sister and her husband came through the door. I was surprised by how much older they both looked.

Wow, I thought. *She's really changed.*

Lydia came over to me and we hugged. "Hi, Jenny," she said.

———————

Grace and I creaked down the stairs of the Coffin House to the second floor. She mixed up a pair of Manhattans, pouring the Irish whiskey and the vermouth and the Tipsy Cherries. We were using Angostura bitters for "bitterness" in the second-floor ritual, but to be honest, the Manhattans weren't all that bitter. Neither were our memories. It was hard, all things considered, to separate the sour from the sweet. As Huck Finn observed, "In a barrel of odds and ends it is different; things get mixed up, and the juice kind of swaps around."

We sat on the floor of the room my parents called "the library." All of its shelves were empty now, its hearthstone cold. We lit a white candle and placed it in a brass candleholder. The sun had set, and the old house had grown dark.

"So what are we reading here, while we drink our bitter Manhattans?" Grace asked, as if there were any question.

I cleared my throat and opened up the Tolkien to the last chapter, "The Grey Havens."

I tried to save the Shire, and it has been saved, but not for me.

When the tears came, Grace took the book from me and read. There had been a lot of tears in this room over the years. I'd fed my father one of his last meals here, back when I'd had to leave Johns Hopkins and tend to him in his final days.

Here at last, Grace read, *dear friends, on the shores of the Sea comes*

the end of our fellowship in Middle-earth. Go in peace! I will not say: do not
weep; for not all tears are an evil.

I blew out the candle, and the smoke rose toward the ceiling.

Out in the hallway, the house creaked. There was one footstep,
then another. Grace and I looked at each other, and then I slowly
went to the door. I looked down the long empty hallway toward the
second-floor landing. I'd once made out with Donna Fierenza on its
deep windowsill on a summer day, when I was young.

"What is it, Jenny?" asked Grace. "Do you see anything?"

———

Melanie, my roommate from surgery in Egypt, called me for advice
concerning the issue of her wedding day. This was in 2006. In lieu
of a caterer, she said, "We could let people select their own veggies,
meats, and sauces, and then we'll stir-fry it, *right in front of them*! It will
be like a cross between Chinese and Mongolian barbecue!"

She went on to sing the praises of frying things in hot oil while
wearing her wedding dress. "It will be flexible, given the weather,"
she noted, "and the food will be fresh and hot!"

We had stayed in sporadic contact, Melanie and I, in the years following the unpleasantness in Egypt. Her family, which had gone out
of its way to belittle her during the time of her greatest desperation,
later swept her up in its arms, gave her a place to stay, and provided
emotional and financial support as she slowly got herself back on her
feet. She'd gone back to school, too, first getting herself a degree in
library science, and later completing her PhD in political science and
public policy. By 2012, Melanie, whom I most clearly remembered
standing in a hospital gown, desperately trying to pee, was now a feared
government professor at a midwestern university. "My students are all
frightened by me," she told me. "That's just how I like it."

Melanie's wedding took place in a Chinese restaurant; the other
bridesmaids and I wore white silk Chinese dresses. Melanie wore red.

The day after the wedding, Melanie took me to the airport, but before she did, she insisted that I "truly experience a real southern breakfast." This, as it turned out, was fried chicken on a biscuit, served at a place called BoJangles'.

As I sat there eating my chicken with the bride and groom and a few other members of the wedding party, it was hard not to think about the journey Melanie had taken over the last few years. If her trouble at the end of *She's Not There* had represented one frame of her life, a morning such as this one represented another, and who could say which moment was infused with more truth? I looked at her, chicken and biscuit in hand, amazed at how far she had come, humbled by her strength.

The day before, after the bridesmaids and the groom had promenaded to the altar, there had been a dramatic pause before Melanie had appeared. For a second we all wondered—*Where is she? What's become of the bride?* And then she appeared, beautiful in her red Chinese dress, holding a bouquet. Her husband-to-be looked upon her and smiled from ear to ear. And on the stereo, someone cued up Etta James singing "At Last." The sweet, sad music filled the air.

———

When I got back to Maine, Grace and I sent Melanie a wedding present. What did we send her? A ham.

———

As the years passed and the newness of femaleness slowly receded, some of my affect—which had been so blissfully feminine when transition was new—slid back into a more androgynous place. My voice, in particular, regained some of its former resonance, meaning that now and again people would mistake me for a man on the telephone.

I wasn't crazy about this, but then, what choice do we have, in the face of all of life's indignities, besides forgiveness?

In those early days, my womanhood was such a fragile thing. It had seemed, at times, as if anything could take it away from me—a stranger's glance, the way I wore a scarf, a breeze coming through an open window.

I had worried back then that my gender was always—as Jeff Probst says of the immunity necklace on *Survivor*—"up for grabs."

I didn't feel that way anymore. At long last, my sense of self seemed firm and fixed. No one else could take my womanhood away from me, and no one thing defined it. At long last I had what other women had—the ability to wake up in the morning and find nothing at all remarkable about the body I was in.

I would never call myself an invulnerable person; it was still all too easy to bring me to tears. But my identity was no longer a matter of debate. I had, to my own enduring joy and surprise, become something solid.

———

Grace and I had reached the ground floor. Now we sat before the hearth of the old fireplace in the empty living room, preparing to eat our salt.

"Do you remember that magic shop?" I said as Grace got out the soft pretzel and slathered it with mustard.

"What?" said Grace. "What magic shop?"

"The one we went to with the boys, right after I finished transition. That guy was showing us all the tricks, and then you and the boys heard voices, and you all walked down the hallway."

Grace nodded. "I remember that. There were all these old guys sitting in a room doing tricks, and the boys and I went to watch. We wondered what had happened to you."

"I was at the cash register, watching you all disappear. I remember thinking at that moment that I was going to lose you, Grace. That I was going to lose you all."

Grace took my hand. "I know," she said.

"That magician who ran the shop was showing me all these tricks. The fake thumb. The disappearing egg."

Grace handed me the pretzel, and I took a bite. Salty.

"We're all still here, Jenny," she said.

I looked with wonder at the woman I had proposed to, in this very room, twenty-four years earlier. She was, as Mary Karr once observed, "still her same self."

I hit play on the iPod and a tune by a group called Sam & Dave began. The name of the tune was "I Thank You."

The music echoed through the empty old house. We got to our feet, and we danced.

I held my hands out to my sides and spun. Faces whirled around me. There were our sons, grown men now, walking across the green quads of college campuses, singing in their low and manly basses. My sister and I, together again, sat at our mother's side as her breathing grew soft, then stopped. Waves crashed on a beach in Surf City, New Jersey, as Gammie and Hilda talked of Spain. A storm approached, and Aunt Nora drove us all away.

It's all right, Jenny, she said. *We're going to be safe now.*

―――――――

We turned out the lights and took our leave. The house was dark now, waiting for its next chapter.

As we climbed into the car, I looked up at my old home for the last time. There on the third floor was the window of my childhood bedroom.

The curtain fluttered, and for a second I thought I saw a pair of eyes, peering down at me through the lace.

James? Is that you?

Grace, following my gaze, looked up at the dark and distant window, where for a single instant I thought I had seen the face of a child.

But he's not there.

Imagining Grace

by Deirdre "Grace" Boylan

January 2012

Jenny is the writer in the family, so I am not totally sure how to do this. Just dive in, I guess.

People have asked me to comment on *She's Not There* since it was first published ten years ago. They ask me all kinds of questions. I haven't responded publicly all that often. Sometimes I feel a little bit like, *I gave at the office.*

I suppose the most important thing I would tell families and spouses is that there are many harder things that families have to endure than having a family member change genders. During the time of Jenny's transition, my sister Katie died of ovarian cancer. Jenny dedicated *She's Not There* to her. At the time it was far more important for us to share our experiences and to support one another as a couple and as a family as we dealt with that loss than it was to separate. It was much more important for all of us to come together than to choose that moment to divide our family.

It was a time of enormous uncertainty, anxiety, and grief. In some ways, it's difficult for me to go back and really remember or describe everything that was going on.

Truthfully, I don't know how I did it. I did what I've always done, which is putting one foot in front of the other. I was anxious. I was scared. I didn't know what my future was going to hold.

I felt like I was riding a freight train. There were no good choices. If I jumped off the freight train, I'd be killed on impact. If I hung on, I had no idea where I was going.

There were a lot of dark moments when I felt like I didn't know what was going to happen, what I wanted, or what would help me answer those questions.

At the same time, Jenny was on a journey of self-discovery and exploration. It could make her quite giddy at times. I was the one hanging back and feeling bereft. I always felt like the children were going to remember me as the sad, depressed, bitchy parent, while Jenny got to be playful and delighted and excited. That was one of my biggest fears—that I would turn into the mean parent.

I think the main thing that got us through the transition was the strength of our love for each other. That never fundamentally changed. It was the internal spiritual connection between us, and our commitment to caring for each other and for the boys, that enabled me to keep putting one foot in front of the other, and to remember the things that have always delighted me about Jenny and our life together.

Our family is united by baking bread and sharing food and drink as a way to be together and to communicate. We don't talk about sex and gender all that much these days. That shouldn't be surprising to anybody who has teenagers. It's a lot of work just to be a family. It takes a lot of coordination, a lot of effort, and a lot of time, which doesn't always leave space to process everybody's life. We're pretty comfortable with one another, the four of us.

Often I forget that our family is different, in terms of gender anyway. But we are extraordinary—extraordinary in terms of the great gifts and talents and love that are embodied in our family. I never forget that.

The lack of physical intimacy is not particularly hard for me. I think it's much harder for Jenny. Like I said, our lives are very full and very busy, and I feel like I have lots of closeness and love.

I've always really enjoyed exercise, and it's a huge stress reliever for me. I have a friend named Patty with whom I walk every morning for an hour before sunrise. The dogs, Ranger and Indigo, come with us. We walk most days of the week unless the temperature is below zero.

I thought *She's Not There* painted a fair enough portrait of our family. I hear sometimes from readers who think I'm a martyr, or that I'm "stuck" with Jenny. I think those aren't particularly accurate descriptions.

Personally, I prefer *saintlike*.

No matter what has happened, I have always had the power to make the decision that has been best for me. I have always seen my choice to stay married to Jenny as positive and strong. I don't feel like I've sacrificed myself or subsumed myself to anything. There were times that it was very, very difficult to make that decision. But now it's ten years later, and I'm happy with our life.

Not every person who finds him- or herself with a transgender partner has to decide what I decided. Everybody gets to make their own decisions. There are things to be gained from working through adversity with the person you love. There are things to be gained from raising a family together. But nobody should stay in a marriage or a family that is not sustaining for them, whether that involves gender or any of the other changes that pull people apart.

We didn't stay together only for the children. We stayed together for each other. If we had stayed together only for the children, we would never have made it through the last ten years. Jenny and I are together for the boys, sure, but we're also together for each other.

I think our boys have learned a lot from having us as parents. I think they've learned that the most important thing is to love each other and to look out for each other. Jenny's mom used to say, "Love will prevail." I think the boys have learned that from us.

I never look at Jenny and see Jim anymore. Not physically, anyway.

On the other hand, she's still the same person she was when we got married. As she has said before, *Same monkeys, different barrel.*

I'm neither a hero nor a martyr. I'm lucky because I'm married to someone I want to be married to, and we have created a life together that both makes us proud and delights us.

If I were to meet my younger self, the person I was ten or twelve years ago, I'd want to tell her that gender journeys—like all journeys—are many and varied. I'd like to tell her that most of the things she's always done, she'll get to keep doing. She'll have lots of adventures. There will be days when the whole family rides their bikes, or hikes up a mountain, or takes a boat ride for ice cream. There'll be cooking and drinking together. There will be family meals, and talking and laughing.

I would want my younger self to know that, truly, it's all going to be okay. That she'll be able someday to look back and know that she has a life she enjoys sharing with the person she loves, a life that's full of good work, good friends, and good kids.

After all these years, I still think that marrying Jenny Boylan was the luckiest thing that ever happened to me.

Notes

This is a true story. In order to make its rendition tolerable, certain moments in it have been gently altered—by compressing or inverting the time line, making various people taller or shorter, blithely skipping over unpleasantness, inventing dialogue, as necessary. All private individuals mentioned in this memoir appear with different names, and some of them have been obscured still further in an attempt to ensure their privacy. Public figures have largely been left to fend for themselves.

The author may be contacted via her Web site, www.jennifer boylan.net; e-mailed via JennyBoylan@aol.com; or written to care of her publisher, Broadway, a division of Random House, Inc.

She's Not There

by Jennifer Finney Boylan

Questions for Discussion

1. Do you feel that Boylan had a choice in becoming a woman to the world?

2. What responsibility does Jenny have for Grace and their children? What responsibility do they have to her?

3. Have you ever known someone who made a gender transition? How did the change affect people who knew the person before?

4. How central a role do you believe gender plays in our identity? How much different, and in what ways, do you believe you'd be if you were a member of the opposite sex? Do you think that some traits are inherent in one gender?

5. Discuss Boylan's experiences buying a car and buying a pair of jeans. Have you witnessed or experienced similar situations? Do you notice the differences in expectations and attitudes in the ways people of other sexes are portrayed?

6. What role does humor play in Boylan's life and in this book?

7. The title of the book, *She's Not There*, is the title of a song that Boylan sings. What do you think the title means in this case? Who is not there, and when?

8. What is revealed about Boylan in her friendship with Richard Russo?

9. As a teenager, Boylan believes that love will cure him of his feelings. In what ways is Boylan saved by love? In what ways do people usually expect to be saved by love? How often is it successful?

10. Discuss the concept of "normal" as it relates to Boylan's narrative, and to your expectations.

11. On her Web site, Boylan remarks, "As I look back at the story of my own life, I occasionally feel that being born transgender was the best thing that could have happened to me. While dealing with this condition made life difficult for me, as well as for my family, it's also true that I have been given a rare gift in life, the gift of being able to see into the worlds of both men and women with clear eyes." Do you feel that you know more about these worlds as a result of reading Boylan's book?

12. Boylan says that her first awareness of being transgender occurred when she was about three. What do you remember about your earliest sense of your identity? How often do you feel that what the world sees in you is at odds with what you know to be true?

13. After reading the book, did you identify with Boylan more or less than you had expected?

FURTHER READING

Chloe Rounsley and Mildred Brown, *True Selves*

Natalie Angier, *Woman: An Intimate Geography*

Kate Bornstein, *Gender Outlaw*

Richard Russo, *Empire Falls*

Julia Serano: *Whipping Girl: A Transsexual Woman on Sexism and the Scapegoating of Femininity*

Leslie Feinberg, *Stone Butch Blues*

Jamison Green, *Becoming a Visible Man*

Deborah Rudacille, *The Riddle of Gender*

Helen Boyd, *My Husband Betty* and *She's Not the Man I Married*

Andrew Solomon, *Far from the Tree*

A NOTE ABOUT THE AUTHOR

JENNIFER FINNEY BOYLAN is co-chair of English at Colby College, in Waterville, Maine, where she has taught since 1988. As James Finney Boylan she authored three novels and a collection of short stories, including *The Planets* (1991) and *Getting In* (1997). Under a pseudonym she has also written a series of four popular young adult novels; she has also written two screenplays for New Line Cinema. Jenny has received a Pennsylvania State Council on the Arts Fellowship in Literature, as well as the Alex Award from the American Library Association in 1998. She was Colby's Charles Walker Bassett Teaching Award recipient in 2000 and holds degrees from Wesleyan and Johns Hopkins, as well as an honorary MA from Colby.

She lives in rural Maine with her family.

Read an excerpt from

Jennifer Finney Boylan's new memoir

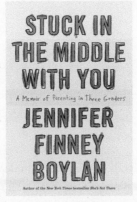

"No other memoirist I've read so perfectly blends intimacy and witty remove, soul-searching and slapstick, joy and pain. As a child—or as a reader—one could not ask for a wiser, warmer, more engaging companion than Jennifer Finney Boylan."
—Mary Roach, author of *Stiff* and *Packing for Mars*

 Available wherever books are sold.

Red Card

She sat alone in the stands as the duel unfolded. Like me, she had no visible husband. I had a lump in my breast. She seemed sad. Our sons had swords.

I slid next to her on the bleacher, put my purse on the floor. Then a group of dads two rows ahead of us leapt to their feet, yelling. A boy was on the ground. His adversary stood above him, foil extended.

"Red card!" shouted one of the dads. "Red-card him, ref!"

The trainer from my sons' school, Kents Hill, stepped toward the ring to protest. But a penalty was not called.

"Are you blind, ref?" shouted one of the dads. He was really upset. I'd never seen a dad all red in the face at a fencing match before.

"They don't understand," said the woman to my right. She was a tiny thing, like a budgie. In her hands she held a copy of *Cooking Light* magazine. "He was flèching him."

"Fleshing?" I said. A lot of the minutiae of fencing was beyond me. Offhand this sounded like the word you'd use if you accidentally encouraged someone to wind up naked.

"Flèche," she said. "That's Ethan's secret weapon."

The dads in front of us were still hollering and booing. The boy who'd been upended was back on his feet, and now I recognized him. This was a young man we'll call Chandler, the smallest boy on the Kents Hill team.

His adversary did a merciless ninth-grade equivalent of Muhammad Ali's victory dance. *I am the greatest.* His facial expression wasn't visible, what with the mask, but it wasn't hard to imagine.

"That's your son?"

She nodded.

"I'm Jenny Boylan?" I said.

"Grenadine Phelps?"[*] she said. It would have been nice to be able to say that this was the first time I'd met a woman named after a liquor, but in Maine, there's a long-standing tradition of naming people after bottles of alcohol. I'd known a Brandy, a Bacardi, and a couple of Sherrys. Brandy had once cornered me in the ladies' room at a blues bar where my band was playing and tried to get me to make out with her. Things like that happened to me more than you'd expect, which at first I'd thought was just my own rotten luck but which lately I'd begun to worry was my fault. On another occasion, for example, I'd accidentally wound up at a convention of ventriloquists, in Kentucky. There'd been this whole scene with this one guy who kept coming on to me using his "muffle voice."

The boys began to fence again, the gigantic Ethan and the tiny, terrified Chandler. Once again, Ethan charged at him, yelling as he advanced like one of the riders of Rohan: "Deaath!" He whacked Chandler's sword and it flew out of the boy's hand and skittered away on the gym floor.

"Flèched him again," said Grenadine wearily, as if irritated that

---

[*] This name, along with some other identifying information, has been changed.

Chandler had not learned that her son only had one trick, and that this was it.

"I'm sorry, what's flèching? You mean that charging thing?"

"Yeah," said Grenadine. "You extend the arm and pounce. Ethan's known for his flèche."

Yeah, well, I thought, Chandler's known for going to the bathroom in his actual pants.

The coach was now out talking to Chandler, who had his mask off. He was sniffing back the tears.

Another boy, an elegant and graceful young thing, picked up the fallen sword and returned it to Chandler with a small bow. He had hair halfway down his back, a huge cascade of blond curls tied in a braid. He patted Chandler on the shoulder, whispered something encouraging to him. Buck up.

"Jeez, look at the hair on that kid," said Grenadine.

"He's got hair all right," I said. My son Zach was admired for his hair in the same way her son Ethan was known for stabbing people.

But before I could explain this, Grenadine said, "My husband would never allow Ethan to have hair like that. He'd send him to military school first."

I shrugged. I didn't feel like defending Zach to a stranger. Was that really what I was here for, a conversation about hair?

Chandler had his mask on again and was back in the ring—more properly known as the *piste,* or strip. Zach stood to one side, watching the boy. He was the team co-captain.

"Kid looks like a girl," said Grenadine. The way she said it, it didn't sound like a compliment.

Zach looked like a lot of things, but a girl was not one of them, unless you were the kind of person who believed *long hair woman, short hair man.* He was tall and broad shouldered, my boy. The hair had made Zach very popular. There were a number of girls—some of them on the fencing team, in fact—who liked to do the braid. It was fairly obvious how much they all adored Zach. It wasn't obvious to him though.

Below us, Ethan extended his arm and went charging down upon little Chandler again. But this time, Chandler parried and then seized right-of-way. He came forward with the riposte and scored a hit off Ethan.

The dads below me shouted their approval. "Atta boy, Chandler!" they yelled. "Push back on him! Slay him!"

"Oh, honestly," said Grenadine.

The boys were now eyeing each other warily. They moved first one way, then the other, looking for an opening. You could feel the tension between them, Ethan looking for another chance to use his trick, Chandler emboldened by the hit he'd scored. There wasn't much chance that Chandler was going to win this match, but you had to give him credit for staying in the game. Very quietly, I began to hope some not-particularly-terrible thing might happen to Ethan, like the roof collapsing, or the boy's having a tiny nonlethal coronary.

At the edge of the strip, my son Zach stood there watching his teammate's progress. The men below me shouted again.

"It's a good thing my husband's not here," she said, listening to the hecklers.

"How come?" I asked.

She sighed. "There'd be trouble."

"Does he come to a lot of the matches? Your husband?"

"Oh, no." There was a slight pause. Then she said, "He's in Iraq."

Ethan got another touch on Chandler, and the dads below me moaned. One of them—was it Chandler's father?—held his head in his hands, as if he'd been called upon to witness his own son's execution for crimes against the state.

"That must be hard," I said.

She pulled into herself and did not respond. For a second it seemed almost as if the stranger were trying to hold back tears.

"It's better with him gone," she said, in a voice that was almost a whisper.

"Seriously?"

She nodded, and a tear brimmed over one of her lashes.

"Sometimes I hope he never comes back," she said. "Sometimes I wish he'd get—"

Gazing upon the gigantic, merciless Ethan below me, I wondered if I could begin to imagine Grenadine's married life. I pictured a menacing Ethan Senior bearing down upon the tiny, birdlike Grenadine Phelps, and winced. Junior had learned that pouncing trick from somewhere, and it wasn't his mom.

She eyed the wedding ring on my finger. "What about you? Where's yours?"

And just like that, I found myself in one of those situations where neither telling the truth nor coming up with a great big lie was going to accomplish anything. What could I say to her? Well, actually, I'm transgender. I used to be a man, but I've been a woman for ten years now. I'm still married to the woman I married twenty-five years ago, back when I was a man. Crazy vorld, huh? Ha! Ha! Ha!

Wow, she'd reply. Isn't your marriage really screwed up then?

I thought about Grenadine's marriage and my own. People looking at my wife, Deedie, and me—two women, not lesbians, legally married to each other—would say we were insane, way out of the mainstream, a threat to traditional American values. And all that. Whereas Grenadine and Ethan Senior were a paragon of all we revere: a heterosexual married couple, a dad serving his country in the war overseas. By almost anyone's measure, Deedie and I are the dangerous outliers, and Grenadine and her husband Mr. and Mrs. Normal. Even though Deedie and I love each other beyond all understanding, and Grenadine's fondest hope was that her husband would be murdered by insurgents.

Sometimes I don't understand the world at all, is my conclusion.

"I don't have a husband right now," I said to Grenadine. I was satisfied by the ambiguity of this, although it had to be admitted that this too was kind of a lie—since it implied that I'd once had one, or that a day would come when I might.

Down on the floor below us, Ethan hollered as he charged

toward Chandler for the match point. The enormous creature bearing down upon the tiny, frightened boy was terrible to behold. Chandler dropped his sword again and raised his hands toward his mask. Ethan wonked him on the chest, and the electronic touch detector—which was automatically scoring the event—registered the hit. Ethan had vanquished Chandler. They took off their masks and shook hands.

"Atta boy, Chandler," shouted his dad. "Way to show character!"

Grenadine rolled her eyes. "Character," she muttered sadly, as if this were something she had heard about once.

Ethan searched the stands and saw his mother there, and then he nodded at her. He had a crew cut and an ingrown smirk.

My own son patted Chandler on the back. Looking down at my boy, I had a strange, nostalgic feeling—wishing that, when I'd been a guy, I'd had half the character now exhibited by my own near-grown son. It's common enough, I guess, a thought such as this, demented though it may be. We look to our children as a kind of cosmic mulligan, our own best hope for a second chance. There were plenty of times I had looked at my son Zach as a better version of me, man-wise. He had the same goofy sense of humor, the same habit of wearing his heart right out there on his sleeve where anyone could crush it, the same buoyant hope that somehow love would prevail over all.

If I had failed as a man—and even those people who loved me most would have to admit this, what with the vagina and everything—then maybe Zach was a last chance to get it right. The man that I had once been clearly lived in him, although this time around we seemed to have been spared the melancholic lunacy.

On the other hand, I knew full well that thinking in this way was a surefire path to frustration. Children are here to live their own lives, not ours, and any parent who looks to her son to right the wrongs of her own past probably ought to get out of the parenting business entirely.

"I'm sorry I said that," said the tiny Grenadine. "About my husband. You must think I'm a basket case."

"Of course not," I said. "I knew you didn't mean it."

"But I did mean it," she said, after a pause.

"Seriously?"

"He's just not a nice guy," she said. "The army changed him."

I shrugged. "People change," I said. Coming from me, this was an understatement.

Something throbbed in my left breast. It wasn't sentiment. An odd, pulsing pain had been lurking in me for a month or two. I'd been doing a self-exam in a shower in a hotel in New York back in December when I'd first found the lump. Incredibly, I'd tried to pretend it wasn't there for the first month or so. But every time I felt for it to see if it was still there, I found it, larger. A mammogram was scheduled for the next day, the morning after the fencing tournament.

I'd begun to do some of the math in my head. Having seen my own father, and then my sister-in-law, slain by cancer, suffering through the chemo and the radiation, and the surgery, only to die agonizing deaths, I'd already decided, if it was cancer I wasn't doing any of that. I'd just go to the zoo and jump into the lions' cage instead.

It wasn't that I didn't love my life—the opposite, in fact. As someone who'd lived a full life as a man, then survived the perilous transition and then lived another ten euphoric years as a woman, I had plenty of things to be grateful for. Quite frankly, I couldn't imagine anyone's having had such a lucky life as my own, in spite of all the tears my condition—and the effects that it had had on others—had engendered. I'd been married for almost twenty-five years to a woman I adored, and who still adored me. I'd had what felt—at times—like the best job in the world, teaching English at Colby. I'd written a bestselling book, been a guest of Oprah Winfrey, even been imitated on *Saturday Night Live* by Will Forte, who, according to some people, did a better impression of me than I did.

I had two brilliant and resilient sons, each of them with amazing and fabulous hair.

Quite frankly, there wasn't a whole lot left on my to-do list. Other than sit back in wonder and see what happens next.

"I hate that," said Grenadine softly. "I hate it, that people change."

I was a father for six years, a mother for ten, and for a time in between I was both, or neither, like some parental version of the schnoodle, or the cockapoo. Of course, as parents go, I was a rather feminine father; for that matter I suppose I'm a masculine mother. When I was their father I showed my boys how to make a good tomato sauce, how to fold a napkin, how to iron a dress shirt; as their mother I've shown them how to split wood with a maul. Whether this means I've had one parenting style or two, I am not entirely certain. I can assure you I am not a perfect parent and will be glad to review the long list of my mistakes. But in dealing with a parent who subverts a lot of expectations about gender, I hope my sons have learned to be more flexible and openhearted than many of their peers with traditionally gendered parents.

I would like to think that this has been a gift to them and not a curse. It is my hope that having a father who became a woman has made my two remarkable boys, in turn, into better men.

Zach learned to shave when he was two years old, by watching me. He says that this is one of his primary memories of me as a man—the morning ritual of the razor and the hot steam from the basin. Zach stood upon a stool so that he could see his face in the bathroom mirror. I used to coat his young, pink cheeks with Gillette Foamy, and then give him a razor with the protective shield still on the blade. As I shaved my face, Zach would shave his. He'd mimic the contortions I'd make with my face in order to keep my skin taut. And he'd shave his own face in the same order I shaved mine—cheeks first, then the neck, then the chin, mustache last.

We stood there before the mirror, the two of us. I wiped the steam away from the top half of the mirror so I could see myself; Zach wiped a smaller hole away for himself at the bottom. Our expressions were so serious as we shaved, as men's faces always are as they undertake this business, as if we are not shaving, but staring out across the bridge of our intergalactic star destroyers.

Afterward, we'd towel down our faces, removing the residual froth and smacking our smooth cheeks lightly with an air of manly satisfaction. "There," he'd say. "I'm clean as a whistle!"

Where he got that phrase I can't tell you. He didn't get it from me.

That Christmas, Deedie bought Zach his own pretend shaving kit, complete with a plastic razor. When he opened this gift, though, he immediately burst into tears. "What?" said Deedie, discouraged that what had seemed like the perfect gift had gone so wrong.

"I don't want a baby razor," Zach wept, looking at me for backup. "I want a real one!"

Twelve years later, when Zach began to shave for real, he did it with an electric razor, one of those contraptions with the "floating heads." I didn't show him how to do it, although I tried. But he stopped me as he headed into the bathroom, and said, "Maddy. I got it from here." A moment later, the door closed, and I sat down in the kitchen and listened to the faint buzzing sound coming through the wall.

I didn't learn how to shave from my father either. Which turns out, I think, not to be so strange. One of the things about manhood I learned from my father is that it's a solitary experience, a land of silences and understatements, a place where a lot of important things have to be learned alone. Whereas womanhood, a lot of the time, is a thing you get to share.

I remember going for a bra fitting once and the saleswoman just waltzing right into my changing room in the midst of things to "check the fit." When she entered the room I was flabbergasted. I wasn't prepared for anyone to barge in while—what's the phrase?—my cups runneth over. But in seeing my astonishment, the saleswoman just laughed. Oh, honey, please, she said. We're all women here.

"How was it?" I asked Zach when he emerged from the bathroom, stroking his face. I was all set to have a big conversation about the experience. Shaving for the first time! A huge rite of passage! Do you remember, my sweet boy, when you were two, and we used to stand before the mirror together, staring through the clouds of steam?

I imagined the two of us sitting down for a moment, in order to take the measure of our rapidly passing lives.

"It was fine," said Zach, with a hint of annoyance in his voice. I recognized that tone. It said, it was what it was and it wasn't all that interesting, and do we have to talk about it as if it was? Not everything in the world, my son was trying to tell me, is worthy of analysis and sentimentality.

"Okay," I said, trying not to be hurt. Zach shook his head and bent down next to me.

"Really," he said. "It was fine." He gave me a hug, to make up for his silence, and I hugged him back, and my cheek brushed against his.

Smooth.

Also by Jennifer Finney Boylan

I'm Looking Through You

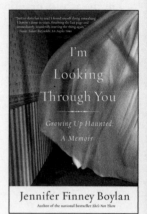

"Jenny Boylan's *I'm Looking Through You* ranks right up there with Mary Karr's *The Liars' Club* and Tobias Wolff's *This Boy's Life* as one of the finest literary memoirs of the last several decades. Like these, it's a haunting revelation of the human heart, its terrible longings, its fears and joys, the secret recesses where we most truly dwell. How alike we all are, down this deep."
—Richard Russo, Pulitzer Prize–winning author of *Empire Falls*

Available wherever books are sold.